THE BOOK OF DAILY PRAYER

MORNING AND EVENING

2004

Kim Martin Sadler

EDITOR

THE PILGRIM PRESS   CLEVELAND

This book is dedicated to

CHINYERE N. WILLIS

"One of God's angels"

July 29, 1985–December 28, 2002

The Pilgrim Press, 700 Prospect Avenue, Cleveland, Ohio 44115-1100
www.pilgrimpress.com
© 2003 by The Pilgrim Press

Biblical quotations are primarily from the New Revised Standard Version
of the Bible, © 1989 by the Division of Christian Education of the National
Council of Churches of Christ in the U.S.A., and are used by permission.
Adapted for inclusivity.

All rights reserved. Published 2003

Printed in the United States of America on acid-free paper

08   07   06   05   04   03   5   4   3   2   1

Library of Congress Cataloging-in-Publication Data

The book of daily prayer : morning and evening, 2004 / Kim Martin Sadler, editor.
p.   cm.
ISBN 0-8298-1531-7 (pbk. : alk. paper)
1. Prayers.   2. Devotional calendars.   I. Sadler, Kim Martin.

BV 245.B586   1997

248'.8—dc80   95-51065
                                              CIP

CONTENTS

"When the prayers go up, the blessings come down." You may have heard these words in your church or maybe you have read them on a bumper sticker as you waited at a red light. These words, seemingly plain, speak truth to so many of our conditions. Prayer works! Lives have been changed by the supplications made through prayer.

During this new year, think about these words when you pray. Pray to God for the blessing of peace in our country and in the world. Pray boldly! Pray with conviction! Pray, expecting a blessing! Be blessed to be a blessing to others.

Peace and Blessings,
Kim Martin Sadler
Editor

The Book of Daily Prayer is to be used for daily devotion in the morning and evening. To use the book as a personal devotional guide, begin
by reading the scripture passage for the day, followed by the opening
morning prayer. Read the meditative prayer next. This prayer is written
in a style known as "praying the scripture." This allows your meditative
prayer to be more than an interpretation of the day's reading.

The intercessory prayer follows. Here, you should offer prayers for
those in need of God's blessings and other personal concerns. You
might find it helpful to maintain a prayer list that can be used during
intercessory prayer. It may be followed by the Prayer of Our Savior or
another suggestion by the author. Both morning and evening devotional times end with a closing prayer.

Those who use *The Book of Daily Prayer* in a group setting can follow the same pattern described for personal use. One person can read
the scripture verses aloud, and another can lead the prayers. The meditative prayer may be said in unison or read silently. You may decide
that each group member will share her or his prayer concerns during
intercessory prayer. The Prayer of Our Savior and the closing prayer
may be recited by the entire group in unison.

You are encouraged to develop your own methods of using this
devotional guide. For example, you may wish to form prayer partner-
ships with others who use this book. You may also choose to sing familiar hymns at the beginning and end in prayer.

1) Form prayer partners with others who use *The Book of Daily
   Prayer*.
2) Insert familiar hymns at the beginning and end of prayer.
3) Maintain a prayer list that can be used during intercessory prayer.

Be creative and prepare to receive God's blessings.

Thursday, January 1

New Year's Day · Kwanzaa ends

(Read Luke 2:41–52)

MORNING

Loving God, I want to meet this day
knowing that you are with me even though
I may be unaware of your presence.

EVENING

Loving God, throughout the day you have been with me,
offering guidance and direction.

Eternal God, how often it is that we become disturbed by the celebration of our traditions and neglect your mission and purpose for our lives. Embrace us, O God, to find our way to your house, where we will find strength, hope, joy, and love.

MORNING

Help me, O God, to seek your guidance
and direction for this day.
(Prayers of Intercession)

EVENING

O God, I thank you for the blessings of today
and for your abiding presence.
(Prayers of Intercession)

IN THE HOUSE OF GOD THERE IS JOY.
(Pray the Prayer of Our Savior.)

MORNING

Now, O God, lead me as I strive
to live for you. In the incomparable
name of Jesus, I pray.
Amen.

EVENING

As I take my rest, grant me
your peace that passes all
understanding. In the incomparable
name of Jesus, I pray. Amen.

Friday, January 2

(Read 1 Samuel 2:18–20)

MORNING
Eternal God, remind me how precious
are the little ones who love you.

EVENING
Eternal God, I give you praise for each child
I have encountered this day.

O God of all people, through your servant Samuel you have shown us
that children can find a place in your service. Help us always to be open
to the ministries that our children render in your church.

MORNING
Bless, O God, each child who seeks
your presence in his or her life.
(Prayers of Intercession)

EVENING
Divine Parent, nurture each child
who is in need of your tender care.
(Prayers of Intercession)

THE INNOCENCE OF CHILDREN IS THE GIFT OF GOD.
(Pray the Prayer of Our Savior.)

MORNING
Dear God, let me be a blessing to
a child this day. In the incomparable
name of Jesus, I pray.
Amen.

EVENING
O God, this night I pray
for children who are hungry and
homeless, that they may find rest
in you. In the incomparable name
of Jesus, I pray. Amen.

Saturday, January 3

(Read Psalms 1, 8)

MORNING

Gracious God, I praise you for your goodness,
your mercy, and your love.

EVENING

Gracious God, this day you have shown me
once again that you are worthy of praise.

You have taught us, O God, through the psalmist that all people should give praise to your name. Help me this day to find new ways to give you thanks and praise.

MORNING

I give you praise this day, eternal God,
because you are worthy.
(Prayers of Intercession)

EVENING

O God of love, help me always
to give you praise.
(Prayers of Intercession)

WHEN THE PRAISES GO UP THE BLESSINGS COME DOWN.

(Pray the Prayer of Our Savior.)

MORNING	**EVENING**
O God, may I this day give you the praise that is due to your name. In the incomparable name of Jesus, I pray. Amen.	I praise you, Loving God, that you watch over me even while I sleep. In the incomparable name of Jesus, I pray. Amen.

Sunday, January 4

(Read Colossians 3:12–17)

MORNING
O God, this morning as I adorn myself
with garments of cloth, may I also put on love.

EVENING
O God, today I have tried to act
as one of your chosen.

O God, the apostle Paul has taught us the importance of wearing a garment of righteousness. Keep us mindful of who we are and whose we are as we strive to live a life pleasing in your sight.

MORNING
This day, dear God, let me walk in a way
that is pleasing to you.
(Prayers of Intercession)

EVENING
If I have failed to be what you wanted me to be this day,
forgive me, eternal God.
(Prayers of Intercession)

CHRISTIANS NEED TO DRESS FOR SPIRITUAL SUCCESS.
(Pray the Prayer of Our Savior.)

MORNING
Wonderful God, may my
deportment this day be a blessing to
others. In the incomparable name
of Jesus, I pray.
Amen.

EVENING
As I find my evening rest,
may I find comfort in your
providential care. In the incomparable
name of Jesus, I pray.
Amen.

Monday, January 5

(Read Isaiah 43:1–4)

MORNING

Holy One, I give you thanks for calling me by name
and guarding me with your love.

EVENING

Holy One, I offer you praise for the ways your love
and care have sustained me this day.

I listen to the words you spoke to the fearful people of Israel, O God. The sound is reassuring. Your people had been in exile so long that the discomfort of being forced to live in a foreign land had given way to habits of ease and routine. But now it was time to return home, to give up what had become known, to begin again. When I am afraid, do not let me become overwhelmed. Let me hear you when you tell me that I am precious in your sight and that you love me.

MORNING

Open me to new possibilities, O God.
(Prayers of Intercession)

EVENING

Remind me of your steadfast love, O God.
(Prayers of Intercession)

WITH LOVE FOR YOU AND ALL CREATION, I PRAY.
(Pray the Prayer of Our Savior.)

MORNING	**EVENING**
Use me this day as a sign of your love. In Christ's love, I pray. Amen.	Help me to recall your saving grace evident in the movement of the Spirit. In Christ's love, I pray. Amen.

Tuesday, January 6 · Epiphany

(Read Isaiah 43:5–7)

MORNING
Saving God, help me this day to navigate through perilous waters
and find joy in your sure promise of salvation.

EVENING
Saving God, may I find my rest and strength in you,
gentled to sleep by your comforting presence.

When I think about what it means to be formed by you, O God, and created for your glory, I am startled by the intimacy that this implies. When I create something, I struggle to give it my essence, my joy, my love. When I form something, I strive to give it shape, care, intensity. To think that you would give this to me in the act of creating and forming me is almost too much to comprehend. But you say these words to me, and your word is true. Help me to trust in this relationship with you.

MORNING
Stir in me compassion for the world you love.
(Prayers of Intercession)

EVENING
Form me, O God, into one who is not overwhelmed by my fears.
(Prayers of Intercession)

TRUSTING YOUR PROMISES, I PRAY.
(Pray the Prayer of Our Savior.)

MORNING
Spur me to compassionate acts
this day, that I may find joy in service.
In Christ's love, I pray.
Amen.

EVENING
Quiet any restlessness within me
this night, that I may awake attuned
to your way. In Christ's love,
I pray. Amen.

6

Wednesday, January 7

(Read Psalm 29:1–6)

MORNING

O God, I begin this day confident of your sustaining presence.

EVENING

O God, I rest from the labors of this day in the assurance
of your gracious love.

Amidst the many competing sounds of life, your voice, Holy One, speaks to me. Will I be listening? Or will everyday distractions lure me to a place of inattentive wandering, of worshiping idols instead of you? Deter my misdirected attention when voices other than yours beckon. Help me to focus on you. Your voice is clear, like the clap of thunder. Your voice is sure, making my heart pulse with delight at the sound. Help me to profess your glory and strength. Keep me safe in you.

MORNING

May the signs of your strength and majesty
encourage me to trust your power in the world.
(Prayers of Intercession)

EVENING

Break open in me with lightning force the desire
to make known to you the prayers of my heart.
(Prayers of Intercession)

IN AWE AND WONDER, I PRAY.
(Pray the Prayer of Our Savior.)

MORNING

God of glory, your voice calls the dawn into being. May I rise to this new day in hopeful anticipation of all that is before me to experience.
In Christ's love, I pray. Amen.

EVENING

God of glory, your voice calls the night to enfold the day with darkness. May I rest in the splendor of your presence this night to dream new dreams.
In Christ's love, I pray. Amen.

Thursday, January 8

(Read Psalm 29:1–2, 7–11)

MORNING

Majestic One, with joy I await your leading this day.

EVENING

Majestic One, with weariness I surrender to you the tumult of this day.

Storms can be frightening: bright flashes of light, roars of thunder, winds that howl. The very thought leaves me feeling tense and uneasy. Like the storms in my life, they rage beyond my control, playing havoc with settled routines and entrenched ideas. And there you are, Creator, shaking my world with storms that shift the landscape of my habits and call me to praise you with a word: Glory! Help me to sense your majesty. Lead me to the place of peace that comes within the voice of the storm, that I might know your sheltering presence.

MORNING

Shake the complacency from my heart with an invitation
to remember the needs of others.
(Prayers of Intercession)

EVENING

Though storms may trouble my existence,
may I trust in your power over the whirling wind and
mighty waters, to bring life, blessing, and peace.
(Prayers of Intercession)

ASCRIBING GLORY TO YOU, I PRAY.

(Pray the Prayer of Our Savior.)

MORNING

May I live this day in faithful praise
of your name. In Christ's love, I pray.
Amen.

EVENING

May I rest this night in the assurance
of your peace. In Christ's love, I pray.
Amen.

Friday, January 9

(Read Luke 3:15)

MORNING
Powerful Messiah, fill me with expectation this day.

EVENING
Powerful Messiah, reassure my questioning heart this night.

Sometimes I feel so troubled by questions. They spin in my mind and heart, and I cannot seem to fend them off. Who are you, God? How do I know you? What are the signs? Where are you in my life? Having the questions without a hint to the answers leaves me feeling frustrated and alone. But you attend to questioning hearts; you send prophets and messengers to point the way. Where are you pointing me, God? Let the chaff of my irritation at not having all the answers burn to ash. Fix in me a patient spirit to live the questions. Help me to look for your signs. Winnow my thoughts and claim the holy ones as rightfully yours. Gather me up, in your bountiful harvest, to nourish and serve a question-filled world.

MORNING
Bring to my awareness in images of water and fire the powerful sweep
of your gathering love. Inspire me to acts worthy of your name.
(Prayers of Intercession)

EVENING
Let me not forget that you are the Messiah, the Anointed One, who both
loves and judges. Forgive me when I question your authority in my life.
(Prayers of Intercession)

IN HUMILITY, I PRAY.
(Pray the Prayer of Our Savior.)

MORNING
Christ, help me to grow in my understanding of you as the one to whom I give my pledge of love and allegiance. In Christ's love, I pray. Amen.

EVENING
Christ, sift through the useless chaff of my sin and hold up for me the goodness you want me to live. In Christ's love, I pray. Amen.

Saturday, January 10

(Read Luke 3:21–22)

MORNING
O God, open me to the fluttering wings of your Spirit this day.

EVENING
O God, as night embraces me, bring me to restfulness
by the murmuring voice of your Spirit.

After his baptism, while Jesus was praying, a wondrous thing happened. The heavens opened and the Holy Spirit alighted on him in the form of a dove. You, O God, proclaimed him your beloved child, with whom you were pleased. In this momentous event, prayer played a crucial part. Time and again, Jesus would withdraw to deserted places and pray. Time with you, O God, was critical to him. Is it so with me? What is it that draws me to prayer? What do I find when I seek you? What more do you want for our time together? In the deserted places, lead me to fresh insights.

MORNING
Help me to be aware of the signs around me that reveal your love,
so that I might bring your good news to a world in need.
(Prayers of Intercession)

EVENING
Set my heart and mind to the rhythms of your way,
calling me to greater faithfulness and love.
(Prayers of Intercession)

TOUCHED BY YOUR SPIRIT, I PRAY.
(Pray the Prayer of Our Savior.)

MORNING
In a mood of watchfulness,
keep me yearning for the signs of your
abiding Spirit this day.
In Christ's love, I pray.
Amen.

EVENING
In the stillness of this night,
keep me searching for new ways
to sense your closeness.
In Christ's love, I pray.
Amen.

Sunday, January 11

(Read Acts 8:14–17)

MORNING

Spirit of Truth, as this day begins, listen to my anxious heart
and draw me into your all-encompassing love.

EVENING

Spirit of Truth, as this day comes to an end,
challenge my wandering mind to focus on you.

When the disciples heard that many in Samaria had accepted Jesus' message and had been baptized, they traveled there to pray for these believers. With the laying on of hands, Peter and John asked you, O God, to touch them with the Holy Spirit. How remarkable, Holy One, that your presence can be conveyed through the touch of another. But is it so surprising? Touch that is wanted, touch that conveys affirmation, touch that embodies all that is good, touch that is healing, is a mark of your love. Help me, O God, that I might be a bearer of your grace to all whom I touch.

MORNING

Loving Spirit, nothing in all creation is beyond the depth and breadth
of your love. Urge me on to ever-widening circles of inclusiveness
in my love and concern for the world.
(Prayers of Intercession)

EVENING

Renewing Spirit, help me to receive you with joy and pray
for creation with inspired love.
(Prayers of Intercession)

FERVENTLY I PRAY.
(Pray the Prayer of Our Savior.)

MORNING

Renew me, O God, in my
commitment to creation and to all
that is good. In Christ's love,
I pray. Amen.

EVENING

Transform my casual concern
for the world into a heartfelt passion
for justice and inclusiveness.
In Christ's love, I pray. Amen.

Monday, January 12

(Read Psalm 36:5–6)

MORNING
Sustaining God, as I awaken, I am aware
of your presence and your faithfulness.

EVENING
Sustaining God, I place myself in your care throughout this night,
resting in the assurance of your steadfast love.

O God, the psalmist glorifies your faithfulness and boundless love. We also hear the truth that your goodness and power are present throughout all creation, from awesome heights to great depths. As I experience tremendous highs and bleak lows in my daily life, guide me lovingly but firmly to do your will so that I may experience your peace. Free me to hear the voice within that allows deep communion with you. Help me realize the wholeness within me that you always see. I continue to be amazed by your incomparable love.

MORNING
Knowing the power of your love, Generous Creator,
I lift to you all those in need of your guidance and care.
(Prayers of Intercession)

EVENING
Precious God, I thank you for your presence this day,
and now I lay before you all my joys and concerns.
(Prayers of Intercesion)

"YOUR STEADFAST LOVE, O GOD, EXTENDS TO THE HEAVENS."
(Pray the Prayer of Our Savior.)

MORNING
I hope that I may recognize you
in the faces of those whom I meet
today. In Jesus' name I pray.
Amen.

EVENING
Allow the hours of rest tonight
to refresh me for the coming day, a
day in which to experience your
companionship. In Jesus' name
I pray. Amen.

Tuesday, January 13

(Read Psalm 36:7–10)

MORNING
Sheltering God, I am comforted by the knowledge
that you will protect me throughout this day.

EVENING
Sheltering God, bless your holy name
for watching over each one of your children.

We all are seeking protection, love, and guidance. The young single mother struggling to balance work and parenting; the abused child trusting no one; the troubled man yearning to escape his prison cell; the drug addict fighting to become sober; the suddenly widowed grandmother searching for peace; the man, separated from his partner, floundering in transition—all are in need of your grace and care, O God. Help us to avail ourselves of your unceasing spiritual nourishment and to experience fully your blessings of peace and prosperity. The awe-inspiring gift of life that comes from you is accompanied by the promise of faithfulness, love, and protection to those who know and accept you. Your light enables us to see new life.

MORNING
Loving Protector, keep us all in your embrace.
Now hear my prayers, especially for those in transition.
(Prayers of Intercession)

EVENING
God of all space and all time, thank you for guarding me this day.
Now I come to you in prayer for those in pain and those in mourning.
(Prayers of Intercession)

"FOR WITH YOU IS THE FOUNTAIN OF LIFE."
(Pray the Prayer of Our Savior.)

MORNING	EVENING
May I go forth this day with confidence, remembering that you abide with me. In Jesus' name I pray. Amen.	O God, I hope my words and deeds today reflected your infinite love and peace. In Jesus' name I pray. Amen.

Wednesday, January 14

(Read Isaiah 62:1–5)

MORNING

Renewing God, as this day dawns, thanks be to you for your glorious power.

EVENING

Renewing God, as the day ends, I thank you for the gift of your strength all the day long.

The prophet vows to continue proclaiming the coming day of vindication and salvation. Eternal God, when I have moments of indecision and uncertainty, help me to possess the commitment and vision of the prophet. During those moments when I question my worthiness, help me to remember that you rejoice in each one of us. Give me the compassion and patience to show others the specialness of your relationship to your people.

MORNING

O God, hear my prayer, as I remember those in need of your grace.

(Prayers of Intercession)

EVENING

Wrap me in your arms, O God, as I share my concerns for others.

(Prayers of Intercession)

GOD NEVER ABANDONS US.

(Pray the Prayer of Our Savior.)

MORNING

Loving God, open my heart and my mind to receive your Word today. In Jesus' name I pray. Amen.

EVENING

My rest this night will be peaceful, O God, knowing that you will never forsake me. In Jesus' name I pray. Amen.

Thursday, January 15

(Read 1 Corinthians 12:1–3)

MORNING
Merciful Savior, inform me of your plan today
so that all my actions will proclaim your salvation.

EVENING
Merciful Savior, I thank you for walking every step with me today.

Each day we encounter excess and irrationality—in ourselves as well as in others. It is difficult to hear the voice of the Holy Spirit within us when our emotions escalate and when we are under duress. We are also challenged when we hear our leaders and loved ones appeal to our raw emotions. Almighty God, grant us the discipline to conduct our lives in such a manner that we will not be swayed by unbridled excitement. Temper our exuberance with direction and loving guidance. Create for each of us a path so that tolerance will be evident everywhere you lead us today. May our speech—and the speech of those who worship differently from us—come from the spirit of love and compassion and not from pettiness and jealousy.

MORNING
Blessed Jesus, hear my prayers, especially for those
who suffer from disease that diminishes the quality of life.
(Prayers of Intercession)

EVENING
Blessed Jesus, I remember those who struggle
to recover from incest, abuse, and all forms of violence.
(Prayers of Intercession)

THANK YOU, O GOD, FOR LISTENING TO ME TODAY AND FOR NOT BEING SILENT.
(Pray the Prayer of Our Savior.)

MORNING
God of this winter morning, I look
for you as I begin my day. Allow your
peace to suffuse my being all day long.
In Jesus' name I pray. Amen.

EVENING
Bless me with rest tonight so I
may awake refreshed and eager to
meet all challenges in the morning.
In Jesus' name I pray. Amen.

Friday, January 16

(Read 1 Corinthians 12:4–11)

MORNING

Generous Spirit, make me mindful of all the gifts that I have received and help me use these gifts for the common good.

EVENING

Generous Spirit, my heart swells with joy when I serve you and my brothers and sisters.

Gracious God, you have blessed me in so many ways and have bestowed gifts of your grace upon me. Empower me to use these gifts to glorify your name and to bring peace and reconciliation to others, and whenever I stumble or fail to reach the mark—as I always do—may your compassionate spirit help my gifts work within me to overcome my self-doubts and fears. Since Paul's words clearly affirm that all gifts come from God, I have no reason to be arrogant or boastful. I remain your humble servant.

MORNING

Living Christ, I bring to you my questions and doubts.
(Prayers of Intercession)

EVENING

Compassionate Christ, I place my concerns before you now, especially for those who are frightened by the responsibilities of life.
(Prayers of Intercession)

THANK YOU FOR YOUR MERCY AND FORGIVENESS, JESUS.
NOW I PRAY AS YOU TAUGHT YOUR DISCIPLES.
(Pray the Prayer of Our Savior.)

MORNING

I attest that God gives me
the strength to manage all crises today.
In Jesus' name I pray.
Amen.

EVENING

I hope I reflected your love
to all whom I met today.
In Jesus' name I pray.
Amen.

Saturday, January 17

(Read John 2:1–11)

MORNING

Almighty God, thanks for pushing me beyond what I can imagine.

EVENING

Almighty God, another day has shown me that,
with you, I experience life in all its fullness.

Beloved Jesus, the first "sign" revealed your glory, and John tells how this "sign" confirmed the faith your disciples had in you. Though I have faith in you, I have moments when I question that faith, and though I know that you are always with me, there are times when I am far from you. Protecting Savior, help me walk the path that you have chosen for me. If I hesitate or lose my way, I know that your still, quiet voice can be heard within me, guiding me and transforming me always.

MORNING

Knowing your constant presence and the power
of your transforming love, I come to you in prayer
for the needs and concerns of others.
(Prayers of Intercession)

EVENING

I pray for your loving guidance for myself
and for my brothers and sisters.
(Prayers of Intercession)

REDEEMER JESUS, I PRAY THE PRAYER THAT YOU TAUGHT YOUR DISCIPLES.
(Pray the Prayer of Our Savior.)

MORNING

When I seek you at "my" center,
may I be reminded to search for you
in the margins. In Jesus' name I pray.
Amen.

EVENING

I hope I helped you work peace
and reconciliation in the lives
of my sisters and brothers today.
In Jesus' name I pray. Amen.

Sunday, January 18

(Read John 2:1–11)

MORNING

Liberating Jesus, as I open my eyes, I relish your gift of new life.

EVENING

Liberating Jesus, I end this day grateful for all the ways
that you enrich my life.

Jesus, by turning water into wine at the marriage at Cana, you gave new life to the wedding celebration. The evangelist John surely intended for us to realize the possibilities for new life that you afford each one of us. Jesus, you bless a life with such bounty—spiritual nourishment, vitality, fullness, and completeness. I will continue to seek you and in heeding the words of your mother—"Do whatever he tells you"—I know that I will experience a new beginning. I will leave the old fears and bad habits behind and, with the confidence of Mary, know that you, Jesus, will help me find my way.

MORNING

O God, I pray now for myself and for all those in need of renewal.
(Prayers of Intercession)

EVENING

Compassionate Creator, I remember those who live
with a thirst for love and peace.
(Prayers of Intercession)

MINDFUL OF THE MIRACLE OF NEW LIFE, I PRAY THE PRAYER THAT JESUS TAUGHT US.
(Pray the Prayer of Our Savior.)

MORNING

Forgive my sins, O God,
and help me to be more like Jesus.
In Jesus' name I pray.
Amen.

EVENING

O God, I hope I fully experienced
and rejoiced in the diversity of your
creation today. In Jesus' name I pray.
Amen.

Monday, January 19 · Martin Luther King Jr. Day

(Read Psalm 19)

MORNING

Glorious God, open my eyes to the full awareness
of your presence in this day.

EVENING

Glorious God, open my heart to full attentiveness
of your presence this night.

Surprising and all-encompassing God, you are everywhere. I ask for re-assurance, expecting words —and you reveal yourself in the sky! In the protective, persistent warmth of the sun! I ask for your guidance, expecting mandates—and you give me the gentle protection of your law. Every day of my life is your sweet message joyously poured out to me, every one of my encounters with the scriptures, a reward.

MORNING

Revive me for this day, sweet God.
Enlighten me to the needs of others.
(Prayers of Intercession)

EVENING

Tonight, I remember and rejoice in the many subtle
revelations of your presence in this day.
(Prayers of Intercession)

CLEAR ME FROM MY HIDDEN FAULTS, O GOD.
(Pray the Prayer of Our Savior.)

MORNING

Let my words reflect you today,
O God, my rock and my redeemer.
In Jesus' name.
Amen.

EVENING

May the meditations of my heart
be acceptable to you, O God, my rock
and my redeemer. In Jesus' name.
Amen.

Tuesday, January 20

(Read Nehemiah 8:1–3, 5–6)

MORNING
Tender and gracious God, I lift my hands to you
this day in praise.

EVENING
Tender and gracious God, I bow my head to you
this night with thanksgiving.

O God, how generous you have been to us—all people, women and men—through all generations. Now, when we stand in worshipful attentiveness, we know that you will speak to us as you once did through Moses and Ezra. We thank you that the loving words you gave them have been preserved for our benefit in scripture. Open our ears to your faithful leaders of this time, too. Show us how and when to say "Amen, Amen" to your living Word today.

MORNING
Let the words of my mouth and the meditation
of my heart be acceptable to you, O God,
my rock and my redeemer.
(Prayers of Intercession)

EVENING
Let the words of my mouth and the meditation
of my heart be acceptable to you, O God,
my rock and my redeemer.
(Prayers of Intercession)

AMEN, AMEN.
(Pray the Prayer of Our Savior.)

MORNING	EVENING
Bless us this day, great God,	We bow our heads this evening
so we might show in all our actions	with thanks to you, great God,
that we are your servants.	for all the blessings of this day.
In Jesus' name. Amen.	In Jesus' name. Amen.

Wednesday, January 21

(Read Nehemiah 8:8–10)

MORNING
Savior God, I greet you on this holy day.
As I read your Word this morning, bless me
with a deeper understanding.

EVENING
Savior God, I bless you for this holy day.
As I read your Word this evening, bless me
with a deeper understanding.

Most loving God, sometimes I am so overwhelmed by my own inadequacies that all I can do is weep. Only your amazing, grace-filled love comforts me in those times. When I remember your love, I see that every day of my life is your holy gift to me. I am then strengthened by the joyful knowledge of your inestimable care for me. Then I am shaken from mournful immobility. Then I can go on.

MORNING
Lead me, God, to those who are unprepared
for your magnanimity. And give me the generosity of spirit
to make their preparations for them.
(Prayers of Intercession)

EVENING
Let me rest this night, O God, reassured that today
I have given sweet portions to others on your behalf.
(Prayers of Intercession)

GOD'S JOY IS MY STRENGTH.
(Pray the Prayer of Our Savior.)

MORNING	EVENING
This day, grant me peace.	This evening, grant me rest.
In Jesus' name.	In Jesus' name.
Amen.	Amen.

Thursday, January 22

(Read Luke 4:14–21)

MORNING

My God, I greet you this morning as my parent,
my love, and my dearest friend.

EVENING

My God, I honor you this evening as my protector,
redeemer, and guide.

Saving God, when I am poor, you provide for me. When I am trapped
by the world's one-sided views and oppressed by its greedy demands,
you set me free. When I am blind to love, you open my eyes. What
great good news you have sent to me in your savior son, Jesus! Fix my
eyes on him that I might know the power of your fulfilling Spirit.

MORNING

Fill me with your spirit this day,
O God, that I, too, might bring good news
to the poor and open the eyes of the blind.
(Prayers of Intercession)

EVENING

Let your spirit rest in me this night,
O God, releasing me and others who worry
from all oppressive thought.
(Prayers of Intercession)

GOD'S JOY IS MY STRENGTH
(Pray the Prayer of Our Savior.)

MORNING

May I walk today in the spirit of
Christ, proclaiming God's great favor.
In Jesus' name. Amen.

EVENING

May the blessings of the triune
God be upon us all this night.
In Jesus' name. Amen.

Friday, January 23

(Read 1 Corinthians 12:12–13)

MORNING
Creator God, I remember and honor
my baptism as I begin this day.

EVENING
Creator God, I thank you for my place in your communion.

God, I marvel at the flourishing complexity of your creation. It is beyond my comprehension. I am stunned by stars, by history, by the many wise leaders you have raised up for us throughout the generations. I am stunned, even, by myself—by my unique body and my distinct personality, which also display your infinite abundance. I am further awestruck that you have made all of this amazing variety One in Jesus Christ. In you, Creator God, wonders never cease.

MORNING
God, you know no boundaries. Open my eyes
to the many, mysterious ways in which your Spirit
moves through all whom I meet this day.
(Prayers of Intercession)

EVENING
God, I have judged others among your children
harshly today. Forgive me.
(Prayers of Intercession)

THE BLESSINGS OF THE TRIUNE GOD BE ON US ALL.
(Pray the Prayer of Our Savior.)

MORNING
Assured in Christ that I am filled
with the power of the Spirit, I go into
this day. In Jesus' name. Amen.

EVENING
Blessed by God through Christ,
I rest assured this night.
In Jesus' name. Amen.

Saturday, January 24

(Read 1 Corinthians 12:14–26)

MORNING
Tender Jesus, I have need of your presence this day.

EVENING
Tender Jesus, I rejoice in your presence this evening.

Teach me your compassion, Christ. All around me, I see others in the body of Christ whom I simply cannot understand. They seem too intolerant or too permissive, too narrow-minded or too loose, too prejudiced or too accommodating. And yet, it is not you, but I, who judge them. You reassure me that you have need of all the members of your body, that, mysteriously, many single members will be needed if your realm is to be made. Let me honor all as you do—with care and love.

MORNING
Compassionate Christ, comfort those
who are suffering today.
(Prayers of Intercession)

EVENING
Compassionate Christ, comfort those
who are suffering this night.
(Prayers of Intercession)

TENDER JESUS, I THANK YOU FOR MY PLACE IN YOUR COMMUNION.
(Pray the Prayer of Our Savior.)

MORNING	EVENING
May I meet the world with your compassion throughout this day. In Jesus' name. Amen.	Bless me tonight, sweet Christ, with the dissolution of all this day's dissention. In Jesus' name. Amen.

Sunday, January 25

(Read 1 Corinthians 12:27–31)

MORNING
God of all good gifts,
I open my heart to you this morning.

EVENING
God of all good gifts,
I thank you for the blessings of this day.

God, you reassure me that I have particular gifts for your realm. But sometimes I wonder just what they are. I see so many other gifted individuals in the world: teachers, preachers, healers, compassionate movers and shakers. What am I compared to them? I feel so inadequate. Show me what you would have me do. And remind me that, through Christ, I have the strength to do it.

MORNING
God, I offer prayers this morning for all the workers
in your realm but most especially for those who seem
confused and disheartened.
(Prayers of Intercession)

EVENING
God, bless all the workers in your realm
and relieve them of this day's burdens.
(Prayers of Intercession)

LET US ALL, TOGETHER, STRIVE FOR GREATER GIFTS.
(Pray the Prayer of Our Savior.)

MORNING
Bless me, God, that I might use
my particular gifts this day for you.
In Jesus' name.
Amen.

EVENING
Thank you, God, for the gift
of this day and for my part in making
it yours. In Jesus' name.
Amen.

Monday, January 26

(Read Psalm 71:1–3)

MORNING

Almighty God, anchor of the universe, today may you
be for me, my "towering crag and stronghold."

EVENING

Almighty God, have the words of my mouth
and the inclinations of my heart been a reflection of you this day?
Forgive me for those things I failed to do that would have
led others to seek your presence.

It is so easy, in the culture in which we live, to invest ourselves in the
promise of wealth and possessions. However, experience and time teach
us that behind all possessions and money is only the illusion of security.
Revealing God, unmask that illusion this day and help me to see you as
the source of all freedom and security.

MORNING

May those for whom I pray, my God, know the assurance
of your presence and the gift of your grace.
(Prayers of Intercession)

EVENING

For any who might have seen "you through me" this day,
I give you thanks and praise.
(Prayers of Intercession)

GOD IS OUR ROCK AND OUR REFUGE, THE ONE IN WHOM I AM SAVED AND SET FREE.
(Sing "If You but Trust in God to Guide You" or another familiar hymn.)

MORNING

Throughout this day, help me
to remember that you are ever present.
May my life this day be a mirror to
your strength and goodness.
Thanks be to Christ. Amen.

EVENING

For your presence with me this day,
O God, I offer you thanks and praise.
Now bring me rest that I may praise
you at the dawn of a new day.
Thanks be to Christ. Amen.

Tuesday, January 27

(Read Psalm 71:4–6)

MORNING
Savior God, once again I lean upon you this day, "my protector
since I left my mother's womb."

EVENING
Savior God, at the end of this day you are the source of my safety
and happiness. Have I truly given you the credit or tried to claim
it for myself? Help me remember you are my hope and my trust.

While I claim you as the foundation of my life, I must confess to the
distractions all about me that insulate me from your assuring presence.
I will soon be busy reading my e-mails and surfing the web, watching
television or listening to the radio, talking on my cell phone or opening my "snail mail." Through all the ding and clamor of my daily ritual, remind me of your presence, O God.

MORNING
O God, continual presence in my life, may those for whom I pray
sense the intimacy of your love this day.
(Prayers of Intercession)

EVENING
Since my earliest childhood, O God, you have been close to me.
Draw close to those for whom I pray.
(Prayers of Intercession)

GOD IS MY HOPE AND MY TRUST, MY COMPANION FROM BIRTH TO DEATH.
(Sing "O Savior, Let Me Walk with You" or another familiar hymn.)

MORNING
Remind me today that the true
source of strength is not in my abilities,
but in your presence. Help me to
remember to lean upon you throughout
this day. Thanks be to Christ. Amen.

EVENING
You have gentled the way for me
yet another day, O God. Keep close
throughout my sleep and be my guide
in the promise of another day.
Thanks be to Christ. Amen.

Wednesday, January 28

(Read Jeremiah 1:4–8)

MORNING

God, you have known me before I was born and have
called me to be your follower. Am I ready to do and say
those things to which you call me today?

EVENING

God, did I say those words that you wanted me to say?
Did I do what you called me to do? Grant that each day I might
grow more and more to be who you created me to be.

Do you not speak to us all, O God, and indicate the ministries to which
we are called? Is it not true that we are all "ministers" of your Church,
each one of us contributing our special word or deed or gift each day?
Help me to recognize the gifts you have given me and grant that I may
share them with others today.

MORNING

I pray this day for those who are confused or do not know
the gifts you have given to them. Grant them new knowledge
and clarity, O God.
(Prayers of Intercession)

EVENING

For all those who gave voice this day to the longings
of your heart, O God, I give thanks.
(Prayers of Intercession)

WHERE ARE YOU SENDING ME THIS DAY, O GOD?

WHAT ARE YOU CALLING UPON ME TO SAY?

(Sing "God, Speak to Me, That I May Speak" or another familiar hymn.)

MORNING

May the words of my mouth
and the meditations of my heart be
those to which you call me this day.
Thanks be to Christ. Amen.

EVENING

Give me rest, O God, that I might
find new energy to be the instrument
of grace to which you call me.
Thanks be to Christ. Amen.

Thursday, January 29

(Read Jeremiah 1:9–10)

MORNING

O God, stretch out your hand and touch my mouth
that my words might speak your truth this day.

EVENING

O God, did I speak the words you called me to speak?
Did I respond to the people around me as you would
have me respond?

How powerful, O God is your word. How great is its authority. Confronted with the world's might, it speaks truth to power, toppling down the Berlin walls of our lives and replacing them with bridges of trust, hope, and love. Confronted by the world's principalities and powers, your one little word can make them fall. Be that word to us today.

MORNING

Hear the names, O God, of those who are called to lead this day.
May they know the authority of your Word.
(Prayers of Intercession)

EVENING

Forgive me, O God, for however I have ignored you this day.
Give new words to my tongue and new actions
to my heart in the day to come.
(Prayers of Intercession)

REALMS CONTINUE TO BE PULLED DOWN AND UPROOTED
AS GOD CONTINUES TO BUILD AND TO PLANT.
(Sing "O God of Earth and Altar" or another familiar hymn.)

MORNING

Give me the courage this day
to say what you would have me say
and do what you would have me do.
Thanks be to Christ. Amen.

EVENING

May the words I speak and the
feelings I feel more truly reflect your
will in the day to come. Grant me
now, O God, your peace.
Thanks be to Christ. Amen.

Friday, January 30

(Read Luke 4:21–30)

MORNING

Loving Savior, help me to see you today in places where I do not
expect you, in people I do not associate with you, and in voices in which
I do not expect to hear you.

EVENING

Loving Savior, how inclusive was I today? Did I say a kind word to those whom
others have marginalized? Did I extend hospitality to those I do not understand?

You are never where we expect to find you, Jesus. Whenever we think
we have the corner on your truth, you show up on the periphery, associating with people who make us uncomfortable, letting in those we
have worked so hard to keep out, and forgiving those we have con-
demned. We are good at closing doors. Teach us how to unlock and
open the door of your grace.

MORNING

You are good at making me uncomfortable, Jesus. You know that I would
rather avoid certain people. Why are you calling me to reach out to them?
(Prayers of Intercession)

EVENING

You keep swimming against the stream, Jesus. Was I beside you
there today? Did I respond to the calls of those rejected and despised,
those forgotten and overlooked?
(Prayer of Intercession)

**IN JESUS WE FIND NOT THE GOD WE EXPECT,
BUT A GOD LARGER THAN WE CAN EVER IMAGINE.**
(Sing "My Song Is Love Unknown" or another familiar hymn.)

MORNING

Help me to see people as you see
them, Jesus. And then help me to act
accordingly, even if others murmur
against me. Thanks be to Christ.
Amen.

EVENING

It is so difficult to confront our culture
—to do and say things that put us out
of favor with the crowd. Grant me rest
and give me courage for tomorrow.
Thanks be to Christ. Amen.

Saturday, January 31

(Read 1 Corinthians 13:1–7)

MORNING

Caring Jesus, do I really have to love people today in a way that is kind and envies no one, that keeps no score of wrongs and does not gloat over others' sins? Do you know how hard that is?

EVENING

Caring Jesus, how did I do today? Was my love patient and kind, envious of no one, not boastful or conceited or rude, not selfish or quick to take offence? Did I improve any today?

You keep thinking "outside of the box," Jesus. With you everything keeps expanding. In a world of centrifugal forces where relationships between persons and nations keep being torn apart and broken, you bring this centripetal force to human history—binding together, healing the wounded, building bridges over brokenness.

MORNING

Help me to hear this day the voices of the loveless and the lost. And may I work for their well-being, even if it is to the detriment of my own well-being.
(Prayers of Intercession)

EVENING

You already know this, Jesus, but there were those I failed to love today as you have taught me to love. Help me to pray for them—and for myself.
(Prayers of Intercession)

THE LOVE OF GOD BINDS THE UNIVERSE TOGETHER AGAINST ALL THE FORCES THAT SEEK TO DESTROY IT.
(Sing "God Our Author and Creator" or another familiar hymn.)

MORNING

In all I do and say, help me to grow this day. Teach me to love as you would have me love. And should I stumble—and I probably will—grant me forgiveness and grace.
Thanks be to Christ. Amen.

EVENING

Is there truly nothing love cannot face? There are things I am frightened to face. Help me now to rest, that tomorrow I might face my fears and learn new ways to love.
Thanks be to Christ. Amen.

Sunday, February 1

(Read 1 Corinthians 13:8–13)

MORNING
Loving Jesus, today is one of those days when I only see "puzzling reflections in a mirror." I cannot see you face to face. Help clear away the clouds about me that I might better sense your presence.

EVENING
Loving Jesus, how childish were my thoughts today?
Did I live up to the mature personhood to which you call us?
Did faith, hope, and love guide my actions today?

You cut to the chase pretty quickly, Jesus. All of the things in which we put our faith and in which we invest our money—prophecy, ecstasy, knowledge—are all illusory. What is really "real" are faith, hope, and love. And love, you tell us, is the most powerful of the three—it is not an emotion, but rather an act of the will. It is not something we are to feel; it is something we are to do.

MORNING
So many cry out to you, O God. Grant that through my heart,
my mind, and my hands, I can be your agent of love in the world this day.
(Prayers of Intercession)

EVENING
O Jesus, author of our faith, hear those who cry out to you. Grant that they might be receptive to your loving presence that heals, restores, and makes new.
(Prayers of Intercession)

THREE THINGS LAST FOREVER: FAITH, HOPE, AND LOVE;

BUT THE GREATEST OF THEM IS LOVE.

(Sing "O Love That Will Not Let Me Go" or another familiar hymn.)

MORNING
Help me not to be fooled this day, O God. Grant that my long-term investment today might be in working for the well-being of others. Thanks be to Christ. Amen.

EVENING
Forgive my preoccupation with the partial; it is so tempting. This night give me new eyes to see and new ears to hear. Thanks be to Christ. Amen.

Monday, February 2 · Groundhog Day

(Read Psalm 138)

MORNING
God of words and deeds, I begin this new day praising your love
and faithfulness. Truly your glory is great and greatly to be praised.

EVENING
God of words and deeds, keep my praise from reflecting
only the words and experiences of others. May my praise spring
from my own knowledge of you acting in your world.

The psalmist begins with a personal burst of praise, which is rooted in
a particular experience of your activity, dear God. You answered a call
for rescue; you gave the psalmist boldness and courage in the face of the
anger of enemies. In light of such a personal experience, how else could
one respond! As I reflect on my personal experience of your activity,
may I, like the psalmist, burst forth in praise.

MORNING
God who acts, hear me as I give you praise for those
specific moments when you transformed my life.
(Prayers of Intercession)

EVENING
God who acts, hear me as I pray for family and friends
and the rulers of the earth, May all praise you, recognizing
your hand at work in moments of transformation.
(Prayers of Intercession)

IN THE MIDST OF ALL THE WORDS AND PHRASES THAT
CAN BE USED TO PRAISE GOD, THE PSALMIST CALLS ME TO ROOT PRAISE
IN MY PERSONAL EXPERIENCE OF GOD'S ACTIVITY.

MORNING
May all that I do today
prompt me to praise you,
O God. Thanks be to Christ.
Amen.

EVENING
I end this day knowing that you
will continue to transform my life and
your world. Thanks be to Christ.
Amen.

Tuesday, February 3

(Read Isaiah 6:11–8)

MORNING

High and Holy One, empower my life as I begin this day.
Frame each moment with the knowledge that your glory
fills the whole earth.

EVENING

High and Holy One, thank you for those moments in this day
when your presence made the ordinary extraordinary, when the
sense of your call to me was heightened and renewed.

The world is full of claims to the spectacular: spectacular special effects in movies, the spectacular nature of space travel. So many are these claims that the spectacular can lose its power to move us, to draw us into a reality greater than our own. In the vision of Isaiah, your awesome presence is revealed. May the depth of the extraordinary flow over my being and permeate my living throughout the day.

MORNING

God of the extraordinary, make me mindful of the signs
of your majesty and glory that fill the world around me.
(Prayers of Intercession)

EVENING

God of the extraordinary, I hear you calling me to see my life
within the framework of your glory. Help me to name how I
might continue to live that calling more completely.
(Prayers of Intercession)

**THANK YOU FOR THE FORGIVENESS AND RENEWAL
THAT ARE PART OF MY LIFE OF FAITH.**

MORNING	**EVENING**
I commit myself to looking	Affirmed by the signs of your presence
for signs of your spectacular presence	today, let me greet tomorrow's new-
in the world around me.	ness with a continuing sense of your
Thanks be to Christ.	greatness in the ordinary moments.
Amen.	Thanks be to Christ. Amen.

Wednesday, February 4

(Read Isaiah 6:9–13)

MORNING
Calling and empowering God, as I begin this day, remind me
of my call to ministry in your world. May I know throughout my
waking hours your power and holiness, which were present to Isaiah.

EVENING
Calling and empowering God, thank you for reminding me that
my call to ministry is centered in you. I do not do it alone.

As a result of his experience in the temple, Isaiah must have felt ready
to take on the world. God, he did not have to wait long for the unveil-
ing of your commission to him. How disappointing it must have been
to learn that it would commit him to a people who would neither listen nor respond. There would be no glory or adulation; instead, his call
would demand faithfulness and perseverance in the face of a lifetime of
seeming failure.

MORNING
Before I engage the world around me, center me, O God,
as I name before you those people and situations that will demand
faithfulness and perseverance today.
(Prayers of Intercession)

EVENING
What I have been a part of today, O God, I now commend
to your care. I ask for forgiveness where I have failed and a
sense of peace in all things.
(Prayers of Intercession)

ISAIAH REMAINED GOD'S FAITHFUL MESSENGER FOR ALMOST FORTY YEARS.

MORNING
I commit myself to ministry,
knowing that failure and success
will be part of this day.
Thanks be to Christ.
Amen.

EVENING
May I awaken to a new day
reconfirmed in my all, ready to
commit myself once again to ministry
in your world. Thanks be to Christ.
Amen.

Thursday, February 5

(Read Luke 5:1–5)

MORNING

Calling God, your call to recommit myself comes anew every morning.
Especially when I experience a sense of futility, you call me.
May this new day find me faithful in my response.

EVENING

Calling God, thank you for those moments in this day
when your call broke through my discouragement.

Sometimes in life, O God, a sense of futility is very strong. Peter's reluctance is easy to understand. He had been out all night and caught nothing, and then he was asked to go out again—out into even deeper water, where the storms could be intense. Why would there be fish now when last night had been such a failure? Peter must have seen only storms, more empty nets, and wasted effort. Yet he went.

MORNING

God, I begin this day mindful that you expect me to look
for new possibilities particularly in the midst of discouragement.
Hear me as I dream those possibilities into reality.
(Prayers of Intercession)

EVENING

God, you ask me to risk in spite of discouragement.
Hear me as I bring to you those things that might render me
unwilling to respond to your call.
(Prayers of Intercession)

PETER WENT BACK OUT EVEN THOUGH THERE WAS NO INDICATION
THAT HE WOULD BE MORE SUCCESSFUL THAN HE HAD BEEN THE NIGHT BEFORE.

MORNING

This day I commit myself to risk,
especially where it might seem most
fruitless. Thanks be to Christ. Amen.

EVENING

I look forward to a new morning that
will call me to things unimagined.
Thanks be to Christ. Amen.

Friday, February 6

(Read Luke 5:5–11)

MORNING
God of hope, I thank you for moments when hope springs to life,
nurtured by every endeavor.

EVENING
God of hope, speak to me words of forgiveness, acceptance, and
commission, which allow me to end this day in hope.

God, Peter had spent the whole night fishing, catching nothing. Your
child Jesus called him to go out again, and the result was beyond Peter's
imagination—a catch so large that the nets began to break; a catch so
large that another boat was filled and both began to sink. Confronted
by the miraculous, Peter was aware of his own insignificance and, like
your servant Isaiah, he needed to hear words of forgiveness, acceptance,
and commission.

MORNING
Hope-inspiring God, in the face of your miraculous presence,
I am conscious of my need for forgiveness. Hear me as I bring before
you those things that prevent hope from springing to life within me.
(Prayers of Intercession)

EVENING
Hope-inspiring God, hear my prayer for signs of hope
where there seems to be no hope.
(Prayers of Intercession)

HEAR JESUS' ASSURANCE TO PETER IN THIS WAY: "DON'T BE AFRAID.
FROM NOW ON YOU WILL DRAW PEOPLE INTO THE NET OF GOD'S LOVING CARE.
YOU WILL DRAW THEM INTO NEW HOPE."

MORNING
This day, as I launch into deeper
waters, I commit all I do and say to
your care. Thanks be to Christ.
Amen.

EVENING
I end this day in thanksgiving,
mindful of those moments in which
hope sprang to life within me.
Thanks be to Christ. Amen.

Saturday, February 7

(Read 1 Corinthians 15:1–11)

MORNING

God of good news, I am mindful of what has been passed on
to me by generations of faithful people. May I live this day
thankful for those essential matters.

EVENING

God of good news, I thank you for that great cloud of witnesses
who have confessed the faith before me.

God, when the Corinthians tried to live the gospel faithfully, a diversity
of viewpoints emerged, a diversity that strained their unity in your
gospel. In responding to this diversity, Paul repeats a very early creedal
statement: that your Child, Christ, died for our sins, that he was
buried, was raised, and appeared to believers. This, says Paul, is the
common ground of all who believe in and preach Christ.

MORNING

God of unity and diversity, I am conscious of those places
here and throughout the world where minds are closed to any
truth but their own. For them, hear my prayer.
(Prayers of Intercession)

EVENING

God of unity and diversity, hear my prayer for those
who live the good news in peaceful places. Hear my prayer
for those whose faith demands great sacrifice.
(Prayers of Intercession)

To LIVE FAITHFULLY, THE BALANCE BETWEEN UNITY AND DIVERSITY
IS PART OF OUR CALLING AS PEOPLE OF THE GOOD NEWS.

MORNING

May I be faithful in living and
speaking your gospel. May I be clear
about its authority and particularity in
my life. Thanks be to Christ. Amen.

EVENING

I end this day thankful for the
communion of faithful people who
continue to enrich my life of faith.
Thanks be to Christ. Amen.

Sunday, February 8

(Read Psalm 138)

MORNING

Loving and enduring God, I begin secure in the knowledge
that you have a purpose for me. This day, may I add my song
to the hymns of others who also have sung your praise.

EVENING

Loving and enduring God, keep praise ever present in my life.

Loving God, the psalmist is leading the community of the faithful to celebrate your presence in their midst at that very moment. The message is not a litany of your past actions but an act of worship, calling forth celebration, dancing, and singing. In that moment of praise their world is changed. May this same call to celebrate, to dance, to sing, to embrace a new world, be my response as I praise you within my community of faith.

MORNING

God who is present now, hear me as I name your activity
in my life. May I know afresh your call to celebrate
all you created me to be.
(Prayers of Intercession)

EVENING

I bring before you all whom you have created, praying
that they may be drawn into praise for your enduring love.
(Prayers of Intercession)

THE PSALMIST DECLARES GOD'S ENDLESS LOVE AND PURPOSE FOR ALL CREATION.

MORNING	EVENING
May each moment of today be a fresh opportunity to praise you. Thanks be to Christ. Amen.	Day in and day out, may my living know celebration and hope. In my faith may I be faithful. Thanks be to Christ. Amen.

Monday, February 9

(Read Psalm 1:1–3)

MORNING

Parent God, in all of our journeys this day, let us travel using your
counsel and guidance. We look to you for all things good.

EVENING

Parent God, you give us a feeling of warmth and love
as we move through this difficult world. We give you thanks
for your tender mercy.

O Loving God, you have provided us a perfect earth and universe in
which to live, yet we live our lives in an imperfect way. Let us not be so
concerned about ourselves, as we are about others. Help us not to be
worried about our earthly security, but rather let us give thanks for our
spiritual eternity. Let us be guided by you each minute of the day. You
are our eternal protector.

MORNING

Help us this day to look for you, in everything we see,
Loving God, and think of you in everything we do.
(Prayers of Intercession)

EVENING

Let us count all of the good things
that you have led us to during this day.
(Prayers of Intercession)

PRAY WHERE YOU ARE BECAUSE GOD IS EVERYWHERE.
(Pray the Prayer of Our Savior.)

MORNING

Nothing brings greater meaning
or depth to life than prayer. Thank you,
Loving God, for being available to us
every second of our life.
In Jesus' name, I pray. Amen.

EVENING

Pray in your resting, as sleep
is the prayer of a person secure in
God's life. In Jesus' name,
I pray. Amen.

Tuesday, February 10

(Read Psalm 1:4–6)

MORNING
Precious Jesus, help me this day to walk in your footsteps.

EVENING
Precious Jesus, may I close this day knowing
that I have served you to the best of my ability.

We realize, Jesus, that we have been given freedom of choice in everything we do, and there is an opposite and equal force tugging at us at each crossroad. Let us choose righteousness over sin at every junction. We know we will definitely have eternal life; help us make the proper choices so that it will be in the right direction. May we constantly be reminded of your commandments and covenant and be able to meet your judgment with joy, thanksgiving, and love.

MORNING
Let us dismiss personal fear and pride from ourselves,
as we go through this morning.
(Prayers of Intercession)

EVENING
Thank you, Jesus, for being our companion throughout this day.
(Prayers of Intercession)

FOLLOWING GOD ALLOWS US TO GIVE UP THE NEED TO CONTROL PEOPLE AND EVENTS.
(Pray the Prayer of Our Savior.)

MORNING
Thank you, Jesus, for being
by our side as we begin this beautiful
morning. In Jesus' name, I pray.
Amen.

EVENING
Jesus, it has been a wonderful day
because of your presence.
In Jesus' name, I pray.
Amen.

Wednesday, February 11

(Read Jeremiah 17:5–8)

MORNING
Loving God, if you can handle eternity,
with your help I can certainly handle today.

EVENING
Loving God, thank you for holding my hand
as I walked through this day.

O Loving God, we pray as Jesus taught us, "Thy will be done." Let us not be upset that your will is not always our desire. We are often selfish in asking for things we may not receive. Let us seek to understand and accept your will in our lives, as only you know what is best for us. Let us turn our daily inconveniences over to you for help and guidance. Thank you for your ever-loving presence.

MORNING
God gives us our first day and our last day,
and what happens in between is up to us.
(Prayers of Intercession)

EVENING
This day ends in peace for us, only because of your blessings.
(Prayers of Intercession)

GOD'S PEOPLE DESERVE A MEASURE OF CHRISTIAN JOY IF THEY HAVE DONE SOMETHING GOOD, BUT THEY SHOULD ONLY LOOK BACK AT THAT DEED IF IT INSPIRES THEM TO DO SOMETHING GREATER IN THE FUTURE.
(Pray the Prayer of Our Savior.)

MORNING
Loving God, as we awake this
morning, we give thanks for the lights
and sounds of nature. In Jesus' name,
I pray. Amen.

EVENING
Loving God, as we end this day
we marvel at your beautiful sunsets,
which bring us divine beauty and
peace. In Jesus' name, I pray.
Amen.

Thursday, February 12 · Lincoln's Birthday

(Read Jeremiah 17:9–10)

MORNING

Gracious God, help us to make the right choices as we begin this
day. You alone know all of our faults and desires.

EVENING

Gracious God, though we have stumbled many times daily, you are
always there to protect us and be our refuge.

Gracious God, we know that your love is eternal even though we fall
short of your expectations. We ask forgiveness for our continued sins.
We know we must also forgive others before we can be forgiven. Help
us to make such actions a permanent attitude rather than just an occa-
sional act. You have told us that you love us as much as the person we
love the least. May the Holy Spirit guide us.

MORNING

May we live this day as you would have us to do.
Keep us from sin and temptation. Give us the strength
of righteousness.
(Prayers of Intercession)

EVENING

It is so wonderful that we can talk to you through prayer.
Thank you for bending down to listen.
(Prayers of Intercession)

THE GOSPEL OF GOD'S GRACE BEGINS AND ENDS WITH FORGIVENESS.
(Pray the Prayer of Our Savior.)

MORNING	**EVENING**
On our very best day,	Loving Parent, help us each day
we are just sinners saved by grace.	to pass on your grace and forgiveness
In Jesus' name, I pray.	to others. In Jesus' name,
Amen.	I pray. Amen.

Friday, February 13

(Read Luke 6:17–26)

MORNING

O Wonderful Savior, on this day let us tell everyone
in our family that, through you, we love them. We share
our family love because you have taught us to do so.

EVENING

O Wonderful Savior, we cross the paths of many people
each day. Some we enjoy and some we do not. We realize that
everyone is equal in your sight. Let us act in the same manner.

Faithful Parent, you have shown that you can heal our physical and mental problems. Our earthly problems are not cured by ourselves or by others. All good things we experience come from you. When we have an especially good day and everything is perfect, it is a gift from you, not of our own making. When we have a difficult day, we know you are our protector and refuge.

MORNING

Faithful Parent, on this day, it is so wonderful
to feel your Holy Spirit within us.
(Prayers of Intercession)

EVENING

Faithful Parent, at this day's end, we know we have made mistakes,
but we give thanks for the continued warmth of your love.
(Prayers of Intercession)

YOU DON'T NEED TO KNOW WHERE YOU ARE GOING, IF YOU KNOW GOD IS LEADING.
(Pray the Prayer of Our Savior.)

MORNING

As we move through this day,
let us pray as if everything depends on
God. In Jesus' name, I pray.
Amen.

EVENING

As this day ends, let us remember
Apostle Paul's request for us to pray
without ceasing. In Jesus' name,
I pray. Amen.

Saturday, February 14 · Valentine's Day

(Read 1 Corinthians 15:12–15)

MORNING

Loving Jesus, you have given us eternal life by your sacrifice
on the cross. Allow us to repent of our sins so that we
may be worthy of such a wonderful gift.

EVENING

Loving Jesus, since repentance means to change,
let our changes be permanent in our lives.

Risen Jesus, there was doubt about your resurrection but only by people who refused to accept your love and receive your grace. Your rising from the dead separates Christianity from any other religion in the world. Your sacrifice on the cross is overwhelming. The event sometimes seems so complex to us, yet it is so simple. We are forgiven of our sins. You are the living God eternal. Your love is eternal. We are eternal.

MORNING

O Savior, your grace has been given to us as a loving gift.
Let us go about this day serving you by helping others.
Let us help to make good things happen in your name.
(Prayers of Intercession)

EVENING

O Savior, we know your grace is given to us because of what
we believe, not because of what we do. By your Holy Spirit,
help us to spread your word daily.
(Prayers of Intercession)

DO NOT BE AFRAID OF TOMORROW BECAUSE GOD IS ALREADY THERE.
(Pray the Prayer of Our Savior.)

MORNING

Dear God, thank you for
sending us into this day with your
love. In Jesus' name, I pray.
Amen.

EVENING

Dear God, as we rest this evening,
help us to prepare for a tomorrow
of serving you. In Jesus' name, I pray.
Amen.

Sunday, February 15

(Read 1 Corinthians 15:16–20)

MORNING
Wonderful Savior, we go through this day giving thanks to you
for your resurrection and the knowledge that we are secure
in eternal life. What a wonderful feeling!

EVENING
Wonderful Savior, let us share the good news of salvation
with family, friends, and strangers. You suffered so much for us.
We must all strive to be your living disciples.

Christ Jesus, there is no doubt about your resurrection. You appeared before the apostles and they spent the rest of their lives telling the story. You appeared before many people, including more than five hundred at one time. History books and the Bible tell of you leaving an empty tomb. You told the apostles they were blessed because they had seen you and believed, and that we who have not seen will be blessed if we believe. I believe.

MORNING
Thank you for giving us another day that we can live in your Holy Spirit.
(Prayers of Intercession)

EVENING
May the Holy Spirit calm our thoughts and continue
to fuel our actions in your name.
(Prayers of Intercession)

GOD LOVES US THE WAY WE ARE BUT REFUSES TO LEAVE US THAT WAY.
(Pray the Prayer of Our Savior.)

MORNING	EVENING
O God, we have wars, floods, and political problems around the world. We also have friendship, love, and beauty. Let us live our lives as a sermon, witnessing for you and striving for peace. In Jesus' name, I pray. Amen.	Dear God, let us continue to find ways to spread our Christian love. We must find it in our hearts to love difficult people. We seek your help. Let us not be afraid to take chances in your name. In Jesus' name, I pray. Amen.

Monday, February 16 · President's Day—U.S.A.

(Read Psalm 99)

MORNING
God, thank you for the gift of a mind
and body refreshed.

EVENING
God, Holy Scripture proclaims your righteousness.
Alleluia.

God, you are great, holy, exalted above the earth. However, you are not "above it all." Creator God, you seek a relationship with humankind. You dispense justice, answer us when we call, have compassion, and forgive us. In the face of this majesty I kneel to worship. God, I ask for new eyes to see as you see, to work for justice, and to have compassion for all people.

MORNING
I pray for the strength and courage to help
and heal the brokenhearted.
(Prayers of Intercession)

EVENING
We can rest in sleep because our God reigns.
For those who cannot find rest, I pray.
(Prayers of Intercession)

IN COMPANY WITH MOSES, AARON, SAMUEL,

AND THE HOST OF SAINTS WHO HAVE GONE BEFORE ME, I PRAY.

(Pray the Prayer of Our Savior.)

MORNING
I pray to keep my eyes focused
on you, Creator. Grant that I may use
my life to give you glory. In the name
of the Christ. Amen.

EVENING
Parent God, you shelter the bird
in its nest. Guard my slumber, I pray.
In the name of the Christ.
Amen.

Tuesday, February 17

(Read Exodus 34:29–35)

MORNING
God of the covenant, you love and forgive your people.
I pray that I too will be empowered to love and forgive
those I meet this day.

EVENING
God of the covenant, you are like no other god.
Reshape me, as I rest, to fit your will for me.

God, Moses talked to you and bargained, asking mercy and forgiveness for his stiff-necked people. Stiff necks are a pain for those who own them and those who must deal with them. How much better to glow and to be radiant because we know you and are working to keep the covenant.

MORNING
God of new beginnings and second chances, you gave Moses
a second set of stone tablets after the first set was broken. This morning
is a new beginning for me. I pray for all who seek a new start.
(Prayers of Intercession)

EVENING
O Divine One, the Israelites were awed and frightened
by Moses' face, which glowed from his encounter with you.
I am filled with wonder that you care for each one of us.
Cradle in your care those who are fearful this night.
(Prayers of Intercession)

GOD SAID, "YOU WILL HAVE NO OTHER GODS BEFORE ME."
(Pray the Prayer of Our Savior.)

MORNING
Our God is holy. On this new day
may holiness shine on all creation.
In the name of the Christ.
Amen.

EVENING
Moses was a bridge between
God and Israel. I fall on my knees
in grateful thanksgiving as I go to my
rest this night. In the name
of the Christ. Amen.

Wednesday, February 18

(Read Luke 9:28–36)

MORNING

Powerful God, you sent visions on the mountaintop.
Nothing could prepare the disciples for the majesty of the transfiguration.
I arise this day not knowing what joy may await me.

EVENING

Powerful God, the end of this day has come and I am weary.
Guard my rest this night and renew my strength.

God, the glory in this passage brings the Old Testament to mind. A pillar of cloud led the Israelites as they fled from Pharaoh, and when the Egyptian army came close the cloud moved behind them to protect them from that army. In your book of Luke, the unnatural brilliance of your Son's appearance and a cloud that overshadowed them were a mystical experience that terrified Peter, James, and John. Some experiences are to be kept in our hearts and pondered.

MORNING

God of the morning, I arise from sleep strengthened for work.
I pray for those who seek meaning in the work they have to do.
(Prayers of Intercession)

EVENING

God of the evening, it is time to sleep. For those who live
in poverty and must sleep on city streets, I pray.
(Prayers of Intercession)

YOU ARE THE CHOSEN ONE, O CHRIST. I THANK GOD FOR THIS ASTOUNDING GIFT.
(Pray the Prayer of Our Savior.)

MORNING

Prepare me for the unexpected
this day. Prepare me for a miracle.
In the name of the Christ.
Amen.

EVENING

Christ, the Son of Humankind,
had nowhere to lay his head. May we
see the face of Christ in the poor.
In the name of the Christ.
Amen.

Thursday, February 19

(Read Luke 9:28–31)

MORNING
God of Grace and Glory,
I am thankful for this beautiful morning.

EVENING
God of Grace and Glory,
grant me release from the labors of this day.

God, I behold the mysterious manifestations of your glory. Jesus speaks with the spirits of Elijah and Moses about his departure, his death. The vision on the mountaintop ends, at last, with silence. The disciples are awed and will ponder this time apart in the days to come.

MORNING
Jesus was God's Chosen One.
I pray for those who do not yet believe;
help their unbelief.
(Prayers of Intercession)

EVENING
O Light, death cannot extinguish you.
I pray for others to see your light in their darkness
on this and all dark nights.
(Prayers of Intercession)

DAZZLING, TRANSFIGURED CHRIST, HAVE MERCY ON ME, A SINNER.
(Pray the Prayer of Our Savior.)

MORNING
Mountaintop God, keep me steady today. I belong to you in good times and bad times. In the name of the Christ. Amen.

EVENING
Jesus, you have experienced all that being human can be. You have known sorrow and joy. Keep me safe. In the name of the Christ. Amen.

Friday, February 20

(Read Luke 9:37–42)

MORNING
Compassionate Jesus, you cast out the demons
from this person's son. Cast out the fears that darken my mind
and send me out into the light of your new day.

EVENING
Compassionate Jesus, I release the cares of this day to you.
You are the great healer. I seek my bed.

Jesus, your love and patience towards us is overwhelming. You left your disciples to care for the crowds of people who followed you everywhere. A father came in sorrow seeking healing for his demon-possessed child, yet your disciples could not cast out the demons—so they turned to you. Loving Jesus, in the midst of your distress over the failure of the disciples, you still had compassion and made the boy well.

MORNING
Jesus, even as you think of your approaching passion, you take pity
on the hurting ones. I pray for the sick. May they be healed.
(Prayers of Intercession)

EVENING
O Righteous One, you alone are holy and worthy of praise.
I know you answer prayer. I pray for all whose minds
and hearts are aching.
(Prayers of Intercession)

KEEP ME, JESUS, FROM FAITHLESSNESS AND PERVERSE ACTIONS.
(Pray the Prayer of Our Savior.)

MORNING
Christ Jesus came that we might
have life abundant. I thank you.
In the name of the Christ.
Amen.

EVENING
Use me to be your hands and feet.
Make me faithful. In the name
of the Christ.
Amen.

Saturday, February 21

(Read 2 Corinthians 3:12–17)

MORNING

Thank you, Risen Christ;
I am filled with hope for this brand new morning.
You are the reason for my hope.

EVENING

Thank you, Risen Christ,
for your hope that gives me power for my life.
No veil obscures my vision of you.

God, Paul says that Jesus is the Spirit and where the Spirit is, there is freedom. Moses was the intermediary between you and the people of Israel. In Christ I can be bold. I can approach your Son directly. There is no veil between us. He said that when we see him, we have seen you, who sent him.

MORNING

With Jesus everything is new.
The old ways and laws do not apply.
I pray for newness for the tired and weary.
(Prayers of Intercession)

EVENING

Hope-bearing Christ, you gave me
this day to serve you. I pray for strength
for those who must work at night.
(Prayers of Intercession)

CHRIST, THE HOPE OF THE ENTIRE WORLD, YOU ARE WORTHY TO BE PRAISED.
(Pray the Prayer of Our Savior.)

MORNING

Glory and honor and praise and
thanksgiving to our Risen Savior.
In the name of Christ.
Amen.

EVENING

As the day ends and the
shadows creep, I remember the
Light who came for all.
In the name of Christ. Amen.

Sunday, February 22

Transfiguration Sunday · Washington's Birthday

(Read 2 Corinthians 3:18, 4:1–2)

MORNING

Omniscient God, changed from glory into glory, it is too much
for this mortal to absorb. Grant me just a small degree of your glory,
Infinite One, so you may use me as your disciple.

EVENING

Omniscient God, degrees of glory, varieties of gifts—with these I
bow in humble adoration and ask to be worthy of such things.

The week leading up to this Sabbath day has been truly one degree of
glory after another as I prayed my way through the scriptures. Paul says
that whenever we look upon the Savior we receive a portion of his glory.
Wow. God, you are greater than our minds can imagine. Love and glory
and hope and power, and you came to earth in the form of the glorious
Christ. I think on these things.

MORNING

Jesus, remember me, when you come into your realm.
I pray for the glorious time when all acknowledge you as supreme.
(Prayers of Intercession)

EVENING

Thank you for this Sabbath day.
May all peoples experience your Sabbath rest.
(Prayers of Intercession)

I TURN TO YOU AND I SEE YOUR GLORY.
(Pray the Prayer of Our Savior.)

MORNING	EVENING
Change me, Christ, so that I may be more like you. In the name of the Christ. Amen.	We have this ministry by the mercy of God. I will not lose heart. In the name of the Christ. Amen.

Monday, February 23

(Read Luke 4:1–4)

MORNING

Great and gracious God, who never abandons us in times of testing,
help me now to recognize and confess where I am most vulnerable to evil's
crafty lures of temptation. May your abundant grace help me to measure up
to the tests and challenges you want me to face today.

EVENING

Great and gracious God, I truly thank you for traveling beside me during
today's ups and downs. Forgive me for times when I may have stumbled.
Thank you for times when your grace enabled me to be steadfast.

I realize that Jesus refused to turn the hard rock of tough survival into quick
and easy "fast food," and I wonder, O God, how I can ever have what it
takes to reject the easy way out. Help me to hang in there and make those
difficult decisions that, with your blessings, can make a vital difference.

MORNING

Guide me during my contacts today with these persons
regarding crucial issues and concerns.
(Prayers of Intercession)

EVENING

Tonight I pray on behalf of special persons who, like me,
need your blessing in facing life's challenges.
(Prayers of Intercession)

**INSTEAD OF THE WORLD'S EASILY AVAILABLE "JUNK FOOD,"
THE BREAD AND THE WINE OF YOUR SPIRIT ARE WELL WORTH WAITING FOR.**

MORNING

When life seems difficult today, may I
turn to your Child, Jesus, who is ever
ready to share his bread and his cup to
nourish my spirit in times of testing.
In the name of the Christ, I pray. Amen.

EVENING

Refresh me this night with the cup
of your overflowing peace, which gives
me joyful confidence to face whatever
tomorrow brings my way. In the name
of the Christ, I pray. Amen.

Tuesday, February 24

(Read Luke 4:5–8)

MORNING
Holy God, who alone is worthy of worship and adoration,
rekindle the flickering light of my fickle devotion into a reliable flame
of joyful and steadfast commitment to you.

EVENING
Holy God, I thank you for guiding me whenever it has been difficult to
recognize clearly what is truly holy or cleverly seductive. Help me sort out my
life's priorities and make a fresh start tomorrow with greater wisdom and courage.

God, I know that Jesus refused to accept evil's glamour of "go for the
gold" but did accept your demands for the highest and best. I can even
recall when I have been tempted to settle for life's mediocre "goodies"
instead of holding out for the best that you would give me. Help me,
O God, to follow your narrow, difficult pathway regardless of how
sweet life in the "fast lane" always seems to be.

MORNING
Give me what it takes in these tempting situations
to choose what you want instead of settling for less.
(Prayers of Intercession)

EVENING
Tonight I pray on behalf of special persons who, like me,
are confronted with tempting choices.
(Prayers of Intercession)

GOD'S MOST DIFFICULT PATH MAKES US SLOW DOWN AND LIVE, IN CONTRAST
TO LIVING LIFE IN THE "FAST LANE," HEADED HELL-BENT FOR A DEADLY COLLISION.

MORNING
With so many wolves disguised
as sheep wherever I go, help me to
hear and follow the voice of the
Good Shepherd today. In the name
of the Christ, I pray. Amen.

EVENING
Use this night's rest, O God, to hush
all the voices clamoring for my
attention and to fine-tune my spirit
to your wavelength. In the name
of the Christ, I pray. Amen.

Wednesday, February 25 · Ash Wednesday

(Read Luke 4:9–13)

MORNING

Almighty God, who protects and rescues your children from peril,
help me reject temptation. May I never take your love for granted but
always seek your approval and guidance before I take action.

EVENING

Almighty God, I thank you for seeking to get me back on track
whenever I have strayed off course. Continue to help me choose
between genuine and ill-advised risks.

I consider how Jesus refused to take the challenge of evil's "bungee jump." I am ashamed of the ways I expect you, Savior God, to bail me out whenever I get myself out on a limb—without ever having asked for your guidance ahead of time. Make me more committed, O God, to keep in touch with you, especially in regard to those life concerns when I might assume it isn't necessary to bother you.

MORNING

Help me today to avoid taking foolish chances in risky situations.
(Prayers of Intercession)

EVENING

Tonight I pray on behalf of special persons who,
like me, can go off the deep end.
(Prayers of Intercession)

GOD IS EVER READY TO HELP ME FIND ANSWERS TO FRUSTRATING OR
BAFFLING SITUATIONS EVEN WHEN I AM TEMPTED TO JUMP TO CONCLUSIONS
WITHOUT TURNING TO GOD FIRST.

MORNING	**EVENING**
Today let me stop trying your patience and instead try responding to your patient efforts to steer me straight. In the name of the Christ, I pray. Amen.	Forgive me for being difficult. Give to me grace, wisdom, and patience to stay in close partnership with you. In the name of the Christ, I pray. Amen.

Thursday, February 26

(Read Deuteronomy 26:1–11)

MORNING

Gracious God, who has blessed me abundantly, may my talents and resources be offered first to you before I consider my own wants and needs. Keep me aware of past generations whose struggles have given me a worthy example to follow.

EVENING

Gracious God, who calls me to give you my very best, thank you for the opportunities to try to make a vital difference in the lives of others. Help me to know the best ways to expend my time and energy for your sake.

Just as the people of Israel needed to be reminded of the hardships of slave labor in Egypt, so we, too, O God, need to be reminded of whoever in our own past had to endure sweatshop working conditions. In these troubled times of corporate downsizing and layoffs of highly gifted people, show us, O God, how to find the most fruitful outlets for our talents.

MORNING

Show me the difference between what is good, better, and best in situations when I will be called to serve you today.
(Prayers of Intercession)

EVENING

Tonight I pray on behalf of special persons who, like me, may wonder what is the best way to give you first priority in the use of our gifts.
(Prayers of Intercession)

WHEN WE SEEK FIRST TO LEARN WHAT GOD WANTS ABUNDANTLY FROM US, WE UNDERSTAND MORE CLEARLY WHAT GOD HAS GIVEN ABUNDANTLY TO US.

MORNING

Help me joyfully to put your "first things first" today. In the name of the Christ, I pray. Amen.

EVENING

Forgive me whenever I failed to make your priorities first. Help me make a vital difference. In the name of the Christ, I pray. Amen.

Friday, February 27

(Read Psalm 91:1–2)

MORNING

Great Protector, I thank you that when life seems overwhelming
and perplexing, my troubled heart can find peace within the shelter
of your steadfast care. Today, be my refuge, so that I can face life squarely,
drawing upon your strength to sustain my spirit.

EVENING

Great protector, I thank you for watching over me today
and helping me to thrive and survive, in spite of my life's baffling twists
and turns. Tonight let me come closer to you and know your
reassurance that you are truly in charge.

Teach me, O God, how to take refuge in you when the storms of life overtake me. Instead of running away from life's challenges, help me to face them and move forward through them until, with your protection, I reach the calm and quiet place at the very center of the storm, where your peace can be found.

MORNING

I need your protection today if a storm breaks loose in these situations.
(Prayers of Intercession)

EVENING

Tonight I pray for these special persons who, like me,
need your help to safely ride out the storms in our lives.
(Prayers of Intercession)

**AS OUR REFUGE AND SHELTER, GOD PROVIDES ONLY THE VERY BEST
TO SEE US THROUGH LIFE'S VERY WORST.**

MORNING

Today when I face life,
let me know, O God, that shelter
is at hand when I need it.
In the name of the Christ,
I pray. Amen.

EVENING

Let me take refuge tonight
within the embrace of your loving
care and discover once again how
great is your love. In the name
of the Christ, I pray. Amen.

Saturday, February 28

(Read Psalm 91:9–16)

MORNING

Savior God, you have promised that I can put my trust in the available power
of your salvation. How glad I am that you will surely answer when I call upon you,
knowing that your vigilant eye is ever on me and on even the littlest sparrow.

EVENING

Savior God, I thank you for being there when I needed you today.
Help me to be gratefully aware of the ways in which you step in quickly at my
time of need. Because your grace has brought me safely through all my toils and
troubles, help me to face the future with greater confidence that you won't quit on
me and that your grace will someday lead me safely to your eternal home.

Today's reading from the Psalms makes it clear, O God, that you want
to establish and maintain a lifelong covenant, reassuring me that you
will indeed deliver and protect me and fill my life with deepest satis-
faction and fulfillment. Help me as a covenant partner to follow your
pathway, keeping the door of my heart open to you, so that nothing can
hinder you from keeping your promise of salvation to me.

MORNING

Here is what is happening today when I will want
to count upon your protection and deliverance.
(Prayers of Intercession)

EVENING

Tonight I pray for these special persons who, like me,
will need your quick hand to rescue them if trouble breaks loose.
(Prayers of Intercession)

**CONFESSING OUR WEAKNESS OPENS THE DOOR FOR GOD
TO SEND US ABUNDANT STRENGTH.**

MORNING	EVENING
May this day give me the satisfaction of living in close partnership with you. In the name of the Christ, I pray. Amen.	May your peace bring reassurance that I am safe in your hands at all times. In the name of the Christ, I pray. Amen.

Sunday, February 29

(Read Romans 10:8b–13)

MORNING

Gracious God, who through Jesus has offered salvation to all,
sometimes I am afraid to believe that you truly love me just as I am.
Help me to know the peace of your presence and the embrace
of your love, which will never forsake me.

EVENING

Gracious God, it seems incredible that simply a heartfelt prayer,
"I want Jesus as my Savior," is enough for me to grasp your outstretched
hand. Thank you for continuing to reach out to me, even when I find it
hard to believe how simple it is to respond to you.

So much, O God, depends upon whether I can believe that Jesus really
was raised from the dead. Whenever I find myself doubting the Easter
miracle of resurrection, I find myself controlled by a fear that takes all
the joy out of life. Help me, Savior God, to meet the risen Christ ex-
tending a hand to me and inviting me on the journey each day.

MORNING

God, here are situations in my life that make it hard for me
sometimes to feel close to you and to Jesus.
(Prayers of Intercession)

EVENING

Tonight I pray for these special persons who, like me, at times are whistling
softly a song of faith in the spirit of anxious doubt instead of singing joyfully
a hallelujah chorus with robust confidence in the risen Christ.
(Prayers of Intercession)

**THE RISEN CHRIST IS SOMEONE I CAN KNOW NOW ON EARTH
AND NOT JUST LATER IN HEAVEN.**

MORNING

Precious Savior, take my hand today
so I know you are real. In the name
of the Christ, I pray.
Amen.

EVENING

God, tonight make it simple for me
to know the presence of you and Jesus
at my bedside. In the name
of the Christ, I pray. Amen.

Monday, March 1

(Read Genesis 15:1–12, 17, 18)

MORNING
Extravagant and Loving God,
I am in awe as I think of your gifts to me.

EVENING
Extravagant and Loving God,
I see the countless stars tonight
and remember your gifts.

God, when I think of our ancestors in the faith, I marvel that they spoke to you so freely. Abram's faith challenges me. But it is your power that astounds me. The one who created the stars knows we can never count them all. Holy God, you are light in the darkness, a shield against danger. When I feel your presence, I am not afraid. Give me courage to follow wherever you may lead.

MORNING
I do not know what challenges this day may bring.
Thank you, God, for being with me.
(Prayers of Intercession)

EVENING
Dear God, thank you for all this day has brought me.
(Prayers of Intercession)

I PRAY FOR . . .
(Pray the Prayer of Our Savior.)

MORNING
Today, help me keep my promises
to you and to the people in my life.
Thanks be to God.
Amen.

EVENING
As I prepare for sleep I will
close my eyes and quietly count the
blessings of this day.
Thanks be to God.
Amen.

Tuesday, March 2

(Read Psalm 27:1–5)

MORNING

Dear God, I woke up this morning and saw the sun rise.
As I see a new day's light, I remember your light and guidance.

EVENING

Dear God, now even as the sunlight begins to fade,
I know that you still give light to my life.

I am fearful. I read and listen to the news. I learn of crimes in my own city, of terror in the nation, of wars and starvation around the world. I am overwhelmed with the evil that seems to thrive. The world is full of angry, violent people. I want to run and hide. I ask, how can I protect myself? Then I remember your presence always with me, God, and I feel your protection. I become calm as I reflect that you are with me in all times and places.

MORNING

I am confident that whatever difficulties I face today,
you will be with me, God. I thank you for your comforting presence.
(Prayers of Intercession)

EVENING

Thank you, God, for being with me today.
You still my anxiety and calm my fears.
May everyone find your peace.
(Prayers of Intercession)

I PRAY FOR . . .
(Pray the Prayer of Our Savior.)

MORNING

As I go about my day,
may I remember that everyone I meet
is your child and that you love us all.
Thanks be to God. Amen.

EVENING

Dear God, today the news
was frightening, but I remember that
the world is in your hands.
Thanks be to God. Amen.

Wednesday, March 3

(Read Psalm 27:6–14)

MORNING

God, can you hear me? I need to know that you are near
and that you will be with me throughout all of this day.

EVENING

God, through this day, I felt your presence many times.
Be with me now as the day ends.

God, how can I praise you as I go about my day? Could I sing as I drive to work? Can I pray before I eat my lunch? Trusting God, as I meet all the different people who will cross my path this day, may a confident smile be the sign of my trust in you? I pray that my path will be smooth today, that the people I have to deal with will be trustworthy, that my friends and family will be on my side. But I know that whatever happens, God, you will be with me. I will be aware of your goodness from morning until night.

MORNING

Help me, God, to use the experience of this day
to learn more about your goodness and love. Make me aware
of your presence every moment.
(Prayers of Intercession)

EVENING

Dear God, I take these few moments to reflect on my day
and to remember the times when I felt your presence.
Thank you for being with me.
(Prayers of Intercession)

I PRAY FOR . . .
(Pray the Prayer of Our Savior.)

MORNING

As my day begins, dear God,
I will look for signs of your holy
presence and I will praise you.
Thanks be to God. Amen.

EVENING

The day has been long and I am
ready for sleep. Help me to slow down
and let go of all that has happened.
Thanks be to God. Amen.

Thursday, March 4

(Read Philippians 3:17–4:1)

MORNING

Loving God, I think of all the examples of faithfulness
recorded in your Holy Scriptures. I pray that, day after day,
you will help me to imitate them and to become like them.

EVENING

Loving God, I come to you now with the experiences of my day.
I know that many times I fell short of the goals I had set
for myself, and I ask for your forgiveness.

I am often torn between the two worlds that claim me. Paul calls on
Christians to be citizens of heaven while the world calls in a louder voice.
Compete! Be successful! Buy this. It will make you beautiful. Wear that;
you will be in style. In the race to succeed at what I do, it is so easy to
neglect time for reading, for reflection, and for prayer. But, Loving God,
when I keep my focus on my faith in Jesus Christ, when I remember with
thanks his dying on the cross, then my priorities seem to easily sort themselves out. I am then at peace with myself and the world.

MORNING

I thank you, God, for your gift of new life in Jesus Christ.
By his death and resurrection I have been made a citizen of heaven.
(Prayers of Intercession)

EVENING

Thank you, God, for this day and for the times when I felt
at peace with my life. I pray that those with whom I had contact
today felt that I treated them with fairness and respect.
(Prayers of Intercession)

I PRAY FOR . . .

(Pray the Prayer of Our Savior.)

MORNING

Just for today, God, may I stop my
busy-ness and tend to my spirit. Just
for today. Thanks be to God. Amen.

EVENING

As I prepare for sleep, let me set aside all
my earthly worries and concerns. May I
always rest in you. Thanks be to God.
Amen.

Friday, March 5

(Read Luke 13:31–33)

MORNING

Good morning, God. As I think about the day ahead of me,
I need to feel the courage and strength that comes from you.

EVENING

Good evening, God; my day is nearly over and I am weary and carrying
many burdens. Please come to me, God, so that I may lay them down.

God, Jesus' courage in this passage astounds me. He called the king a fox—a sly vicious killer. This is not "gentle Jesus meek and mild"; this is not a cooing baby in a manger. This is an angry prophet who speaks the truth clearly and without fear. Jesus is so firm in his calling and purpose. I long for that same certainty. I long for the courage to name and to speak against all that is hindering your realm. It is so easy to confuse being Christian with being nice. It is so easy to confuse working for your peaceable realm with simply "going along to get along." Oh, I long for courage.

MORNING

God, I know that you will be with me this day and that
your presence will guide me and give me strength. Thank you.
(Prayers of Intercession)

EVENING

God, I thank you for the times during the day when you gave me
the right words to speak and the courage to speak them.
(Prayers of Intercession)

I PRAY FOR . . .

(Pray the Prayer of Our Savior.)

MORNING

Today, may I speak truth with
courage and with love. And may my
words also be received with courage
and love. Thanks be to God.
Amen.

EVENING

God, as my day closes,
I think about tomorrow and I place it
in your care. Thanks be to God.
Amen.

Saturday, March 6

(Read Luke 13:34–35)

MORNING
Loving God, I know I can come to you as a
protective mother and loving father. I put my whole trust in you.

EVENING
Loving God, I feel safe and secure when I rest
in the shadow of your wings.

I watch ducks in a pond near my home. They follow their mother so
closely, looking only at her. They trust that she will lead them to food
and away from danger. As evening comes they return to the spot she has
chosen and they gather close to her for warmth and shelter. Parent God,
how often I have wished for a guide to lead me through my days, for
someone to watch for danger and make sure I find what I need. I know
that I have such a guide—if I trust and follow, looking only to you.

MORNING
I thank you, God, knowing that as I begin this day
I may look to you for everything I need.
(Prayers of Intercession)

EVENING
I thank you, God, that I am one of your children
and have felt your shelter and protection all through this day.
(Prayers of Intercession)

I PRAY FOR . . .
(Pray the Prayer of Our Savior.)

MORNING
As I am carrying out many
responsibilities today, remind me that
I am your child and I am in your care.
Thanks be to God. Amen.

EVENING
Dear God, night has come and
I am weary. I nestle in the comfort of
your love and care. Thanks be to God.
Amen.

Sunday, March 7

(Read Luke 9:28–36)

MORNING
Great God, as my day begins, keep me awake and
watchful for signs of your presence and glory.

EVENING
Great God, I know that I often go through my day
noticing only the humdrum and missing your miracles.
Please forgive me.

Imagine almost sleeping through the Transfiguration! Luke says "Peter and his companions were weighed down with sleep." They came too close to missing this wonderful revelation of who their leader really was. Omnipotent God, Jesus stands clearly in the tradition of your chosen, Moses and Elijah. What do we miss when we "sleepwalk" through our days?

MORNING
God, I thank you for the ways you reveal your glory each day.
Today, may I be alert to the signs of your presence.
(Prayers of Intercession)

EVENING
I thank you, God, that I was able to "see" you today—in the kind
smile of a stranger, in a hug from my child, in a brilliant sunset.
(Prayers of Intercession)

I PRAY FOR . . .
(Pray the Prayer of Our Savior.)

MORNING
As this day unfolds before me,
let me find time for rest, for worship,
and for basking in the dazzling light
of Jesus. Thanks be to God.
Amen.

EVENING
I feel at peace as this day ends.
Guard me through the night; my trust
is in you. Thanks be to God.
Amen.

Monday, March 8 · International Women's Day

(Read Psalm 63:1–8)

MORNING

God of new beginnings, with your help,
with your strength, I will face this day.

EVENING

God of new endings, I pray for your perspective
as I lay my burdens down for the shelter of your word.

Sometimes we lie frozen as we face the trials of the new day, or we toss and turn as precious sleep eludes us as our problems circle about us. Your Psalms, God, remind us that the faithful have faced mornings of uncertainty and evenings in despair praying the same words we now speak aloud. God, you are our sanctuary in dry places. You are our feast in famine. Your steadfast love shelters us. We are not alone.

MORNING

Nourishing God, I pray for those whose life
seems to be a desert without rain.
(Prayers of Intercession)

EVENING

For all who toss and turn in restless torment,
I raise my prayer to you, never-sleeping God.
(Prayers of Intercession)

IN THE SHADOW OF YOUR WINGS I SING FOR JOY.

(Pray the Prayer of Our Savior.)

MORNING

In the shelter of your wings,
God of the new day, I resolve to live
your presence. Blessed be the Christ.
Amen.

EVENING

My God, I offer my burdens
to you to bear these precious hours.
Grant me rest, solace, and peace.
Blessed be the Christ. Amen.

Tuesday, March 9

(Read Isaiah 55:1–5)

MORNING
God, open my heart and hands today that I might gladly give.

EVENING
God, open my heart and hands that I might gladly receive.

Giving God, for the past two decades—on the same day—our family has made a point to invite everyone to dinner who has been associated with the churches we have served. We've patterned the meal after today's scriptural passage. We call it the Fiesta. People cannot bring anything with them and they cannot pay. Moreover, we have always encouraged our guests to bring people we do not know to the meal so that we may introduce them to the body of Christ. Inevitably, we never have enough money to pay for things before the meal, yet by the time it's all over the money's arrived. God, we need to learn to freely receive as well as give. It is through giving and receiving that you help us call unknown nations to you. We incline our ear to you so we might live.

MORNING
Generous God, I pray for these who struggle to receive your blessings.
(Prayers of Intercession)

EVENING
Christ who sacrifices, I pray for these who struggle to look beyond themselves.
(Prayers of Intercession)

SOMETIMES IT IS JUST EASIER TO GIVE THAN TO RECEIVE.
(Pray the Prayer of Our Savior.)

MORNING
God, open my heart and hands
that I might gladly receive.
Blessed be the Christ.
Amen.

EVENING
God, open my heart and hands
that I might gladly give.
Blessed be the Christ.
Amen.

Wednesday, March 10

(Read Isaiah 55:6–9)

MORNING

This day, God, I will seek you where you may be found,
and call upon you while you are near.

EVENING

This evening God, have mercy upon me,
as together, we reflect upon this day.

God give me strength. / The night is barely cool. / The heart of darkness' reign is still ahead. / Though kindness shields us from nature's duel / when sun shall battle shade and take her stead. / The list of tasks is laden with the trite / and I will labor with the necessary. / Forgive me if, with solid work in sight, / I sigh for every time my plans miscarry. / For though you set your royal stars ablaze / and every orb is by your power moved. / No sparrow falls unnoticed by your gaze. / Each hair is counted, every human loved. / No love so large it could not find me too, / no task too small for me to do for you.

MORNING

God, so many struggle with so much.
I lift up these troubled souls to you today.

(Prayers of Intercession)

EVENING

God, these whom I love, you love as well.
Set their lives ablaze like stars.

(Prayers of Intercession)

GOD FOUND US. GOD LOVES US.

(Pray the Prayer of Our Savior.)

MORNING

God, you are already waiting
for me at the end of this day. I resolve
to walk with you and towards you.
Blessed be the Christ. Amen.

EVENING

Thank you for today's blessings,
and for the purpose you have granted
to my struggles. Bless me this evening.
Blessed be the Christ. Amen.

Thursday, March 11

(Read Luke 13:1–5)

MORNING
God, despite all distractions I turn my heart towards repentance.

EVENING
God, this day is yours. Your salvation can still be mine.
I repent and ask your forgiveness.

Current events define the boundaries of our life's landscape. The assassinations of two Kennedys and the Rev. Dr. Martin Luther King Jr., along with the explosion of the space shuttle *Challenger* and the shattering maelstrom of September 11, 2001, define in part my days. God, when your son Jesus was asked about a current event, he countered with another and reminded us that it is even more important that we keep your plan of wholeness and peace at the center of our lives. It's not that shattering events such as the fall of the Tower of Siloam—or the Twin Towers—matter any less. It is that your love is even more powerful.

MORNING
God, for these who might be distracted by all that swirls about
in their lives, I pray that your righteousness and peace should
abide within them.
(Prayers of Intercession)

EVENING
Gracious God, help these for whom I have concern to shed
the cares of this day, that they might feel the power of your love.
(Prayers of Intercession)

LOVE GOD'S PEOPLE. LOVE GOD EVEN MORE.
(Pray the Prayer of Our Savior.)

MORNING
God of history, I repent of my sins
and put my trust in you this day.
Blessed be the Christ. Amen.

EVENING
God over history, I give this day
back to you and receive your peace.
Blessed be the Christ. Amen.

Friday, March 12

(Read Luke 13:6–9)

MORNING

God, my eyes have opened. You have given me
yet another chance to be your willing servant.

EVENING

God, I thank you for this day of discipleship and prayer.

As a beekeeper I know the literature suggests that each spring one should kill the queen and replace her with a younger insect, full of energy and life. Yet it is hard not to remain loyal to one who has served well, and to grant her another season of life with hope and in honor of good service. Because of their native sympathy for creation, many beekeepers I know rarely replace queens. God, your Gardener is the Word made Flesh, whose sympathies stem from having shared our infirmities. Thank you for one more chance, one more year, with a pledge of hard work from the Gardener, that we may yet bloom in your garden.

MORNING

God, these, your children whom I lift up,
are flowers in your garden.
(Prayers of Intercession)

EVENING

I call to mind at close of day these, your children,
who in you live and move and have their breath and being.
(Prayers of Intercession)

EACH DAY BRINGS ANOTHER CHANCE TO BLOOM IN GOD'S GARDEN.
(Pray the Prayer of Our Savior.)

MORNING

God and Gardener, let this
be a day that I may help you bring
forth the fruit of your realm.
Blessed be the Christ. Amen.

EVENING

Your patience, God, astounds me.
As a flower closes with the setting sun,
close my eyes with your peace.
Blessed be the Christ. Amen.

Saturday, March 13

(Read 1 Corinthians 10:1–12)

MORNING

God of history, open my heart to the lessons your people lived.

EVENING

God of history, what have I gleaned today from my life,
the people of faith, and your wisdom?

The [God] who blesses, God who shares shalom, / who keeps, whose face with glory makes to shine. / Whose graciousness would lead these people home / if they would only follow Love as kind— / But spies are daunted. Can they not recall / the plagues of Egypt, cloud and flame as guide, / the minha and the quail? Still they fall / and cling to desert's breast though it is wide, / eschewing risk, embracing safety's lure. / [God] despairs and means to end the pact, / and states that liquidation is the cure / and raising other peoples a new tact. / But Moses reasons, begs, implores, / and leads as God intended, and the doom recedes.

MORNING

God, for these I pray that they might from your holy history
learn their trials are not new.
(Prayers of Intercession)

EVENING

Forgiving God, I lift up these your gentle servants
who struggle still.
(Prayers of Intercession)

GOD IS PATIENT AND GOD'S MERCY IS SURE.
(Pray the Prayer of Our Savior.)

MORNING

God, let me learn from the story
of your people so I do not repeat my
old errors. Blessed be the Christ.
Amen.

EVENING

God, I stand or fall by you.
The day was yours. The day is through.
Blessed be the Christ.
Amen.

Sunday, March 14

(Read 1 Corinthians 10:13)

MORNING

God, I pray for your strength as I face today's journey.

EVENING

God, I reflect on today's pilgrimage, on all I have endured today.

On a trip out west we stopped to see Felipe Gonzales, a friend of my wife's family. Over the course of her life she has endured many tragedies, including a daughter who contracted polio just before the vaccine was made available; the death of a grandchild at birth; debilitating illnesses among the several members of her family; and now confinement to a wheelchair with crippling arthritis that has left her helpless. The attending nurse smiled when we told her who we had come to visit at the nursing center. We were told Felipe is always filled with joy, with the gentlest spirit and kindest heart. How is this possible? God, your Word tells me what seems impossible is true.

MORNING

God, mold me into an instrument of your peace
for all who struggle in times of trial.
(Prayers of Intercession)

EVENING

God of peace, grant rest to those restless souls
I lift up to you now.
(Prayers of Intercession)

GOD, LEAD US NOT INTO TEMPTATION, AND DO NOT PUT US TO THE TEST!
(Pray the Prayer of Our Savior.)

MORNING

Glorious God, I praise you in
the midst of trouble, trial, and testing.
With your help I will face the day.
Blessed be the Christ. Amen.

EVENING

I thank you for your constant
presence through the length of this
day's testing. Blessed be the Christ.
Amen.

Monday, March 15

(Read Psalm 32:1–5)

MORNING

I commit this day to you, my God and Savior.
May I see all those I meet through your eyes of compassion.

EVENING

I commit this night to you, my God and Savior. Help me to know
the freedom of sins forgiven. Break any bonds of sin that yet bind me,
as I confess that sin in the strong name of Jesus.

You are God of all creation, yet you have time to hear my prayer. Thank you, my loving God. Teach me that honest confession brings relief. The psalmist says the reason his spirit groaned and his body wasted away was because of his unwillingness to acknowledge his sins. Your hand was heavy upon him. With an act of will, the writer decides to make full confession. What a burst of joy followed. God, you forgave him, forgetting his transgression.

MORNING

God, I thank you for the privilege of living another day
in your world. Help me to do only those things that please you.
(Prayers of Intercession)

EVENING

It is evening again, my loving God. Help me to commit
the night to you that my sleep may be unmarred by fruitless
recollections of the day's imperfections.
(Prayers of Intercession)

**"HAPPY ARE THOSE WHOSE TRANSGRESSION IS FORGIVEN,
WHOSE SIN IS COVERED . . . IN WHOSE SPIRIT THERE IS NO DECEIT."**
(Pray the Prayer of Our Savior.)

MORNING

God, please keep me from wronging anyone today. But if I do, help me to readily confess it both to you and to the other person. In Jesus' name. Amen.

EVENING

O God most holy, may I go to my rest this night with no unconfessed sin that may mar my relationship with you. In Jesus' name. Amen.

Tuesday, March 16

(Read Psalm 32:6–11)

MORNING

Loving God, I praise you because you have forgiven me. Although
my judgment may sometimes be mistaken, may this day be lived
with perfect motives toward you and toward all whom I meet.

EVENING

Loving God, you invite all who are faithful to offer prayer to you.
May I be found in that number as I turn to my rest tonight.

My Divine Teacher, your promise in this psalm is that you will teach me
the way I should go. Although you are God of all, exalted in the heavens,
you are also El-Roi, the God Who Sees. You promise to keep your eyes
upon me, instructing, teaching, counseling. Thank you for your steadfast
love that surrounds me. Help me to rejoice in you, knowing that even in
a time of distress you can preserve my spirit from hopelessness.

MORNING

Loving God, your promise (v. 8), your admonition (v. 9),
and your warning (v. 10) are here in your word, bound together
with your promise to preserve me in trouble.
Walk with me through this day.
(Prayers of Intercession)

EVENING

Thank you for the return of quiet, the prospect of rest.
Be my hiding place this night.
(Prayers of Intercession)

"BE GLAD IN GOD AND REJOICE, O RIGHTEOUS,
AND SHOUT FOR JOY, ALL YOU UPRIGHT IN HEART."
(Pray the Prayer of Our Savior.)

MORNING	EVENING
Even early in the morning, can my heart shout for joy? I will rejoice in you, and go out with praise. In Jesus' name. Amen.	Preserve me from trouble and surround me with your mercies through the night. In Jesus' name. Amen.

Wednesday, March 17 · St. Patrick's Day

(Read Joshua 5:9–12)

MORNING
God, our lives are filled with many unforeseen changes.
Whatever this day holds, may I face it in your strength.

EVENING
God, the day is ended. It was filled with the familiar and the new,
the good and the uncomfortable. Help me to commit it all to you
knowing that nothing takes you by surprise.

Your record, our faithful God, contains a remarkable testimony. The manna stopped. Some persons must have panicked. For forty years after leaving Egypt, your people had moved about Sinai, never growing crops, fed by your manna that fell fresh every day. You provided, God. Now they had to plant and harvest crops. What would they do? It was just more work. But something else was gone, the disgrace of Egypt. They were no longer slaves, but free people moving ahead with you, Provider God.

MORNING
May I go to my duties invigorated with the knowledge
that you will provide what I need this day.
(Prayers of Intercession)

EVENING
My gracious God, I come again with gratitude to the end
of another day. You gave me these hours. Whatever was good
or bad in them I now commit to you.
(Prayers of Intercession)

"TODAY I HAVE ROLLED AWAY FROM YOU THE DISGRACE OF EGYPT."
SO THEY NAMED THE PLACE GILGAL, DERIVED FROM A WORD THAT MEANS "TO ROLL."
(Pray the Prayer of Our Savior.)

MORNING	EVENING
Precious God, may I honor you today in all I do. In Jesus' name. Amen.	Loving God, roll from me the weight of mistakes and imperfections of the day just ended. In Jesus' name. Amen.

Thursday, March 18

(Read Luke 15:1–3, 11b–19)

MORNING
Precious God, save me from launching into this day
in self-assurance. Give me your directions.

EVENING
Precious God, show me if there has been a time in this day
when I have left your presence. If so, help me to do better tomorrow.

Jesus, you are God. That fact did not excuse you from criticism. "This fellow associates with bad people," the church leaders said. Our God, you did not give them copies of your résumé to prove your identity. You told a simple story about a boy who began in cockiness and ended in humility, all pretenses gone. Help me to learn.

MORNING
God, your word says that you lead the humble in what is right
and teach the humble your way. Help me to humble myself before you,
thus qualifying for your instruction.
(Prayers of Intercession)

EVENING
Our God, help me to come before you with as much candor
as the lost son displayed. Left to myself, I am lost and hungry.
With you, I am found and filled. Stay with me through the night.
(Prayers of Intercession)

"I WILL GET UP AND GO TO MY FATHER."
(Pray the Prayer of Our Savior.)

MORNING
God, help me to realize my need
of your help in every part of my life.
If anyone I meet today is a prodigal,
help me to deal with that person in
your love. In Jesus' name. Amen.

EVENING
Loving God, thank you for this day.
Thank you for giving me food,
clothing, shelter—the necessities of
life the prodigal son lacked.
In Jesus' name. Amen.

Friday, March 19

(Read Luke 15:20–24)

MORNING

God, your love is unending. As I meditate today on the prodigal son's homecoming, help me to marvel at the depths of your love for us sinners.

EVENING

God, thank you for the many evidences of your love for me that I have seen today. Thank you for friends and family, for work and play.

Caring and loving God, yesterday you showed me the prodigal son's humility. Today you illustrate your love by this father's example, conveyed to us entirely by what the father does. You did not record for us one word the father said to his younger, sadder-and-wiser son. But what he did speaks clearly. He ran to him, hugged him, kissed him. Then he said to the servants, "Let's celebrate!"

MORNING

God, is there someone to whom I should speak words of love and encouragement today? Help me to recognize the opportunity when it comes.
(Prayers of Intercession)

EVENING

Most merciful Christ, thank you for loving me, even when I was ungrateful and unlovable. You humbled yourself to become one of us to show us your love. Thank you.
(Prayers of Intercession)

"BUT WHILE HE WAS STILL FAR OFF, HIS FATHER SAW HIM AND WAS FILLED WITH COMPASSION."
(Pray the Prayer of Our Savior.)

MORNING

Matchless Christ, you told this story to illustrate God's love for me. Thank you for loving me when my heart was far from you.
In Jesus' name. Amen.

EVENING

O God, please accept my sacrifice of praise for your watchful care over me this day. In Jesus' name.
Amen.

Saturday, March 20 · Spring begins

(Read Luke 15:25–32)

MORNING

God, help me never to be jealous when you show your love
for someone else.

EVENING

God, as you and I gather the loose ends of this day, help me to reach out in love
to any who need to hear your gospel message of redemption.

Our God, you have shown me the younger son's crassness turning to humility. I have seen the father's love. Now comes the elder brother's anger. Why didn't you tell us that the older son was mollified, went indoors, greeted his brother warmly, and they all lived happily ever after? You did not do that. We are left instead with the focus on the father's pleading love. God, have you changed? I don't think so.

MORNING

God, I read that all that you have is mine.
Open my heart and mind to receive what you want to give.
(Prayers of Intercession)

EVENING

My loving God, I will rejoice this night for the privilege
of another day lived under your mercy, with the knowledge
that my life is precious to God.
(Prayers of Intercession)

**"O GIVE THANKS TO THE GOD, FOR [GOD] IS GOOD, FOR [GOD'S]
STEADFAST LOVE ENDURES FOREVER" (PSALM 136:1).**
(Pray the Prayer of Our Savior.)

MORNING	**EVENING**
Send me out this morning,	Like the son in Jesus' story, I have
Loving Christ, with the quiet confidence	sinned. But what glad news it is to find
that comes from knowing who I am as a	that God loves me and welcomes me
redeemed, forgiven, loved child of God.	back when I come in true humility.
In Jesus' name. Amen.	In Jesus' name. Amen.

Sunday, March 21

(Read 2 Corinthians 5:16–21)

MORNING

God, help me this day to maintain Christ's point of view
in all my activities.

EVENING

God, you say that it is my responsibility to spread the word that we have
been reconciled with you. Show me my part in this adventure.

Savior, the psalmist found release from the weight of sin. Ancient Israel found freedom from the stigma of slavery. The wayward son discovered the profound truth that God is ready to forgive. Paul saw you initially, Jesus, as a personally ambitious Jewish leader. But after Paul's encounter with you on the Damascus Road, he no longer saw from this human point of view. Help me, like Paul, to become a new creature in you.

MORNING

You, the sinless Christ, gave yourself for my sin.
Help me to go out this day as your ambassador to tell others
about this great reconciliation.
(Prayers of Intercession)

EVENING

This is your work, not mine, my God, to do away
with my old sinful self. Renew me in your likeness.
(Prayers of Intercession)

**"FOR OUR SAKE HE MADE HIM TO BE SIN WHO KNEW NO SIN,
SO THAT IN HIM WE MIGHT BECOME THE RIGHTEOUSNESS OF GOD."**
(Pray the Prayer of Our Savior.)

MORNING

God of all glory, what a high calling
you have given me. Help me as I face
this day to discover what it means
for me to become the righteousness
of God. In Jesus' name. Amen.

EVENING

May I not accept your grace in vain,
but learn more about God each day.
In Jesus' name. Amen.

Monday, March 22

(Read Isaiah 43:16–21)

MORNING
Gracious God, make a way for my soul today
so that I might find you in the wilderness.

EVENING
Gracious God, with praise for your holy name I put my day
before you. May you open my heart anew to your presence.

In ever new ways you make yourself known to us. The river of your grace lets abundant life spring forth even in the most forlorn desert. And yet so often my soul is thirsting for you because I fail to ask for the drink of living water that you so freely give. So often I stumble around on my own, not thinking to look for the way that you have made for me. Help me today to be aware of your presence.

MORNING
Help me reach out to others today. I pray for our family of faith.
(Prayers of Intercession)

EVENING
In other people, loved ones and strangers,
I have encountered you today. Give peace to all who hope for you.
(Prayers of Intercession)

HOLY GOD, I PRAY IN THE NAME OF THE ONE THAT YOU SENT TO BE AMONG US.
(Pray the Prayer of Our Savior.)

MORNING	EVENING
I will go out into this day to glorify your name. Thanks be to you. In Jesus' name. Amen.	Peace you have given to me, and you have blessed me with your grace. Thanks and praise be to you, my God. In Jesus' name. Amen.

Tuesday, March 23

(Read Psalm 126:1–2)

MORNING
O God, awaken my spirit to your splendor
and make me a messenger of your good news.

EVENING
O God, I offer myself to you in prayer
and give you thanks for this day.

God, you have not left me alone but placed me among the family of your children. You have given my life a destination and you have guided my path. You have sent me on a journey of faith. You offer me a hand when my step is timid and insecure. You have called me by name and you give me a voice to praise you. I want to go through this day as your servant. O gracious and faithful God, let what I say and do be a worthy testimony to your love.

MORNING
God of gentle love and tender care,
I lift up to you all who are in need of your presence.
(Prayers of Intercession)

EVENING
I pray for those who are worried and anxious tonight
and for all who are longing for peace.
(Prayers of Intercession)

IN THE PRAYER THAT JESUS TAUGHT US, WE ARE CONNECTED WITH ALL YOUR CHILDREN, IN PRESENT, PAST, AND FUTURE.
(Pray the Prayer of Our Savior.)

MORNING
May there be shouts of joy
on my lips today, for this is a day that
you, my God, have made.
In Jesus' name. Amen.

EVENING
I pray for rest and peace tonight,
here and in all places. May the peace
of Christ be ever present.
In Jesus' name. Amen.

Wednesday, March 24

(Read Psalm 126:3–4)

MORNING

O God, let nothing keep me from being aware
of your presence today.

EVENING

O God, this was a day that you have made.
Let my heart rejoice in you.

We are thirsting for you, O God. In the midst of demands that are brought to us, we thirst for meaning and purpose. In the midst of a hectic day, we thirst for a moment of quiet reflection and prayer. In moments of loneliness, we thirst for your love to greet us in others. Even our faith can become routine and leave us thirsting for an outpouring of your Spirit. We pray that you may restore to us the river that brings life and life everlasting.

MORNING

How can I bring living water to others today?
I pray for all who are thirsting.
(Prayers of Intercession)

EVENING

Tonight, bless all who are a blessing to me.
I lift up their names with gratitude.
(Prayers of Intercession)

LET THE FAMILIAR WORDS OF THIS PRAYER BE A WELLSPRING OF YOUR SPIRIT.
(Pray the Prayer of Our Savior.)

MORNING

God, make me an instrument
of your promise today.
In Jesus' name.
Amen.

EVENING

Let me rest tonight
in your peace, O God.
In Jesus' name.
Amen.

Thursday, March 25 · The Annunciation

(Read Psalm 126:5–6)

MORNING

Caring God, wherever I go today, you will go with me.

EVENING

Caring God, I come to you at the end of the day
so that my spirit may find renewal and my soul may be at peace.

Restore the fortunes in my soul, O my God. Bring to life in me the riches of faith that are a gift from your Holy Spirit. You know when I am overwhelmed—when my smile is but a sad attempt to keep up a happy face. Sometimes I can let tears flow; other times I just hold my breath and clench my teeth. Gracious and merciful God, I confess the times where prayer seems an effort, when I would rather hold on to my fears than allow your embrace. May you lead me back to the wellspring of your love that brings forgiveness and peace.

MORNING

Make me a vessel of your grace. I pray for all who struggle
with sickness, of mind and soul and body.
(Prayers of Intercession)

EVENING

May your spirit restore the souls of all who cry
for grace and forgiveness.
(Prayers of Intercession)

I PRAY WITH THE WORDS THAT CHRIST GAVE US.
(Pray the Prayer of Our Savior.)

MORNING

God of grace, I want to let go
of all that holds me back and offer
myself to your promise today.
In Jesus' name. Amen.

EVENING

I simply give thanks, O God,
and ask your blessing for this day
and for the night ahead.
In Jesus' name. Amen.

Friday, March 26

(Read Philippians 3:4b–10)

MORNING

Faithful God, let me be bold in the speaking
and doing of my faith today.

EVENING

Faithful God, there is no day when I am without you.
Help me open my heart to the wondrous gift of your faithful love.

Once in a while we find something in which we seem to recognize ourselves: work that is rewarding; a relationship that speaks to the depth of who we are; children who teach us about our capability to love; friends who make us better at being ourselves. Through faith, we not so much find ourselves as we are found in Christ Jesus. Gracious and merciful God, help us surrender the struggle for identity to you who called us into being and then called us by name to be your children. Help us be most fully ourselves through you who loves us for who we are.

MORNING

I pray for those who struggle to accept and love themselves.
God, let them know your love.
(Prayers of Intercession)

EVENING

Holy One, may your blessing tonight be
on all who struggle in their relationships.
(Prayers of Intercession)

I PRAY THE PRAYER OF YOUR SON, OUR SAVIOR,

IN THE COMMUNION OF SAINTS OF ALL TIMES.
(Pray the Prayer of Our Savior.)

MORNING	EVENING
May this day bring me closer to you and put me at peace with myself. In Jesus' name. Amen.	Bless me tonight, O my God, for in you my life is at peace. In Jesus' name. Amen.

Saturday, March 27

(Read Philippians 3:11–14)

MORNING
Praiseworthy God, help me be a faithful servant today.

EVENING
Praiseworthy God, let there be praise to you for this day.

I want to know Christ, the one who came to us to join in the mess of our humanity. I want to know Christ, the one in whose death the gates will open to life everlasting. I want to know Christ, who called disciples, who wept for his friend. I want to know the one who offered healing in his words and his touch. I want to know Christ, who went to be alone with God—the one who stilled the forces of nature and upset the established ways of faith of his people. I want to know Christ, the preacher, the savior, the sacrificial lamb. Give me faith, O God, and patience, and understanding.

MORNING
I pray for my fellow human beings, friend and foe,
beloved and stranger, near and far.
(Prayers of Intercession)

EVENING
Let there be peace tonight, O God, in the places
where people fight over matters of faith and religion.
(Prayers of Intercession)

I FIND REASSURANCE IN THE WORDS THAT JESUS TAUGHT US TO PRAY.
(Pray the Prayer of Our Savior.)

MORNING	**EVENING**
Gracious and merciful God,	I am yours, O God, this day and
help me follow Jesus' call into	all days. Give me your peace tonight.
discipleship today. In Jesus' name.	In Jesus' name.
Amen.	Amen.

Sunday, March 28

(Read John 12:1–8)

MORNING

Come, Holy Spirit, come! Open my heart to the presence of God.

EVENING

Come, Holy Spirit, come! My mouth will glorify our God always,
and God's promise will be on my lips.

On this Sabbath day, may we use a time of rest to recognize and celebrate the ways in which Christ is present with us. May we see Christ in one another. May we find him revealed in scripture. May we find him in the stranger who asks for help. May we encounter Christ in the loving touch we give to a loved one. Each moment is a gift that we can cherish. Let us worship our God, the creator, redeemer, and sustainer, the one who was, and is, and forever will be, alpha and omega, beginning and end.

MORNING

Today I thank God for the diversity of all God's children.
I pray for all persons who are facing discrimination.
(Prayers of Intercession)

EVENING

Tonight I pray for all who go to bed worried how they are
going to make it through the next day. Pour out your gift of peace
and strength over them, O God.
(Prayers of Intercession)

JESUS IS WITH US WHEN WE PRAY IN THE WAY THAT HE TAUGHT US.
(Pray the Prayer of Our Savior.)

MORNING

What are ways in which
we can honor God's gifts to us today?
In Jesus' name. Amen.

EVENING

Help me, God, that I may let go
of all that troubles me, and find rest
and peace in you.
In Jesus' name. Amen.

Monday, March 29

(Read Psalm 118:1–2, 19–29)

MORNING

Faithful God, I thank you with all my being because your love
endures. You have made this day. I will rejoice and be glad in it.

EVENING

Faithful God, your love has been with me throughout this day.
May the gates of my heart open wide so that I may
give you thanks. You have answered me.

God of all comfort, in my moments of joy and in my times of difficulty,
your love is there. When my love wavers, you are steadfast. When I
squander my gifts, you are steadfast. When I am distracted from you,
you are steadfast. Thank you, God, for your immense love.

MORNING

Faithful God, I am mindful of your love for people I care about,
for people whom I will never know, and for people I dislike.
I am mindful of your love for creation so often abused by humankind.
(Prayers of Intercession)

EVENING

Faithful God, I thank you for your amazing presence in my life
today. You are my God. Your love of me endures forever.
I pray for all who do not know your love.
(Prayers of Intercession)

GOD'S LOVE KNOWS NO LIMITS. REALLY.

(Pray the Prayer of Our Savior.)

MORNING

May I find your steadfast love
in many surprising places this day.
In Jesus' name.
Amen.

EVENING

Rejoicing in this day, I rest now
in you. Thank you, Faithful God;
you are good. Your steadfast love
endures forever. In Jesus' name.
Amen.

Tuesday, March 30

(Read Philippians 2:5–11)

MORNING

Exalted God of Highest Heaven, I rise this morning
thankful for Jesus Christ. May the same mind be in me
this day that was and is in him. Amen.

EVENING

Exalted God of Highest Heaven, I thank you for every moment
in this day when I was mindful of you. Help me to recall
those moments now in reverence and gratitude.

In our day, God of Glory, we find humility a difficult virtue to experience. Christ's humility comes out of his great love of you. Bless me with that kind of love that I may know faithful humility.

MORNING

Exalted God, as Jesus was in human form so long ago,
so he is present to me this day. Help me to see him in all I meet
that all might see him even a little, somehow, in me.
(Prayers of Intercession)

EVENING

I thank you for my faith in Christ, however strong
or wavering it was today. I pray for all who do not and
cannot bow in awe at the name of Jesus.
(Prayers of Intercession)

GOD GIVES GRACE TO THOSE WHO ARE HUMBLE.
(Pray the Prayer of Our Savior.)

MORNING

Exalted God, whenever I hear
the name of Jesus Christ today,
whether in swearing or in praise,
help me pause and give you thanks
for him. Amen.

EVENING

I rest now, grateful for the life
of Christ. Bless me with restoring
sleep that I may wake to praise
him again. Amen.

Wednesday, March 31

(Read Psalm 31:9–16)

MORNING

God of Life, I trust in you. You are my God.
Be gracious to me. Be my comfort and my guide this new day.

EVENING

God of Life, you have been gracious to me this day.
With heart and mind and soul, I thank you. Night has come
and I am weary. Deliver me into your peace.

Our bodies wear out. Grief brings us low. People speak unkindly to us.
Some misjudge us, and even abuse us. At times we feel afraid. Yet I will
trust in you, letting you guide me, knowing my times are always in your
hands.

MORNING

God of Life, terror sometimes seizes the world and us.
Let your love radiate this day. Let insight, generosity, and compassion
overflow in me and in people throughout your beloved world.
(Prayers of Intercession)

EVENING

God of Life, you continue to hold us all in your steadfast love.
I pray for those I love, for people in difficulty around the world,
and for your creation so often misused.
(Prayers of Intercession)

GOD'S LOVE CAN HEAL EVERY BROKEN VESSEL.
(Pray the Prayer of Our Savior.)

MORNING

I place this day now into your hands.
May your face shine upon me
and all I am and all I do.
In Jesus' name. Amen.

EVENING

Even as I sleep, I trust in you.
Deliver me from harm. Restore my
body, mind, and soul, that I may
rise and praise you again.
In Jesus' name. Amen.

Thursday, April 1

(Read Isaiah 50:4–9a)

MORNING
God, Jesus was a teacher; am I a teacher, too?
What would you have me teach today? To whom? Guide me,
that I might teach faithfully even when I least expect it.

EVENING
God, you call us to sustain the weary. I am weary now.
The day is ending and I must rest. Hear me as I pray.

Deep within me, Holy One, I know you are helping me. Whatever happens to me, I am not a disgrace in your eyes. It is you who stand with me and walk by my side. I will not be afraid. You are always near to me.

MORNING
Awaken my ear to listen well. Let me hear you sing
in the song of a bird, speak in the voice of a friend,
and call in the heartbeat of a stranger.
(Prayers of Intercession)

EVENING
Holy One, I did not have to give my cheek today to those
who pull the beard. I did not have to hide from spitting.
But others did; they may have to do so tonight.
(Prayers of Intercession)

INSULTS CAN BRING BLESSINGS.

(Pray the Prayer of Our Savior.)

MORNING
In all I hear today, may I be
mindful of you. Keep my ear open.
Grant me the tongue of a teacher.
For I long to stand truly with you.
In Jesus' name. Amen.

EVENING
Holy One, you grant me
rest and sustain me in the night.
You bless me. I am yours.
In Jesus' name. Amen.

Friday, April 2

(Read Luke 19:28–40)

MORNING

God of Processions, Palm/Passion Sunday is coming,
Day of Foreshadows. Yet today will unfold with amazing signs
of your walk among us. Help my eyes to see you.

EVENING

God of Processions, you passed so lovingly near me today
in so many ways. I thank you. Help me become aware
of those sacred moments now.

Why do you come into my life, Holy God? Can it be that you yearn for
me? As you journey with me, may I praise you more joyfully for your
great deeds. Blessed are you!

MORNING

There will be stones in my day, God of Processions.
As I encounter them, help me listen for you. I pray for all whose
lives feel only hard and barren, with no shouts of joy today.
(Prayers of Intercession)

EVENING

God of Processions, blessed are you! Peace is yours and glory!
Peace is ours because of you. Thank you, Holy One.
I pray for those who do not understand you and your ways.
(Prayers of Intercession)

ASK QUESTIONS. GOD MAY NEED THEM.
(Pray the Prayer of Our Savior.)

MORNING

Jesus, help me to recognize you
amid the loud voices and the calls
for silence today. In Jesus' name.
Amen.

EVENING

Jesus, even the stones can praise you.
So do I in the dark and quiet of this
night. Continue always to go ahead
of me that I may follow with growing,
ever-greater love and praise of you.
In Jesus' name. Amen.

Saturday, April 3

(Read Luke 22:14–53)

MORNING
Jesus, Palm/Passion Sunday is almost here,
Day of Foreshadows. At any table today, help me find you sitting
there. For any bread is your bread. And any cup is yours.
Every meal is sacred because you are there.

EVENING
Jesus, thank you for your nourishing of me, your guidance,
and your grace. For you, may I be one who serves.

Jesus, you knew how it would unfold: Peter would not stand the test;
Judas would betray; the others would be confused. May I be so mindful of you that I may stand the test, and not betray nor be confused by
your ways. Is this possible for me?

MORNING
You invite many others to your table, Jesus.
Those who are hungry. Those who have known you all their life.
Those filled only with pain or questions. Those whom I dislike.
(Prayers of Intercession)

EVENING
Jesus, you left the Upper Room well nourished, then went out
to pray in anguish, for your hour had come. May we not feel we
fail when our hour comes, despite our prayers and faithful living.
(Prayers of Intercession)

ALL DARKNESS IS FILLED WITH GOD'S LIGHT.
(Pray the Prayer of Our Savior.)

MORNING
Jesus, you gave them bread
and passed a cup. Help me remember
you through the large and small
gestures that I see today.
In Jesus' name. Amen.

EVENING
Unlike the disciples, may I
sleep well throughout the night,
safe in your loving care.
In Jesus' name. Amen.

Sunday, April 4

Palm/Passion Sunday · Daylight Savings Time begins

(Read Luke 23:1–49)

MORNING

Searcher of hearts, Palm/Passion Sunday has come again,
the day that begins so hopefully and ends so sorrowfully. May I be
sensitive to all my emotions and to the feelings of those around me.
Help me to watch and understand.

EVENING

Searcher of hearts, today had moments of delight and moments
of despair. Thank you for all I saw and felt within my heart.

"Save yourself and us!" That was a desperate plea so long ago. It rings
within our hearts today. Why is there so much suffering? Why so much
destruction and pollution of your earth? Why so much cruelty, man to
man, woman to woman, child to child? Do you hear our cry? More
faithfully, perhaps, I should ask, "Do we hear your heartfelt reply?"

MORNING

Searcher of hearts, you know me better than I know myself.
Help me to forgive as you did and to pray for others who need
to feel your compassion today.
(Prayers of Intercession)

EVENING

Searcher of hearts, let us hear your promise of paradise.
Speak to us! Then help us weep within our souls for all your children.
(Prayers of Intercession)

WATCHING CAN BE A SACRED ACT.
(Pray the Prayer of Our Savior.)

MORNING	EVENING
In this Day of Wonder, the wood is green; I am so very blessed. Help me be faithful, even when noontime darkness covers my inner land. In Jesus' name. Amen.	Into your hands I commend my spirit. Grant me holy rest. In Jesus' name. Amen.

Monday, April 5

(Read John 12:1–11)

MORNING
Creator of all things and Bestower of every grace and goodness,
today as I begin the pilgrimage of Holy Week, I offer my costliest treasures and
the totality of my being to you to whom I owe all that I am in Jesus Christ.

EVENING
Creator of all things and Bestower of every grace and goodness,
too often today I have questioned the costly expressions of love by others to your
honor and glory. As I retire, help me celebrate generous actions I have seen
in others and commit my life to serve you better tomorrow.

Beneficent God, you have given me daily opportunities to serve the poor
in the name of Christ and to offer my talents, time, and treasure, to bring
glory and honor to your name. Help me commend all living to the life
of Jesus Christ, and generously give from the gifts with which I have been
gifted. Thank you for opportunities to lavish your grace through my life.

MORNING
Thank you, God, for Jesus—for memories of him,
his message, and his mercy. I pray for all who have special need
of your grace, which I have discovered in the Savior.
(Prayers of Intercession)

EVENING
Dear God, thank you for the expressions of love that I received
this day. I pray for all who have demonstrated a generous character.
(Prayers of Intercession)

O GREAT CREATOR, I PRAY IN THE NAME OF JESUS, WHO GAVE EVERYTHING FOR ME.
(Pray the Prayer of Our Savior.)

MORNING	EVENING
Will I demonstrate generosity	As I close my eyes in sleep
this day? I pray in Jesus' name.	let me rest in your gracious care
Amen.	for me. I pray in Jesus' name.
	Amen.

Tuesday, April 6

(Read John 12:20–36)

MORNING

Dear God, "The hour has come for the Son of [Humankind] to be glorified."
May the crucified one draw people from every ethnic group and station to
worship him, serve in his name, and share the new order that he brought about.

EVENING

Dear God, as darkness gathers, I celebrate the inner light.
As Christ moves toward sacrifice, I rest in what Christ did and
what he does, and anticipate what more he will do.

God of Grace, you gave Jesus Christ in death. I praise you that this
death draws people in some mysterious way. No one has shown greater
love! None have given their all for the worst of sinners. Help me embrace the light shining in the darkness. Help me become a child of light
that the world may be a brighter place.

MORNING

O God, I thank you for the way your cross has become a blessing.
Help me be one who follows the crucified One and find in him the divine glory.
(Prayers of Intercession)

EVENING

O God, I thank you for the crucified one. I pray for those who
suffer or who bear some cross and need some special grace.
(Prayers of Intercession)

O GREAT CREATOR, I PRAY IN THE NAME OF THE ONE CRUCIFIED,
WHOSE CROSS INVITES PRAYER.
(Pray the Prayer of Our Savior.)

MORNING	EVENING
Help me know that if I hoard my life, I will lose it. But remind me that if I lose my life in service for Jesus, I will discover it in a fresh way. I pray in Jesus' name. Amen.	A seed is planted in the earth and it seems to die. But, behold, it is transformed! As I fall into sleep, transform my inner thoughts by your divine Spirit. I pray in Jesus' name. Amen.

Wednesday, April 7

(Read John 13:21–32)

MORNING

O God, I anxiously begin this day knowing that I might
betray Jesus Christ. Yet I know that Christ's glory will triumph.
I now begin my day.

EVENING

O God, it is night. I review my life to ask if it has contributed
to darkness. I reconnect my life to the glorified Christ.

Eternal One, nothing occurs unless you allow it. All things are taken
and ultimately changed in your divine plan. Evil brings about darkness.
Jesus eventually transforms it into glory. I find it hard to imagine. I sorrow in the cruelty I witness and the sorrows brought upon others. I
thank you that your plan is greater than mine.

MORNING

God of life and liberty, I pray that I will not betray Jesus Christ.
Hear me as I pray for the world.
(Prayers of Intercession)

EVENING

Creator of memory, how have I betrayed Jesus today?
(Admit the sins of your day.) Giver of hope: how have I witnessed Christ's
glory in the events that have taken place since this morning?
(Rejoice in the graces demonstrated before you today.) I now pray for others.
(Prayers of Intercession)

**O GREAT CREATOR, I PRAY IN THE NAME OF THE ONE WHO GIVES ME DAILY BREAD,
EVEN IF I INTEND BETRAYAL.**
(Pray the Prayer of Our Savior.)

MORNING	**EVENING**
Will the bread offered to me by Jesus Christ be spurned? Will I leave the table of Jesus' love? I pray in Jesus' name. Amen.	I rest, O God, in the care of Jesus. Allow something of his glory to visit my dreams. I pray in Jesus' name. Amen.

Thursday, April 8 · Maundy Thursday

(Read John 13:1–17, 31b–35)

MORNING

Divine Love, on this Maundy Thursday, I consider that last meal
of Jesus, when he took the role of a servant and washed the feet of
God. I ask that pride will not interfere with my life today.

EVENING

Divine Love, how have I loved you?
Have I "washed the feet of others" as if I were a servant?

God, I thank you for the servant example of Jesus evidenced in his last
meal with his disciples. I rejoice that Jesus gave an example for how I
should live my life. We keep the commandment of the table to "do this
in remembrance" of Jesus Christ. We ask that we keep the commandment to love one another.

MORNING

God of Communion, I thank you for every opportunity
to have fellowship with you. I anticipate the table of love.
Hear me as I now, in prayer, include others at the board of grace.
(Prayers of Intercession)

EVENING

God of Communion, I thank you for today's events
that have brought me into table community with others.
Hear now my prayers for those I know that have some need.
(Prayers of Intercession)

O GREAT CREATOR, I PRAY IN THE NAME OF MY SAVIOR.
(Pray the Prayer of Our Savior.)

MORNING	EVENING
In what ways can I wear	Again I pray,
the towel of a servant today?	"Our Father in heaven, hallowed be
I pray in Jesus' name.	your name, your kingdom come, your
Amen.	will be done, on earth as in heaven."
	I pray in Jesus' name. Amen.

Friday, April 9 · Good Friday

(Read John 18:1, 19:42)

MORNING
"When I survey the wondrous cross on which the
Prince of glory died, my richest gain I count but loss,
and pour contempt on all my pride."

EVENING
"Were the whole realm of nature mine,
that were a present far too small: Love so amazing,
so divine, demands my soul, my life, my all."

"Forbid it, [God], that I should boast, save in the death of Christ my
God; all the vain things that charm me most, I sacrifice them to His
blood."

MORNING
"See from His head, His hands, His feet, sorrow and love
flow mingled down; did ever such love and sorrow meet, or thorns
compose so rich a crown?" Hear me as I bring such love
to the sorrows of the world that I know.
(Prayers of Intercession)

EVENING
"To Christ, who won for sinners grace by bitter grief
and anguish sore, be praise from all the ransomed race forever
and forevermore." Hear me as I pray for those I know.
(Prayers of Intercession)

O GOD, KNOWN IN THE SACRIFICE OF OUR SAVIOR,

I PRAY THE GREAT PRAYER OF THE ONE WHO GAVE HIS LIFE FOR ME.

(Pray the Prayer of Our Savior.)

MORNING
As I survey the wondrous cross,
I rejoice in a love that conquers all
fear and evil. I pray in the name of
Christ. I pray in Jesus' name. Amen.

EVENING
I retire this evening in the sorrow
of the death of Jesus. I rest in the
Savior's love. I pray in Jesus' name.
Amen.

Saturday, April 10

(Read John 19:38–42)

MORNING
God, this is a day of waiting. The events of yesterday fill me
with terror and dread. In faith I anticipate those events that I await.
Allow me to deal with earthly cares with a God-given hope.

EVENING
God, I come to the end of this day aware of my limited
understanding, trusting only in your providence.

God, we sometimes act as if Jesus Christ were an entombed good person that deserves our admiration. "I believe; help my unbelief!" Accept my devotion.

MORNING
God of all things made new and God of hope, in hope I pray for
those people and those events that awaken sorrow within my heart.
(Prayers of Intercession)

EVENING
God, you are always with me even in times of waiting and
uncertainty. I pray for all those seeking an answer to deep needs.
(Prayers of Intercession)

"O GOD, THE [REALM], THE POWER, AND THE GLORY ARE YOURS
NOW AND FOREVER." I BELIEVE THIS EVEN WHEN I DOUBT. HEAR ME NOW
AS I PRAY THE PRAYER JESUS GAVE ME.
(Pray the Prayer of Our Savior.)

MORNING
I trust in my hope in Christ
to get me through all events of this
day. I pray in Jesus' name.
Amen.

EVENING
"Now I lay me down to sleep.
I pray, dear Lord, my soul to keep.
If I should die before I wake.
I pray, thee, Lord, my soul to take."
I pray in Jesus' name. Amen.

Sunday, April 11 · Easter Sunday

(Read John 20:1–18)

MORNING

"Hail, Thou once despised Jesus! Hail, Thou Galilean King!
Thou didst suffer to release us; thou didst free salvation bring.
Hail, Thou universal Savior, Who hast borne our sin and shame!
By Thy merits we find favor; life is given through Thy Name."

EVENING

"Jesus, hail! Enthroned in glory, there forever to abide;
all the heavenly hosts adore Thee, seated at Thy Father's side.
There for sinners Thou art pleading; there Thou dost our place
prepare; thou for saints art interceding till in glory they appear."

O God, we rejoice in this day of resurrection glory. We delight in the providence that brought about eternal life from the grave.

MORNING

"Paschal Lamb, by God appointed, all our sins on Thee were laid;
by almighty love anointed, Thou hast full atonement made.
Every sin may be forgiven through the virtue of Thy blood;
opened is the gate of heaven, reconciled are we with God."
I pray especially this day for sinners, including myself.
(Prayers of Intercession)

EVENING

In resurrection joy I intercede for the world's needs.
(Prayers of Intercession)

I PRAY IN THE NAME OF THE RISEN SAVIOR.
(Pray the Prayer of Our Savior.)

MORNING	EVENING
Bring to this day the brightness of resurrection glory. I pray in Jesus' name. Amen.	Before I go to sleep, hear my praises, "Worship, honor, power, and blessing Christ is worthy to receive; loudest praises, without ceasing, right it is for us to give. I pray in Jesus' name. Amen.

Monday, April 12

(Read John 20:19–23)

MORNING
Loving God, in joy we greet this day,
newly aware of the grace of resurrection light.

EVENING
Loving God, on the evening of his resurrection,
Jesus came to his friends and offered peace. With gratitude
I receive his gift of the Holy Spirit's presence and peace.

Some of the disciples met in fear and locked the doors. Deliver me, O Christ, from the fears that cause me to barricade myself from the world. As the risen Christ was able to transcend those barriers, I pray that he may be present to me now, in spite of my defenses. I pray for the gentle breath of your Holy Spirit to bring peace and forgiveness, so that I may rejoice. Then send me out, transformed by the power of your peace.

MORNING
In your grace, O God, cradle those who live in fear,
and bless us all with peace.
(Prayers of Intercession)

EVENING
You have been bold to overcome the fear-locked doors
of human hearts, gracious God. Pour out your peaceful Spirit
on all those in circumstances of conflict this day.
(Prayers of Intercession)

THE RISEN CHRIST HELD NO GRUDGE AGAINST THOSE
WHO HAD DESERTED HIM; RATHER, HE BREATHED PEACE.

MORNING
How may I bring the healing
of forgiveness this day? Guide me,
risen Christ, to speak and act as you
have taught me. In the name
of the Christ, I pray. Amen.

EVENING
As night falls, we can give up
our fears to Almighty God, who sends
peace through the risen Christ and the
Holy Spirit. In the name
of the Christ, I pray. Amen.

Tuesday, April 13

(Read John 20:24–25)

MORNING
Risen Christ, as I share my faith, not all may believe.
Give me patience for this and all obstacles I encounter.

EVENING
Risen Christ, sometimes I am a witness, and sometimes a doubter.
Wherever I am in my faith journey, I know you travel with me.

God of second chances, like Thomas I may not be in the right place at the right time every time. Be patient, I pray, when I insist on seeing things with my own eyes. Grant me the imagination to hear the words of others and see the truth that gives life. May trust and respect grow so that your community of faith may grow.

MORNING
I remember again that we each come to you in our own way,
in our own time. Be with those who struggle to believe;
may the frustrations of doubt fall away so all may sing your praise.
(Prayers of Intercession)

EVENING
Patient God, I lift up to you those situations where one person
judges another. May truth and integrity permeate your people.
(Prayers of Intercession)

GRANT EACH PERSON WHAT WE NEED TO BELIEVE AND TRUST IN YOU, O GOD.

MORNING
I would not like to be branded "Doubting Thomas"; I will resist branding others, recognizing each one's potential to be transformed by Christ's love. In the name of the Christ, I pray. Amen.

EVENING
Thank you for the opportunities you gave me this day to bring the good news of your peace. May I be open to your surprises. In the name of the Christ, I pray. Amen.

Wednesday, April 14

(Read John 20:26–29)

MORNING
Patient Jesus, even if I have not seen, by my faith I am blessed!
Glory to the God of wondrous surprises!

EVENING
Patient Jesus, thank you for meeting us where we are, welcoming
our inquisitive touch. Your peace is our hope.

Compassionate Jesus, you tenderly encourage us saying, "Do not doubt but believe." If only it were so easy! Yet here you stand, willing to give me what I need to take that leap of faith. Lead me and shepherd me, gentle Christ. Build on what I know to be true. Breathe your peace on me. As Thomas joyfully proclaimed his faith, I too offer my own proclamation, in my own words . . .

MORNING
In your peace I find the courage to face uncertainties and doubts. I
lift up those who yearn for such courage and strength.
(Prayers of Intercession)

EVENING
Each day brings new challenges whether we are full of faith or
dogged by doubt. I pray God's blessings on those who struggle to
cope day to day.
(Prayers of Intercession)

GIVE ME WORDS TO PROCLAIM MY FAITH.

MORNING
Help me to reflect Thomas' delight
as he affirmed the presence of the living Christ. Open my eyes to new
truth and light that may bring
welcome confidence and faith.
In the name of the Christ, I pray.
Amen.

EVENING
Thank you for your presence
and peace in the ebb and flow
of this day, O God. Bless the night
with rejuvenating rest that I may wake
to serve you well tomorrow.
In the name of the Christ, I pray.
Amen.

Thursday, April 15

(Read John 20:30–31)

MORNING

O God, I give thanks for my ancestors in faith, who shared the
good news and witnessed boldly so that people of every generation
might hear and believe that Jesus Christ gives life.

EVENING

O God, brimming with gratitude for the Gospel message and the
witness of people of faith, I begin to see where I fit into the
scheme; I have a legacy of faith to carry on.

God of all generations, you link us together across the ages. We can
only imagine the fervor of the disciples once they had experienced the
risen Christ, his forgiveness and peace. They told their amazing story,
some daring to record it for posterity, so we would have holy scripture
to hold in our hands. Praise to your empowering Spirit!

MORNING

Believing in the new life Christ gives brings hope to each new day.
When the shadows threaten to overpower us, Christ is our light. I
pray for all who yearn for light to break through.
(Prayers of Intercession)

EVENING

Imagine the stories that were not recorded in scripture! I lift up all
who have a story to tell, and who long to tell it.
(Prayers of Intercession)

I CELEBRATE LIFE IN THE STRONG NAME OF THE RISEN CHRIST!

MORNING

By my words and my actions
·I will witness to you today, God of
life. May the resurrection light shine
in me and through me. In the name
of the Christ, I pray. Amen.

EVENING

My words and my actions
spoke loudly today, God of life.
Rekindle your light in me each day.
In the name of the Christ, I pray.
Amen.

Friday, April 16

(Read Acts 5:27–32)

MORNING

Steadfast God, the disciples dared to follow your Spirit's lead
as they shared the good news. At times they risked, at times
they were imprisoned, at times they were set free.
You did not desert them and you will not desert me.

EVENING

Steadfast God, your Spirit has blessed me today. You did not desert me.

Our ancestors in faith risked much for your sake, O God! We benefit from their energetic mission, as they surged undaunted into new places and withstood the threats of those who tried to unravel the Christian movement. May we hear you calling us out from the prisons that confine us, so we may fill the world with the teaching that will bring forgiveness and resurrection hope.

MORNING

Empowering Spirit, you gave stamina to the disciples
in their ministry. I pray for those who are weary and burdened,
feeling imprisoned, or hopeless.
(Prayers of Intercession)

EVENING

We are not alone on the faith journey. Others have gone before,
rehearsed the stories, and prayed for us. Now I pray for those yet
to come, that the Holy Spirit may empower their journey.
(Prayers of Intercession)

IGNITED BY THE HOLY SPIRIT, WE ARE WITNESSES.

MORNING

God has released the prison doors
and given us yet another chance to
teach the way of life. This day is a
new opportunity. In the name
of the Christ, I pray. Amen.

EVENING

Whatever I have done for you today,
O Christ, I have done in love.
Bless the night. In the name
of the Christ, I pray. Amen.

Saturday, April 17

(Read Psalm 150)

MORNING
God of Glory, may everything I touch today,
be it harp or cymbal, pencil or plow, become an instrument of praise!

EVENING
God of Glory, as this day comes to a close,
may the echoes of our praise ring throughout your Creation.

God of petal and leaf, cloud and soil, turtle and cheetah, praise to you! Be as present to me as air—so life-giving, heart-enhancing, mind-clearing. With each long breath may I join all creatures in praising you, our Creator. With the in-breath may I enrich myself with your Spirit; with the out-breath utter praise for your goodness. In this cycle of breathing may I be mindful of my oneness with all creation as we rely on the precious air we share. Bless this sweet earth with sun and rain in good measure this day.

MORNING
The new day vibrates with life. Lift up all creatures and creation,
that life in all its fullness may abound.
(Prayers of Intercession)

EVENING
As evening comes and breath comes long and deep,
may your Holy Spirit bless the sleeping and dreaming
of all creation, until the new day dawns.
(Prayers of Intercession)

WITH EACH BREATH, MAY I PRAISE THE GOD OF ALL LIFE!

MORNING
May the music of the universe invoke harmonies of praise to your name, mighty God. May I join the cosmic orchestra with sounds of joy! In the name of the Christ, I pray. Amen!

EVENING
Breathe through me into the night, Holy Spirit, and inspire my sleeping and my rising. In the name of the Christ, I pray. Amen.

Sunday, April 18

(Read Revelation 1:4–8)

MORNING
Eternal God, we cannot hear it enough: Jesus loves us and frees us
from our sins. That good news makes each day a fresh start.

EVENING
Eternal God, who was and who is and who is to come,
we thank you for our niche in history.

God of all the ages, Alpha and Omega, we stretch our thinking to imagine how eternal you are. You are the Alpha, the beginning, the source of all life. Your Holy Spirit moves through history like wind—here a breath, there a gale—inspiring all creation with the divine spark. You are the Omega, the end, the culmination in a perfection beyond our capacity to envision. Humbled to be included in this magnificent history, I praise you!

MORNING
Jesus' love lifts me out of my dead-end plodding,
into the saving light of forgiveness. For those who feel mired
down, discouraged, and uninspired, I offer prayers.
(Prayers of Intercession)

EVENING
Has anyone been touched by my resurrection hope today?
I pray that the Christ-light will embrace them in healing love.
(Prayers of Intercession)

GOD IS THE ONE WHO WAS AND WHO IS AND WHO IS TO COME.

MORNING	EVENING
Just as you are the Alpha and the Omega, God of eternity, you are with us in the beginning of this new day. In the name of the Christ, I pray. Amen.	Just as you are the Alpha and the Omega, God of eternity, you are with us in the ending of this blessed day. In the name of the Christ, I pray. Amen.

Monday, April 19

(Read Psalm 30:1–5)

MORNING

O Bringer of Joy, awaken my heart; pour out your love and your blessings.

EVENING

O Bringer of Joy, you have graciously given me your love and blessings today . . . especially those I haven't recognized.

O God, may this day reflect the renewal of my spirit, a gift new every morning. Though fear pursues me, and may crush me, with your light veiled in the darkness, yet I cry to you. And you help me to rise again. Will I forget my joy? Will I once again weep? Then restore me again that I may share the joy of my faith with everyone who sees my actions. And they shall know that weeping does come, but is followed by joy in the morning. Let me sing praises to you all day.

MORNING

Holy One, your faithfulness empowers me to bring my sincere requests and helps me believe you have already answered me.
(Prayers of Intercession)

EVENING

Gracious God, I end my day by singing your praise.
(Prayers of Intercession)

REMEMBER, GOD RESTORES THOSE WHO HAVE
DESCENDED INTO THEIR OWN HELL OF FEAR AND PITY.
(Pray the Prayer of Our Savior.)

MORNING
O Bringer of Joy, now fill me
and grant me power to love and serve
your people this day.
Thanks be to God. Amen.

EVENING
Loving God, grant me rest.
Restore me to life once again.
Thanks be to God.
Amen.

Tuesday, April 20

(Read John 21:4–14)

MORNING
O God, my Beloved, your grace renews me every morning. Let me
sing your praise.

EVENING
O God, my Beloved, if I failed to be faithful today, forgive me and
grant me rest from my fears.

God, you are so generous in helping us recognize your presence in our
lives. But so often I ask, "Who are you?" to avoid responsibility. At
times I am embarrassed because I fall short. Sometimes I am angry because you don't judge others as harshly as I do. Occasionally I am frightened because you know me too well. Too often I don't dare to ask because you might expect more of me than I am willing to give. But
repeatedly you simply invite me to the table to share in a meal of reconciliation. Help me share the abundance of your grace this day that
others may recognize Christ through me.

MORNING
O God, may Christ appear to those for whom I now pray.
(Prayers of Intercession)

EVENING
O God, you came for me in Christ. Come again, I pray.
(Prayers of Intercession)

**JESUS GAVE BREAD AND FISH TO THOSE WHO NEEDED TO SEE HIM ALIVE.
DO WE ALSO NEED PROOF?**
(Pray the Prayer of Our Savior.)

MORNING
Loving God, may I share
my bread today as generously
as I have received it from you.
Thanks be to God. Amen.

EVENING
Lead me into the safety
of your arms, Gentle Beloved,
as I rest from the stress of today.
Thanks be to God. Amen.

Wednesday, April 21

(Read Acts 9:1–6)

MORNING

Creator God, you awakened me to your light this morning.
May I now rise to do your will.

EVENING

Creator God, you have darkened the skies to end my day
in stillness. Now my soul rests in gratitude.

God of Justice, have I ignored the needs of your people? Have I neglected my health? Do I pursue peace and seek reconciliation? Have I breathed threats of persecution against those I don't like or with whom I am frustrated? Do I just want to give up? Shine your light upon my heart that I may turn from the road to apathy to the Way of selfless love. May I hear your voice speak a word of truth and an invitation to discipleship. Help me to get up to do as you tell me to do.

MORNING

For those who feel persecuted by their illness or relationships,
I offer these prayers of hope, O God.
(Prayers of Intercession)

EVENING

Unbind those who feel cut off from your grace,
O God, especially those for whom I pray.
(Prayers of Intercession)

WILL OTHERS KNOW WE BELONG TO THE WAY?
GRANT US STRENGTH TO BE FAITHFUL TO CHRIST.
(Pray the Prayer of Our Savior.)

MORNING

O God, may a light
from heaven guide us today. Let the
voice of Jesus bring us good news.
Thanks be to God. Amen.

EVENING

God of the Way, I give thanks
that you kept me safe today.
Tomorrow I will once again
get up to do your will.
Thanks be to God. Amen.

Thursday, April 22 · Earth Day

(Read Psalm 30:6–12)

MORNING

O Bringer of Joy, awaken my heart. As you have turned
night into day, let my morning become a dance of praise.

EVENING

O Bringer of Joy, the winds blew hard, the earth quaked,
the storms raged, but you had established me as a mountain and,
by your faith in me, I come tonight to give you thanks.

I praise you for your goodness, Great God of Love. When I was weighed down by depression, you clothed me with joy. When I took credit for my accomplishments, you showed me the mountains you called forth. So search my heart, cleanse my soul, and grant me the joy of your presence. If I refuse to live with power from on high, bring me up from false humility to bold faithfulness. O God, you have turned my sadness into dancing so that my soul may praise you and not be silent.

MORNING

Each morning we may cry to you for help.
Be gracious to me as I ask these petitions.
(Prayers of Intercession)

EVENING

Each evening we are reminded of today's miracles.
Hear my gratitude in these prayers.
(Prayers of Intercession)

MY PROSPERITY IS NOT MY OWN.
(Pray the Prayer of Our Savior.)

MORNING

Through the dust and toil
of this day, with your help, Loving
God, I will remain secure. At the end,
I will tell of your power.
Thanks be to God. Amen.

EVENING

God of peace, I ask for rest.
In the morning I shall once again
serve your people with joy.
Thanks be to God. Amen.

Friday, April 23

(Read John 21:15–19)

MORNING

Great God of Love, open my mouth to sing your praise
and my will to serve your people.

EVENING

Great God of Love, I pray my life today has reflected your light.

"Do you love me?" Jesus asks. In fact, Jesus asks "Do you love me more than these . . . ?" (We can fill in the blank!) Love without expectations allows our words to be empty phrases. But we are not told, "I will love you if . . ." The truth is that if we love, it must show. The hurting and mournful of humanity only ask that Christians live as though they love Christ. So, let us answer the call to feed and tend the people to whom Christ came to offer abundant life. Instruct me in your divine way, O God. May my life be an example of faithful loving. In so doing, I shall love myself.

MORNING

God of all people, we have faith in you.
Guide us into prayer for one another.
(Prayers of Intercession)

EVENING

Very truly, God, you have simply asked us to love.
Hear my prayers.
(Prayers of Intercession)

DO I LOVE YOU MORE THAN THESE? AM I BEING HONEST?
(Pray the Prayer of Our Savior.)

MORNING

May you be glorified today,
O God of Grace. Give me courage to
witness to your love.
Thanks be to God. Amen.

EVENING

Most Holy and Compassionate God,
feed me the love that shall calm my
fears and anxieties so I may rest and
rise to love your people once again.
Thanks be to God. Amen.

Saturday, April 24

(Read Revelation 5:13)

MORNING
Compassionate God, may I rise to offer
blessing and honor and glory and strength to you,
my Beloved.

EVENING
Compassionate God, as I reflect upon this day,
may I judge my actions according to your will.

You are the Creator of all that was, and is, and is to be. You have bestowed upon us your trust that we will care for all of creation. May we all live together in harmony to sing your praise. To you and to Christ the Lamb, our Savior, may every creature live to eternally honor the gift of our lives. May our lives be a blessing in the sight of all, for your sake and for our world.

MORNING
If I boldly ask these prayers according to your will,
you hear me, Generous God.
(Prayers of Intercession)

EVENING
I thank you for interceding on behalf of those I love today.
Hear my prayers once again, Gracious God.
(Prayers of Intercession)

CHRIST IS WORTHY!
(Pray the Prayer of Our Savior.)

MORNING
Thank you, God, for making me
worthy to be Christ's disciple.
You believe in me. Help me live as
though I believe in me too.
Thanks be to God. Amen.

EVENING
I am humbled this evening to realize
how blessed I am. Grant me awareness
tomorrow, in your name I pray.
Thanks be to God. Amen.

Sunday, April 25

(Read Revelation 5:11–12, 14)

MORNING
God of Revelation, awaken my heart;
pour out your love and your blessings.

EVENING
God of Revelation, if I failed to be faithful today,
forgive me and grant me rest from my fears.

God of Creation, all those with breath sing your praises. If I had a thousand tongues, I would not be able to give you the praise of which you are worthy. Let me worship you and praise with my "Amen!" on this Sabbath day.

MORNING
O God, may Christ appear to those
for whom I now pray.
(Prayers of Intercession)

EVENING
O God, you came for me in Christ.
Come again, I pray.
(Prayers of Intercession)

ALL GLORY AND HONOR BELONG TO GOD.
(Pray the Prayer of Our Savior.)

MORNING
O God, may a light
from heaven guide us today.
Thanks be to God.
Amen.

EVENING
God of the Way,
I give thanks that you
kept me safe today.
Thanks be to God.
Amen.

Monday, April 26

(Read Psalm 23:1–3)

MORNING
Caring God, you are my compass and guide.
I look to you for direction . . .

EVENING
Caring God, I rest in the safety of your presence.
Lead me into stillness.

Dear God, the psalmist reminds me that you, my Shepherd, are the one who knows what I need and leads me to it. In the hurry and heat of my days, I can be tempted to ignore or skip over my need for rest, nourishment, direction, or community. I can get caught up in accomplishing my goals and completing all on my agenda—forgetting that I am part of a wider community of your people. Overload can also come from the time and energy it takes to communicate and cooperate with others. God, you allow me to know when there is a time of "being" as well as "doing." Today and every day, lead me to timely pauses for re-creating, remembering, and realigning myself with you and your people. Show me what is needed.

MORNING
Compassionate God, Refresh those in leadership
and the communities they serve.
(Prayers of Intercession)

EVENING
Re-creating God, gather in your stressed ones
and lead them to a place of rest.
(Prayers of Intercession)

GOD CALLS FOR "TIME-OUT."

MORNING
Dear God, in the living of today's possibilities, remind me of my relationship with you and others. In Jesus' name, I pray. Amen.

EVENING
Refreshing God, I come to you for the rest I need to replenish my spirit this night. In Jesus' name, I pray. Amen.

Tuesday, April 27

(Read Psalm 23:4–6)

MORNING
Faithful One, I stand on the threshold of this day with you.
Strengthen me for what lies ahead.

EVENING
Faithful One, I come home with the joys and struggles
of this day to share them with you.

Shepherd God, you know how quickly darkness can transform the landscape of life into a dangerous place. In dark valleys, uneven ground, tree roots, and rocks become hazards, and landmarks are hard to see. Enemies can sneak up on me. I need direction and protection. It is such a gift to know that you are with me in dark times to provide not only light but also a table overflowing with grace—a table where I can meet my enemies face to face. O God, give me courage to meet my enemies in the power of your transforming love.

MORNING
Dear God, I bring my prayers for all
who find themselves in despair today.
(Prayers of Intercession)

EVENING
O God, I bring my enemies one by one into your loving embrace.
(Prayers of Intercession)

GOD LEADS ME FORWARD THROUGH DIFFICULT TIMES.

MORNING
Dear God, protect and encourage
me as I face the challenges of this day.
In Jesus' name, I pray. Amen.

EVENING
Generous God, my heart overflows
with thanks for your unconditional
love, which I experienced today.
In Jesus' name, I pray. Amen.

Wednesday, April 28

(Read Acts 9:36–39)

MORNING
Ever-present God, help me to be still enough
to recognize your calling for me this day.

EVENING
Ever-present God, I recall your messengers and my response.
Help me to hear your affirmation and/or forgiveness.

Peter responded to the message to come quickly. He drew near to death and listened to the people, the situation, and you, Patient God. I, too, have found myself in grief-filled scenes. The sense of loss can be overwhelming and tearful with the transition between the death of what was, and the birth of what is yet to be. Time is needed to listen with compassion; to remember and cherish life; and to share in the longing for new life. I, like others, am tempted to short-circuit, limit, discount, stay away from, or put off this prayerful pause. God of All Seasons, help me to be present to seasons of change, loss, and death. Teach me to listen carefully and to cherish stories for the sake of new life.

MORNING
O God, Comfort those who grieve losses
(loved one, relationship, job, health, youth).
(Prayers of Intercession)

EVENING
O God, I pray for families of those who have lost
someone or something dear today.
(Prayers of Intercession)

IN TIME AND BY THE GRACE OF GOD, DEATH AND GRIEF WILL OPEN INTO NEW LIFE.

MORNING
Dear God, help me to cherish
and affirm the people in my life today.
In Jesus' name, I pray. Amen.

EVENING
O God, thank you for the gift
of a community in times of life,
death, and new life. In Jesus' name,
I pray. Amen.

Thursday, April 29

(Read Acts 9:40–43)

MORNING

Dear and Gracious God, I come to you humbly
to connect with your power to bring new life.

EVENING

Dear and Gracious God, bring to my awareness
prayers spoken and unspoken this day.

Peter cleared the room to be alone with you and a seemingly impossible situation. O God, help me to clear prayer space today so that I may come to you to offer my deepest concerns. Peter looked at the lifeless form of Tabitha and fell to his knees in heartfelt prayer. Believing in your resurrection power, he asked you for new life out of death. O God, encourage me to pray your hope, peace, joy, love, and new life into the impossibilities of my life and the lives of others. In this case, Peter saw the answer to his prayer, but it is not always given to me to see or to understand the unfolding of your response to my prayers. Gracious God, help me to be faithful in prayer even when I cannot see the outcome.

MORNING

Loving God, I ask your healing for those facing death and loss.
(Prayers of Intercession)

EVENING

Gracious God, encourage your people to ask
for what they need for new life.
(Prayers of Intercession)

JESUS' PRAYER-FULL MINISTRY CONTINUES IN ME.

MORNING

Dear God, I go forth
into this day to pray and live boldly.
In Jesus' name, I pray.
Amen.

EVENING

Gracious God, thank you
for the loving way you answer prayer.
Keep me praying. In Jesus' name,
I pray. Amen.

Friday, April 30

(Read John 10:22–25)

MORNING

Faithful and Loving God, I come in faith,
acknowledging my doubts and fears.

EVENING

Faithful and Loving God, thank you
for your love offered, received, and passed on today.
Forgive me and help me to forgive others.

The religious gathering in the temple challenged Jesus, "If you are the Messiah, tell us plainly." O God, I see my own doubts and fears reflected here. There are times when I too want your identity and your leading written in big letters on a big sign so there is no mistaking that it is you. You know the times when I choose to back away and the times when I choose through loving service to declare the ongoing presence of Jesus the Christ. You know my frustration and discouragement with those who reject ministry in your name. Forgive my hesitation, O God, and challenge me to deeper faith. Make me more aware of your presence every day. Give me courage to name and share in your ministry of love.

MORNING

Dear God, I pray for those in the church and world struggling
with unbelief.
(Prayers of Intercession)

EVENING

O God, I pray for those who struggle to teach and for those who
struggle to learn.
(Prayers of Intercession)

MY LIFE IS LIVED IN JESUS' NAME.

MORNING	**EVENING**
Dear God, may my living today point to Christ's ongoing ministry and mission. In Jesus' name, I pray. Amen.	Generous God, thank you for Christ's ministry of love, which I experienced today. In Jesus' name, I pray. Amen.

Saturday, May 1 · May Day

(Read John 10:26–30)

MORNING

Shepherd God, I come as one known and loved by you,
to listen for your voice.

EVENING

Shepherd God, I come this night to meditate
on your loving care. Thank you.

Sheep recognize the loving concern of their shepherd's voice and they follow where he leads. There are many voices (friends, family, teachers, leaders, coworkers, children, and my own voice within) that I hear daily. I also hear the voices of strangers. Sometimes I hear the voice that short circuits my best intentions saying, "You can't do that!" or "You're hopeless!" At other times, I hear the voice that says, "You can do it!" Assuring God, help me to discern your loving voice in scripture, situations, people, and in the silence of my heart. I want to make sure it is you whom I am following.

MORNING

Dear God, I pray for the church to hear
Jesus' voice in their decision making.
(Prayers of Intercession)

EVENING

Loving God, I pray for lost and lonely ones,
that they may know you are with them.
(Prayers of Intercession)

I LISTEN FOR CHRIST'S LEADING.

MORNING

Dear God, I enter this new day
committed to following your lead
in Jesus. In Jesus' name, I pray.
Amen.

EVENING

Thank you God, for the joy and the
pain of belonging with others in your
family of faith. In Jesus' name, I pray.
Amen.

Sunday, May 2

(Read Revelation 7:9–17)

MORNING
Almighty God, I join with disciples
around the world today, to sing your praises.

EVENING
Almighty God, I reflect on your presence
in the challenges of this day.

Almighty God, in this reading from Revelation, I see a wonderful vision of a congregation of Christians gathered from all around the world. They are not present to debate or defend their holiness, their theology, or their differences. They are there as one body in their experience of journeying in faith through painful and difficult times with Christ and for Christ. They are gathered at the throne of grace to sing and praise you because they know what you have done for them. Loving God, where in my life have I experienced such moments of faithful celebration of your presence and provision? O God, bring me in touch with what enables and what hinders worship for me. Draw me into community and communion as I worship you with my faith family today.

MORNING
Dear God, give courage and hope in Christ to those facing crises.
(Prayers of Intercession)

EVENING
O God, I pray for the worldwide Christian Church
that we may be faithful.
(Prayers of Intercession)

I COME TO THIS PLACE TO WORSHIP GOD.

MORNING	EVENING
Dear God, lead me to a place of belonging and loving service. In Jesus' name, I pray. Amen.	Thank you for today's gathering, God. I continue to celebrate your saving grace. In Jesus' name, I pray. Amen.

Monday, May 3

(Read Psalm 148:1–6)

MORNING
God, explode into my consciousness this morning,
through the thunderous evidence of your magnificent creation!

EVENING
God, in the sun, the moon, the shining stars—the highest heavens
and the work of your hands—you have spoken eloquently
to my soul today. I offer you my praise.

In 1961 when Yuri Gagarin became the first person in space, he was reported to have scoffed that he could see no evidence of God. A couple of summers ago, on a trip to Bryce Canyon National Park with my family, we all lay on our backs on a rocky outcrop to watch the celestial map come out. The clarity was amazing. We saw a shooting star neatly dissect the Big Dipper; we observed light that had traveled at 186,000 miles per second for several years in order to reach our gaze. We looked out, from the limits of our terrestrial lives, into the vast cosmos that yields—thanks to inventions like the Hubble Telescope—more and more evidence of God's glory every day. God, you are truly an awesome God!

MORNING
Accept the praise of my humble and grateful heart, God. May the witness
of this day lead the unbelieving into the realm of your grace.
(Prayers of Intercession)

EVENING
God, did I point the way to your glory?
Did I illuminate other paths? I am your humble servant.
(Prayers of Intercession)

IF THE MAGI HAD FOLLOWED MY STAR, WOULD THEY HAVE FOUND JESUS?

MORNING
Thank you, Powerful God, for the gift of this new day. The evidence of your majesty overwhelms my senses. May it saturate my experience, too. Thanks be to Christ. Amen.

EVENING
Take my offering of this day, God, and accept it as my living act of worship. Thanks be to Christ. Amen.

Tuesday, May 4

(Read Psalm 148:7–14)

MORNING
Dear God, when I understand the imperative of your truth,
there is hope for this world.

EVENING
Dear God, I have such a deep yearning in my heart
that this world will live your law of love.

Creator God, King David realized how critical it was to recognize your sovereignty, and such a confession permeates every breath of his prayers. There is no constitutional mandate for a U.S. president to likewise acknowledge his or her creator. In 1789, however, having completed the oath of office, George Washington spontaneously added the phrase, "So help me God." Since that moment, almost every U.S. president has followed suit. Oh, the potential power of a cadre of world leadership who not only praise your name but also live lives and make policies that submit to your marvelous law of love! Guide our prayers of petition, Loving God, as we hold the politicians of this world before you.

MORNING
Loving God, today, help me to translate the power
of your authority into the details of my day.
(Prayers of Intercession)

EVENING
As I watch the evening news, I feel a heavy burden.
Use that burden, dear God, to direct my prayers.
(Prayers of Intercession)

DO I PRAY FOR THE GOVERNMENT WITH AN INTENSITY COMMENSURATE TO MY CRITICISM?

MORNING
Dear God, it is a privilege to work
out the details of my day knowing
that you are ruler. Thank you for your
trust. Thanks be to Christ. Amen.

EVENING
Thank you for the opportunity
to live another day as your humble
servant. Thanks be to Christ.
Amen.

Wednesday, May 5 · Cinco de Mayo

(Read Acts 11:1–14)

MORNING

Loving God, each day is an opportunity to see how
I will respond to your truth as revealed in scripture.

EVENING

Loving God, not only is your grace sufficient,
but it is my ever present guide.

Our lives as believers have always engaged this great struggle, since Peter first reached out to the Gentiles, between the admonition, "Go into all the world," and our natural tendency to be suspicious of anyone who does not look or act just like us! The gospel is good news, a revelation that is too precious to filter through our selective cultural prejudices, as if the message were invented exclusively in mainstream North America. God, forgive us for our arrogance when we seek to trap salvation in a political or cultural bottle. Lower such a sheet onto our rooftops, dear God, and then lead us into the places where we, too, can deliver the message of salvation.

MORNING

As I begin this day, I pray that you will challenge
my prejudice and all bigotry by the law of love.
(Prayers of Intercession)

EVENING

You wept, God, when you looked over Jerusalem.
I weep this evening in response to the injustice I have seen today.
(Prayers of Intercession)

WHAT PARTICULAR CHALLENGE HAS GOD HIGHLIGHTED FOR ME TODAY?

MORNING	**EVENING**
How gentle is your voice in directing my paths, God. Show me the way. Thanks be to Christ. Amen.	Grief and shame work together in my soul as I contemplate my divergences from your path of love, God. Teach me your way. Thanks be to Christ. Amen.

Thursday, May 6 · National Day of Prayer—U.S.A.

(Read Acts 11:15–18)

MORNING
God, what power do you have in store for me today?
And how might I serve you through my life?

EVENING
God, it is with a sense of gratitude and completion
that I consider your work through my life this day.

As a classroom teacher for almost twenty years, I always invited God to be a part of my work. Often moving from desk to desk before the day began, I would pray for each child by name. Once the students were in class I could sometimes feel the power of the Holy Spirit move through me as I would rest a hand on the shoulder of a troubled youth and offer a silent prayer. Caring and Gracious God, one reason that I believe so solidly is the tangible evidence of God's presence that the Holy Spirit provides. I know the power of your active presence and I am deeply grateful that you have never left me alone. May my life reveal that truth to the world.

MORNING
There is so much to face today, and I have so little strength.
Fill me anew with your powerful love.
(Prayers of Intercession)

EVENING
I was weak, and you strengthened me; I was broken,
and you healed me; I was happy, and you filled me with more joy.
(Prayers of Intercession)

WHAT MEASURE OF GOD'S POWER HAVE I LEFT UNTAPPED?

MORNING
God, with humility I ask for more.
More of your grace, more of your
love, more of your spirit.
Thanks be to Christ. Amen.

EVENING
I have been filled so that I might
empty myself for your sake. Now it is
evening; restore me, and hold me in
your love. Thanks be to Christ. Amen.

Friday, May 7

(Read John 13:31–35)

MORNING
Newness God, dawn is breaking, the night is over, and the newness
of your love surprises me once again with its freshness and glory.

EVENING
Newness God, no shadow, no storm, no intrusion of darkness
can displace the personal focus of your love, my friend and Creator.

God, this glory, this God-kissed radiance that defined and clarified
Christ's relationship to the Almighty, was demonstrated and fleshed out
in the form of love. Jesus loved these men and women deeply, with a
completeness they were only beginning to understand. In going away,
he was initiating a process whereby that love could be exemplified in
their relationships to one another . . . in our relationships, today, in the
church. Wow! You have entrusted us with the privilege of following you
in the way of love; you are counting on us to love one another, "Just as
I have loved you." We can be the evidence of your incarnation! Thank
you for this confidence, and for believing in us this much.

MORNING
This new day holds such possibility for a world starved of love.
Please multiply your love through your church.
(Prayers of Intercession)

EVENING
There are many, yet, to love; strengthen me.
There are many I cannot love; please heal us all.
(Prayers of Intercession)

IN MY LOVING, IS THERE AN END OF MYSELF, AND A BEGINNING OF GOD?

MORNING
The possibilities of this day
are only limited by the extent of my
immersion in you, dear God.
Thanks be to Christ. Amen.

EVENING
Thank you, Gracious God,
for loving the world through me
today. I am blessed. Thanks be
to Christ. Amen.

Saturday, May 8

(Read Revelation 21:1–4)

MORNING
Great God of purpose and promise, please inspire me today
with your vision of what is possible through your power.

EVENING
Great God of purpose and promise, while there is a distinct gulf between
the earth and your glory, I am grateful for what you have revealed to me today.

God, we read the great passages of scripture that speak of the future and become discouraged by the reality of this broken world. But then we become caught up in the vision of a time when tears will be wiped away, crying and pain extinguished, and your presence experienced in all of its joy. We will never understand the way that you propose to break into this temporal world with your redefinition of time and space. Yet, here in this particular day, May 8, 2004, it is your intention and your promise to enter my personal experience and to live profoundly through me. I am at once both honored and humbled by your commitment to this day, and to my particular life.

MORNING
Whatever the future holds, dear God, you have given this day.
I pray for all those who accept your gift.
(Prayers of Intercession)

EVENING
There has been death today, mourning, and crying.
Comfort your people, God, throughout this world.
(Prayers of Intercession)

WE ARE GOD'S EMISSARIES IN THIS BROKEN WORLD.

MORNING
It is hard to see the future, God;
be our today. It is hard to dry the
tears. Grant us strength. Thanks be
to Christ. Amen.

EVENING
Thank you, dear God,
that you are a present reality as well
as a future hope. Thanks be to Christ.
Amen.

Sunday, May 9 · Mother's Day

(Read Revelation 21:5–6)

MORNING
Alpha God, be the Alpha of this day
and make a newness in me that translates into life.

EVENING
Omega God, be the Omega of this day.
Please complete the experience of this day in the fullness of my devotion.

I have awakedned thirsty, God, eager to drink from the spring of the water of life. The newness of your love almost surprises me, sometimes, catching me off guard as I stumble sleepy-eyed into your Word. And then I am equipped for the expression of worship that is my life. The scripture speaks of the completion of all things, the beginning and the end vested in you. My life speaks of my yearning to find such completion in my discipleship. This moment, every moment of this day, I sing praise and gratitude because of your great love.

MORNING
Sovereign God, complete your work of redemption this day
in the lives of all your servants. Use even me.
(Prayers of Intercession)

EVENING
Your truth was rejected by so many today, and the evidence
of your love was not perfected. Restore us all in grace.
(Prayers of Intercession)

WHOM HAVE I DIRECTED TO THE SPRING OF THE WATER THAT GUSHES OF LIFE TODAY?

MORNING
Alpha fresh in daybreak fair,
be present in my morning prayer.
Renew my thirst, don't satisfy simply
because I cry. But, instead, because I
give, so through my life your love may
live. Thanks be to Christ. Amen.

EVENING
Alpha and Omega, greet the day
complete in love replete;
I now entreat, with God retreat,
with Jesus meet. Thanks be
to Christ. Amen.

Monday, May 10

(Read Psalm 67)

MORNING
Gracious and Loving God of new beginnings,
be my first awareness today.

EVENING
Gracious and Loving God of new endings,
I have joined with all nations and people to sing your praise.

God of starlight and sunshine, like a moth we are attracted to your brilliance. Melt hatred of nation against nation, brother against sister. How can we truly love you if our hearts hold even the smallest hate?

MORNING
Gift-giver God, thank you for the gift of life. For our brothers
and sisters who face terror and death daily, I pray. For terrorists
who do horrible deeds in your name, for enemies even when my
very being rebels against reaching out to them, grant mercy.
(Prayers of Intercession)

EVENING
Great Provider, you have blessed my day. As I sleep, others wake.
For these I pray. May those who wake begin with joy in your
name. You are God of every religion, yet not contained by any.
(Prayers of Intercession)

PRAY THE PRAYER OF OUR SAVIOR.

MORNING
May my living be a joyful
song to you! In the name of the
Christ. Amen.

EVENING
May my breathing into sleep
join the rhythm of those now waking
singing your praise. In the name
of the Christ. Amen.

Tuesday, May 11

(Read John 14:23–27)

MORNING

Newness of Life, open my eyes to the joy of obeying your word.
Help me win the struggle of ego as my will clashes with your teaching.

EVENING

Newness of Life, thank you for surprises of your grace this day
and rewards of peace and love for my small efforts.

Obeying your word is all you ask of us. You promise to come and dwell in our home, blessing us with your presence. You promise love and peace to those who listen. Open our ears so that we may hear. Set our feet on the path of righteousness.

MORNING

Your promise of love empowers me to claim partnership with you
in seeking those who do not know love. May our love spill over, spreading love
where there is none. I pray for those considered untouchable by society
and church. I pray for those who will not touch them.
(Prayers of Intercession)

EVENING

I pray for those who seek protection from all causes of anxiety especially those
who struggle with fear of abandonment and shame, those with mental illness,
those who contemplate suicide, for those whose tangled lifestyle gives little hope
of obeying your word. God of calm, grant your peace to these, your people.
(Prayers of Intercession)

PRAY THE PRAYER OF OUR SAVIOR.

MORNING

May my feet walk in the ways
of your teaching. In the name
of the Christ. Amen.

EVENING

Bless my sleeping
with your presence, allowing my sleep
to praise you. In the name
of the Christ. Amen.

Wednesday, May 12

(Read John 14:28–29)

MORNING
Spirit of God, each day is a Pentecost.
Sensitize me to the breath of your coming this day.

EVENING
Spirit of God, may the Pentecost you begin in me
spark the flint of craving a love where all are one in one another.

Praise to you, Primal Fire and Eternal Flame! On that first Pentecost your spirit rushed through the house and shook it. Shake us out of complacency. Kindle a burning desire to live in your new creation where generosity is defined by the times we gather the lost and nurture those despised by society, church, and family.

MORNING
God of fiery sunrises, allow dawn's blush to kiss the heart
of humanity, awaking a yearning for you. For those in denial
of sunrises, I pray.
(Prayers of Intercession)

EVENING
You have tested me by fire and I have caught the spark.
Allow my flame to mingle with other fires, becoming a bonfire
of praise. I pray for those not yet ignited. Set the blaze of love
in all people until this world becomes a living fire, destroying the
darkness of loneliness, bigotry, and social "isms."
(Prayers of Intercession)

PRAY THE PRAYER OF OUR SAVIOR.

MORNING
Fire in me new beginnings,
Holy Spirit! In the name
of the Christ. Amen.

EVENING
In the warm glow of embers,
I thank you for "Pentecosting" me!
In the name of the Christ. Amen.

Thursday, May 13

(Read Acts 16:9–15)

MORNING

O God, you come to me through Lydia, your servant, this morning.
Allow me to find in her story you, who are blind to gender.

EVENING

O God, thank you for the gift of Lydia and her believing household.

God of surprises, you bring the story of a woman for reflection. What are we to learn of her business acumen and ministry within the apostolic church? Is this a story for today, or only one of the past?

MORNING

I delight in your reminder that women were a blessing in the spread
of your word throughout the world. I pray for all women in ministry
and those who support them. For our sisters in religious traditions denied
full participation in ministry, I pray. I also pray for those who believe
women cannot be copartners with men in ministry.
May Lydia's acceptance by Paul become a model for all.
(Prayers of Intercession)

EVENING

God of all who labor, you came to us in a woman this day. I pray
for those who set barriers for women in the workplace, whether home or
church. For all who struggle for balance; for single mothers; for working
mothers; and for women whose work is creating a nurturing home, I pray.
(Prayers of Intercession)

PRAY THE PRAYER OF OUR SAVIOR.

MORNING

May the challenges of women
be instructive. In the name
of the Christ. Amen.

EVENING

The day is at an end.
God of all humanity, never let the
lessons of this day come to an end.
In the name of the Christ. Amen.

Friday, May 14

(Read Revelations 21:10)

MORNING

O God of mystery and intimacy, who is close
and yet far away, forever ancient and yet new,
open my eyes to discovery of you this day.

EVENING

O God of mystery and intimacy, you have touched me
through your poetry. Continue to teach me through the wonder
of your revelation.

You swept humanity to the highest mountain for a glimpse of what can
be—the new Jerusalem, here now and not yet. You created each of us
to help fulfill that wondrous day when all will be well. Remind me of
my role in preparing this world for transformation.

MORNING

Creating and re-creating God, what a blessing
and responsibility is ours! I pray for those who seek justice,
walking together in pilgrimage. I pray for those with potential,
hovering on the brink of decision.
(Prayers of Intercession)

EVENING

God, our architect of forever, thank you for building lessons.
I pray for those in power to use it wisely building bridges
instead of fences.
(Prayers of Intercession)

PRAY THE PRAYER OF OUR SAVIOR.

MORNING

May the beginnings of the new
Jerusalem start with my waking.
In the name of the Christ.
Amen.

EVENING

May sleep come easily
after this day's labor. Revealing God,
thank you for this day of discovery.
In the name of the Christ. Amen.

Saturday, May 15

(Read Revelation 22:5)

MORNING

Creator God, what joy to wake to possibilities
of no national boundaries, no labels, no focus but the promise
fulfilled. My heart is filled with your fullness!

EVENING

Creator God, thank you for broadening my vision,
allowing me to taste the future in the now.

We are being lured to a time and place where there is no artificial light. The only light we will need is the reality of our relationship with one another in you. Help me bring about this reality in my everyday world.

MORNING

Thank you for the opportunity to work with you in building
a new tomorrow. For all that is lacking in me, I rely on your strength.
I pray for our churches to welcome all cultures, all clans and families, so
they find room in our hearts and in our lives. I pray that our country
cherishes the aging and the young, the disenfranchised, the differently able,
minorities of any kind, so that we honor our part of the covenant.
(Prayers of Intercession)

EVENING

Thank you for insights and a day well spent. I pray for those
not yet aware of our task. For those whose world is too small, whose vision
is limited, for those whose attitudes are too rigid and whose assumptions
are too simplistic, I pray for challenge and change.
(Prayers of Intercession)

PRAY THE PRAYER OF OUR SAVIOR.

MORNING

May we become inclusive in our
worldview, O God of humanity!
In the name of the Christ.
Amen.

EVENING

My sleep is peaceful
knowing you are God!
In the name of the Christ.
Amen.

THANK YOU FOR YOUR INTEREST IN BOOKS FROM THE PILGRIM PRESS.

Title of book purchased _____

What comments do you have? _____

Why did you purchase this book? (Check all that apply)

❑ Subject ❑ Recommendation of a friend ❑ Information on cover ❑ Gift
❑ Author ❑ Recommendation of reviewer ❑ Appearance of cover ❑ Other _____

If purchased: Bookseller _____ City _____ State _____

I am interested in the following subjects (check all that apply):

❑ African American Resources   ❑ Evangelism and Church Growth   ❑ Personal Growth/Spirituality
❑ Biblical Studies   ❑ Lectionary and Worship   ❑ Seasonal Resources
❑ Children's Sermons   ❑ Meditation and Devotion   ❑ United Church of Christ Identity
❑ Confirmation/Baptism   ❑ Multicultural/Multiracial   and History
❑ Education: Christian, Theological   ❑ Pastoral Resources   ❑ CURRENT CATALOG

Name _____ Phone _____

Date _____ Fax _____

Address _____ City, State & Zip _____

_____ E-mail address _____

BOOKS AT THE NEXUS OF RELIGION AND CULTURE

THE PILGRIM PRESS

700 Prospect Avenue ■ Cleveland, Ohio 44115
Phone: 1-800-537-3394 ■ Fax: 1-216-736-2206
E-mail: pilgrim@ucc.org ■ Web sites: www.pilgrimpress.com

CALL OUR TOLL-FREE NUMBER, LOG ON TO OUR WEB SITE,
OR VISIT YOUR LOCAL BOOKSTORE.

TO ORDER

{ 1.800.537.3394 }

THE PILGRIM PRESS

Sunday, May 16

(Read Revelation 21:22)

MORNING

Sunrise God, bless those who sing your praise
rather than destroy others. May our harvest
be abundant love for all people.

EVENING

Sunset God, may the many names
that are yours become a symphony of joyful song
and healing balm for those who suffer.

Creator God, you are the truth and the way. No walls can hold your glory and power. You are the temple that I seek. Allow my voice to praise you.

MORNING

Never leave me, O Blessed One,
for it is you who work through me.
(Prayers of Intercession)

EVENING

For those whose seek you in all the wrong places,
I pray that they will seek you in truth, love, and justice.
(Prayers of Intercession)

PRAY THE PRAYER OF OUR SAVIOR.

MORNING

For those who labor,
birthing peace and compassion,
wisdom and justice, I pray. Take these
bricks and mortar of our intentions
and build a new Jerusalem.
In the name of the Christ.
Amen.

EVENING

Those who empower others,
who liberate, who live with integrity
and dignity, those who live as
faithful stewards, I pray you
bless with abundance.
In the name of the Christ.
Amen.

Monday, May 17

(Read Revelation 22:12–14)

MORNING

Dear God, as I brush the cobwebs of sleep from my mind,
I give thanks to you. As you are the beginning of this day,
I thank you for life.

EVENING

Dear God, from the Alpha of life you have kept me
in your care. Thank you.

Most precious and loving God, I come before you remembering that you were in the beginning, that you are in the present, and that you will be in the end. I thank you for being with me from my beginning, and I pray that you will continue to walk with me as I open my heart to your perfect will.

MORNING

Holy God, as I start this day, keep me mindful
of others who do not know you and are in need of your love.
(Prayers of Intercession)

EVENING

God, as the Omega of this day approaches, I thank you
for your presence. Be with me this day and every day
until the Omega of my life comes.
(Prayers of Intercession)

AS JESUS CHRIST TAUGHT, I PRAY.
(Pray the Prayer of Our Savior.)

MORNING

Come, dear God, fill me
with your Spirit, that I may do your
will this day. In Christ, I pray.
Amen.

EVENING

Thank you, gracious God,
for your presence with me this day.
In Christ, I pray.
Amen.

Tuesday, May 18

(Read Acts 16:16–34)

MORNING

Dear God of freedom and liberation, free me from the prisons
of selfishness as I greet those who have not been exposed to your love.

EVENING

Dear God of freedom and liberation, help me to keep
my covenant with you by sharing your forgiveness of sins
with others as you have shared it with me.

God of love and life, who has been with us as we live in diaspora, struggle, and oppression, send another earthquake to free us from our prisons of hate and self-doubt. God, you would not have allowed us to remain if you did not have plans for our freedom. Have mercy on me this day, Savior God. Allow me to share your love and your freedom with someone who has lost hope in life.

MORNING

Dear Jesus, free me from my apathy as I see the need
to help others in their quest for liberation and freedom from sin.
(Prayers of Intercession)

EVENING

Thank you, God, for giving me the courage
to share your gospel with one who was in spiritual bondage,
as you shared it with me in my bondage.
(Prayers of Intercession)

WITH HOPE I PRAY.
(Pray the Prayer of Our Savior.)

MORNING

Dear saving God, keep me free
from my addiction of selfishness.
In Christ, I pray. Amen.

EVENING

Dear holy God, thank you
for your power, which has been my
strength this day. In Christ, I pray.
Amen.

Wednesday, May 19

(Read Psalm 97)

MORNING
Dear God, I awake today fresh in the knowledge
that no matter what I am confronted with,
you are in control of the situation.

EVENING
Dear God, thank you for being the sunshine of my day
and for making my enemies like wax in your light.

O God, I thank you for the knowledge that you are with me. As I engage with those who seek to hinder my service to you, I can take comfort that you are in control. As long as I keep steadfast and do your will, then all things will work out to your glory and honor.

MORNING
Dear Jesus, thank you for your presence in my life.
Holy God, as you control the flow of time, control me,
and keep me from going against your will.
(Prayers of Intercession)

EVENING
Thank you, God, for this day of freedom in Christ.
Keep me in your way of freedom.
(Prayers of Intercession)

EVER-PRESENT GOD, I PRAY.
(Pray the Prayer of Our Savior.)

MORNING
Dearest God, control my thoughts
and actions this day and always.
In Christ, I pray. Amen.

EVENING
Dear God, your mercy was evident
in my life today. Thank you
for loving me. In Christ, I pray.
Amen.

Thursday, May 20 · Ascension Day

(Read Revelation 22:16–17)

MORNING

Good morning, loving God, who watched over me as I slept.
Thank you for your touch this morning—a touch that allowed me
to wake in the land of the living.

EVENING

Good evening, loving God. As this day fades into night, my soul is buoyed
by your light. You have smiled upon me and made me glad. Thank you.

Gracious and generous God, thank you for being the wellspring of love in my life. God, I acknowledge that I stand in need of your love as I go through this wilderness journey. In the middle of the desert of difficulty, you are there with a refreshing offering of "come and drink." Without you in my life I would dry up and burn out. But you are there, always ready to comfort and console me. I am coming to drink from the well that offers the water of life. Thank you, thank you, thank you.

MORNING

Good morning, God; thank you for waking me with the cool running
waters of life this morning. I pray that during the heat of this day
I will come to you to quench my thirst.
(Prayers of Intercession)

EVENING

Thank you, Jesus, for your presence in my dealings today. I was truly in need
of spiritual refreshment and you provided me with all that I needed. Thank you,
Jesus. May I always have the good sense to call on you when I am thirsty.
(Prayers of Intercession)

REFRESHED, I PRAY.
(Pray the Prayer of Our Savior.)

MORNING

Good morning, Jesus. Truly this
will be a blessed day because you
are the bright and morning star.
In Christ, I pray. Amen.

EVENING

Jesus, I end this day in the comfort
of being blessed by your love.
In Christ, I pray. Amen.

Friday, May 21

(Read John 17:20–26)

MORNING

God, as I come to consciousness, I feel bathed in the light
of your revelation that Jesus is the Christ and that if we
acknowledge Jesus then we can be one with you.

EVENING

God, today I saw the beauty in the diverse quilt
of humankind and not in the blanket of sameness.

Dearest God, you created us in your image of love and planted in our collective hearts the seeds of inclusiveness. Allow our love for one another to grow, so that we may be one in your sight. And may we be one in our sight as well—not one in the sense of clones, but one in the spirit of Christ.

MORNING

Sovereign God, who looks upon those called by your name,
I pray that I will be able to look beyond our differences
to see the beauty of our diversity.
(Prayers of Intercession)

EVENING

Loving God, you created us in your image, equal yet not same,
like a tapestry as beautifully woven as a field of wildflowers.
Jesus, let us see the world through different eyes today.
(Prayers of Intercession)

IN AWE OF YOUR MERCY, I PRAY.
(Pray the Prayer of Our Savior.)

MORNING

Dear God, let me see myself in the lives of those whom I normally pass by on the streets. In Christ, I pray. Amen.

EVENING

Thank you, God, for letting me see myself—and you—in the face of a hungry child, in the outstretched hand of a person asking for money, in a person who was challenged. Praise be to you. God. In Christ, I pray. Amen.

Saturday, May 22

(Read Acts 16:16–34)

MORNING

Dear God, I awaken this morning comforted
by the knowledge that I know in whom I believe. Thank you for
caring enough about me to allow me to be one of your children.

EVENING

Dear God, thank you for keeping me out of harm's way.

Saving God, who threw me a rope of hope in a sea of despair, I come as humbly as I know how to say thank you. If I had been left to my own devices, I would have self-destructed. You entered my life in a mighty way. You shook me like you shook that jail. You rocked the foundations of my foolishness and brought me into a right relationship with you. You freed me from a prison of self, and freed me to live in relationship with you. God, I love you and I thank you for caring so much about me. Help me to share the message of what it takes to be saved with others whom I encounter.

MORNING

Good morning, Jesus, I take comfort in being rescued
from sinfulness and shame by your love.
(Prayers of Intercession)

EVENING

God, you are the architect of the household of my life.
Thank you for your presence today.
(Prayers of Intercession)

BOLDLY I PRAY.
(Pray the Prayer of Our Savior.)

MORNING

Dear God, may I feel
your guiding hand in every place
that I venture today.
In Christ, I pray. Amen.

EVENING

Thank you, God. You protected me
from harm. Empower me to share a
message of love from Christ Jesus:
Don't harm yourself; instead choose life,
choose Jesus. In Christ, I pray. Amen.

Sunday, May 23

(Read Revelation 22:20–21)

M O R N I N G

Good morning, God. I awaken with anxiety today
knowing that you could come back at any moment or that I could
leave this place at any moment. Regardless, help me to live
this day in a manner that will be acceptable to you.

E V E N I N G

Good evening, God. Thank you for your mercy in my life.

Jesus, today is your day. Today I will try to live my life as completely as possible. Come into my life, Lamb of God, and you will see that the table has been set for your arrival. There is room in the inn of my soul for you to reside. Jesus, I pray that I will be able to help make this world as ready for your coming as I am ready for you to come back.

M O R N I N G

Help me, God, to make the world a better place in which all can live.
(Prayers of Intercession)

E V E N I N G

Well, Jesus, it is the end of another week, and I thank you for having been
with me. By your grace I have made it through, and by your grace I look
forward to the next week. Your grace has sustained me through the narrow
passageways of difficulty and has guided me to the pastures of peace.
May your grace continue to be all that I need.
(Prayers of Intercession)

CONFIDENTLY I PRAY.
(Pray the Prayer of Our Savior.)

M O R N I N G

God of life, I take great pleasure
in waking in your arms this day.
In Christ, I pray. Amen.

E V E N I N G

Perfect and loving God,
I am blessed because I am your child.
In Christ, I pray. Amen.

Monday, May 24 · Victoria Day—Canada

(Read Genesis 11:1–9)

MORNING

God of order, when I pray in the language of confusion,
all understanding comes to a halt. Teach me this day to listen
only for what I need to hear.

EVENING

God of order, thank you for those moments today
when I heard your quiet voice in the midst of confusing times.

When all appears to go well and our towers fall upon us, you, O God, show us a new way of speaking. With clarity of purpose, you meet our yearning for oneness of human dignity and fair-spirited respect. You give us a common language of compassion and the new choice of practicing a tenacious hope rather than allowing fear to reign.

MORNING

My prayer for a sense of wholeness and continuity
goes to all who rise this day with spirits still scattered
and confused by the disruption of their plans.
(Prayers of Intercession)

EVENING

My prayer for healing patience goes to all for whom
night time awakens the lament of grief because toppled towers
have caused a temporary Babel of their lives.
(Prayers of Intercession)

GOD SCATTERS OUR MISGUIDED EFFORTS,

THEN PROVIDES A WAY TO REBUILD UNDERSTANDING.

(Pray the Prayer of Our Savior.)

MORNING

As I rise from my bed this day,
God, before wrongful reasons shout,
I would listen to my first nature to
understand and to be understood. In
the mighty name of the Christ. Amen.

EVENING

As I turn into bed this night, God,
I would give over to you the regretful
misunderstandings and lack of communication that I prompted today. In
the mighty name of the Christ. Amen.

Tuesday, May 25

(Read Psalm 104:24–26)

MORNING

Holy One, when I pray in the language of creation, I greet your new day
with a spirit that sings. Curious about what great or small creations my own
wisdom might engender, my imagination dances with anticipation.

EVENING

Holy One, thank you for the song of each small and great work
that I have created today, each an expression of your gift of creativity.

Creating God, from toenail to thumb, from wonder to imaginative
vigor, from chuckle to tear, in wisdom you have made them all. Today,
may I use the vigorous living sea of my mind with the renewed strength
of a creating and purposeful spirit.

MORNING

Dear God, may all who first meet this day with a lack of enthusiasm
become curious about the possibility of some small or great accomplishment.
May fullness of life flow through your spirit.

(Prayers of Intercession)

EVENING

I pray for all who have begun to hope, turning their energy
toward shaping productive ideas. Thank you, God, for all creative
thought and work of this day.

(Prayers of Intercession)

GOD IS ALWAYS AWAKENING POSSIBILITY WITHIN US,

AROUND US, AND THROUGH OUR BEING.

(Pray the Prayer of Our Savior.)

MORNING

Dear God, may I see your creative
hand in all that I produce today and
be grateful. In the mighty name
of the Christ. Amen.

EVENING

Thank you, God, for each small
or great act of creation, each a gift
from you that I have uncovered today.
In the mighty name of the Christ.
Amen.

Wednesday, May 26

(Read Psalm 104:27–30)

MORNING
God, you who engage, when I pray in the language
of your rhythm, may I be receptive to the life-giving offerings
of your extended hand.

EVENING
God, you who release, as this day dies and turns to memory,
may I let go of all that has completed its season in the gift of today.

From the linden's greening to the dusting from its leaves, from the possibility of a child's being to that living adult's commencement, from the hint of a relationship to its conclusion, throughout creation you teach the rhythm of engagement and release. In the turning point of this week, may I open my hand with as gracious a spirit for both moments of receiving and of letting go throughout the seasons of today.

MORNING
Engaging God, fill with expectancy all those who have mislaid
hope of receiving life-giving blessings from your open hand.
(Prayers of Intercession)

EVENING
Releasing God, fill with hopeful wonder all those who are gloomy,
having become aware of some letting go of their being.
(Prayers of Intercession)

BECAUSE GOD STANDS READY WITH RENEWING SPIRIT,

EVEN LETTING GO IS AN ACT OF CREATION.
(Pray the Prayer of Our Savior.)

MORNING
This new day frees what is new
about me. I go forth with a thankful
heart for your gifts of the season
called today. In the mighty name
of the Christ. Amen.

EVENING
Day's end frees what about me
has been completed. I rest thankful
anticipating your benediction and
tomorrow's renewal. In the mighty
name of the Christ. Amen.

Thursday, May 27

(Read Psalm 104:31–35)

MORNING

Holy One, I hear a quiet humming within my soul this morning
and know that, today, I will pray in the language of song. Thank you.

EVENING

Holy One, have you heard my song today? In every action, I have sung
you a song of hope. In every pause, I have sung you a song of adoration.

A song of keening, a song of peace, a song of doggedness, a song the
color of yellow; a song of freedom, a song of trust, a silent song—you
hear them all, God, and sing your Amen.

MORNING

Lyric God, for all who have forgotten how to sing,
awaken a new rhythm—one that first sways then breaks
into a voice as life-full as that of May's nesting birds.
(Prayers of Intercession)

EVENING

Give to all who end this day without a song,
the memory of having once sung and the certainty that you,
dear God, heed the yearned for but yet silent note.
(Prayers of Intercession)

LISTENING FOR THE FIRST NOTE WITHIN MY SOUL,

THE SPIRIT OF GOD OFFERS AT ONCE A COMPOSITION FOR TWO VOICES.

(Pray the Prayer of Our Savior.)

MORNING

With tomorrow having
become today, my song is a spirited
refrain. For as long as I live, God,
I will meet your morning song with
mine. In the mighty name
of the Christ. Amen.

EVENING

As Thursday modulates
into Friday, my song is telling tranquil
tones. For as long as I have being, God,
I will sing with you an evening song.
In the mighty name
of the Christ. Amen.

Friday, May 28

(Read Acts 2:1–4)

MORNING

Dear God, when I pray in the language of understanding,
I first greet your new day by listening.

EVENING

Dear God, thank you for those times today that I heard the quiet,
native tongues of grief, pain, injustice, or serenity.

You always have something in mind for us, Holy One—a new way of connecting, a new way of speaking even if a stroke has taken our voice or a disease has muddled our thought. As the language of my prayer continues to change, you show the way for new clarity, new voice, new listening, a new language.

MORNING

Gracious God, I pray for the opening of your spirit among all for whom communication is thwarted so that they might recognize that tending a garden, listening to the language of silence, touching a hand to another's arm, and playing the harmonica are among the languages of prayer.
(Prayers of Intercession)

EVENING

Gracious God, as their language of living and praying continues to change,
I give thanks for all who spoke and found understanding this day.
(Prayers of Intercession)

SPIRIT-FILLING GOD, ALWAYS FIND A PATH FOR ALL TO SPEAK AND TO BE UNDERSTOOD
EVEN IF THAT WAY IS SITTING IN THE OPENING SILENCE AND SIMPLY BEING.
(Pray the Prayer of Our Savior.)

MORNING

I set about this new day
with a new listening beyond words to
the spirit-filled language of the heart.
In the mighty name of the Christ.
Amen.

EVENING

I put away this day grateful that I
heard you, Kind One, in those listening moments of compassion, patience,
and forgiveness. I am amazed. In the
mighty name of the Christ. Amen.

Saturday, May 29

(Read Acts 2:5–21)

MORNING
Accepting God, when I pray in the language of one who has been
understood, may I greet those whom I may meet this day with the
leverage of an understanding heart.

EVENING
Accepting God, thank you for those moments of this day when my native
tongue became a bridge instead of a barrier to my neighbor's understanding.

Through the gift of your accepting spirit, the Babel of many native
tongues gains the possibility of becoming understandable. Your affirmation of my differences opens my heart to speak with a welcoming
voice, accessible to others within our diverse human family.

MORNING
I pray this morning, God, for all who feel invalid,
unaccepted, or less than whole because of relationships with faulty
communication. Open these hearts to an awareness of your
presence as spirit nudging all toward greater understanding.
(Prayers of Intercession)

EVENING
Thank you, God, for those moments throughout the day when the presence
of your spirit revealed a greater understanding among those whose ears once
could comprehend nothing beyond their own native tongue.
(Prayers of Intercession)

GOD'S ACCEPTING, VALIDATING, AND AFFIRMING PRESENCE IS CONTAGIOUS.
(Pray the Prayer of Our Savior.)

MORNING
Today, Gracious One, may I speak
with understanding that conveys a
recognition of my neighbor's unique
value as part of the human family.
In the mighty name of the Christ.
Amen.

EVENING
I end this day, God,
with a grateful heart for those
moments that one to whom I spoke
received the gifts of understanding
and having been understood. In the
name of the Christ. Amen.

Sunday, May 30 · Pentecost Sunday

(Read John 14:8–17)

MORNING
Indwelling God, today I pray in your language.
I begin this special day of Pentecost with less wandering and
greater moral vigor because of your persistent, present spirit.

EVENING
Indwelling God, in the difficult decisions of this day,
in the moments of celebration and relief, in the midst of the routine,
I recognized the gift of your lively spirit and gave thanks.

You understand when my belief stammers. I need more than an historical memory. You offer the presence of your spirit in my innermost depth. I perceive your steadfastness as a trusted friend. Spirit of truth, you are present as the clarion ring of a right decision, as the integrity of my actions.

MORNING
My prayers encircle all for whom belief comes hard.
May your sustaining presence become obvious today in acts of justice,
fair play, honorable relationships, and trustworthy friends.
(Prayers of Intercession)

EVENING
God who remains with us, strengthen the trust of those
who dared to believe today in the advocacy of your Holy Spirit. Amen.
(Prayers of Intercession)

GOD IS ALWAYS SEEKING WAYS TO MAKE GOD'S PRESENCE UNMISTAKABLE.
(Pray the Prayer of Our Savior.)

MORNING
God who remains with us,
may my actions tell that I choose to
love God and my neighbor as myself.
May I gain strength from knowing
your presence. In the mighty
name of the Christ. Amen.

EVENING
Thank you, God, for your quiet,
persistent voice of truth that guided
the truth of my actions today.
In the mighty name of the Christ.
Amen.

Monday, May 31 · Memorial Day—U.S.A.

(Read Proverbs 8:1–4)

MORNING

God of wisdom, as day dawns, open the ears of my heart to hear
the word you will speak to me in the persons and events of this day.

EVENING

God of wisdom, as night falls, let my heart ponder the words
you have spoken to me in all I have encountered today.

For those who have ears to hear, Wisdom still cries out upon the heights. God, does not everything that exists speak of you, the one who called it into being? The order of creation proclaims your intelligence, you who gave it the laws of nature; each person announces your love in whose image he or she is created. God, in every situation, you call us to respond in faith, hope, and love; in every decision, Christ himself says, "Come, follow me." Yet, God, your voice often comes to us in a whisper, as it did to the prophet Elijah.

MORNING

God, I praise you for calling me to you each new day.
I pray for all those who will be too busy to hear you speak today.
(Prayers of Intercession)

EVENING

God, I thank you for all you have said to me today.
I pray for all those who are afraid to hear your voice.
(Prayers of Intercession)

GOD, I PRAY IN THE WORDS THAT YOU YOURSELF HAVE TAUGHT US.
(Pray the Prayer of Our Savior.)

MORNING

O God, may I be both a hearer
and doer of your word.
In Jesus' name. Amen.

EVENING

O God, may the word
of Christ dwell within me.
In Jesus' name. Amen.

Tuesday, June 1

(Read Proverbs 8:22–31)

MORNING

Christ, wisdom and power of God, as the sun rises,
illuminate my day with the light of your truth.

EVENING

Christ, wisdom and power of God, as the sun sets,
dispel the darkness of my night with the light of your truth.

God, from generation to generation, humans pass on their accumulated wisdom in their institutions and customs, stories and songs, laws and rituals. But with the passage of time, their original insights often become distorted, irrelevant, or lost. God, your wisdom, however, existed before time began and will exist after it has come to an end. Yet, there is no "before" and "after" in the divine wisdom; it exists in the timelessness of your eternal "now," but is present to every moment of human time and history. This eternal wisdom has entered time in Christ and continues to enlighten us through his Word and his Spirit.

MORNING

God, I thank you for Christ, the light of the world, and pray
for all those who will be tempted to follow a lesser light today.
(Prayers of Intercession)

EVENING

God, I thank you for Christ, who has lit our way to you,
and I pray for all those who have walked in darkness today.
(Prayers of Intercession)

GOD, I PRAY WITH THE WORDS OF YOUR HOLY WISDOM.
(Pray the Prayer of Our Savior.)

MORNING	**EVENING**
O God of all truth, may your eternal wisdom inspire all my thoughts, words, and actions throughout this day. In Jesus' name. Amen.	O God of all truth, may your eternal wisdom stand guard over my mind and heart throughout this night. In Jesus' name. Amen.

Wednesday, June 2

(Read Psalm 8:1–5)

MORNING
God of glory, you who make all things new,
I praise you at the beginning of this new day.

EVENING
God of glory, you who bring all things to fulfillment,
I praise you at the close of this day.

Creator God, scientists have calculated that our expanding universe is over ten billion light years across and is between ten and fifteen billion years old. How insignificant is the planet Earth, and how incomparably small are we individual humans! Yet, we are the objects of your special care: You call each of us by name and have even numbered the hairs on our heads. Not only have you created us out of infinite love and redeemed us through the life, death, and resurrection of Christ, but you dwell in our hearts through the Holy Spirit, closer to us than we are to ourselves.

MORNING
God, I praise you and pray for all those who have not yet
come to know you through the things you have made
and through the revelation of Christ, your Son.
(Prayers of Intercession)

EVENING
God, I praise you and pray for all those who, even though they
know you, do not give you the glory and honor that is your due.
(Prayers of Intercession)

GOD, I HALLOW YOUR HOLY NAME IN THE WORDS OF CHRIST HIMSELF.
(Pray the Prayer of Our Savior.)

MORNING
O God, may I praise you throughout
this day, you who are always with me.
In Jesus' name. Amen.

EVENING
O God, may I praise you this evening,
you who care for me even
while I sleep. In Jesus' name. Amen.

Thursday, June 3

(Read Psalm 8:6–10)

MORNING

God of all the earth, help me to use well
all that you have entrusted to my care.

EVENING

God of all the earth, thank you for all the gifts
and blessings of this day.

We have polluted our air, water, and land; allowed the deforestation of woods, the erosion of soil, and the extinction of species; and consumed nonrenewable resources. Yet, in giving us dominion over the earth, God, you call us not to domination and exploitation but to care and conservation. Creator, the things that you have made are available for our use, not our abuse, and ought to serve our need, not our greed. No amount of hoarding or consumption will ever fill our empty hearts, which hunger until we are fed by you. May we see your presence in all things and prove ourselves good and faithful stewards of all that you have given us.

MORNING

God, I praise you for your creation and pray for all
who lack the things they need.
(Prayers of Intercession)

EVENING

God, I thank you for your gifts and pray for all
whose hearts are closed to those in need.
(Prayers of Intercession)

GOD, I BEG MY DAILY BREAD FROM YOU IN THE WORDS OF CHRIST.
(Pray the Prayer of Our Savior.)

MORNING

O God, you have given me
more than I need. May I be generous
in sharing with others today.
In Jesus' name. Amen.

EVENING

O God, how can I give to others
as you have given to me? Forgive all
my failings and help me to grow in
your love. In Jesus' name. Amen.

Friday, June 4

(Read Romans 5:1–2)

MORNING
Faithful God, help me to be true to you today and,
in doing so, to be true to myself and to others.

EVENING
Faithful God, thank you for your steadfast love for me today.
Let me rest in you tonight.

Caring God, my relationship to another human person becomes truly personal when I receive, in belief and trust, his or her good will towards me. Likewise, when I receive your acceptance of me, I enter into right relationship with you. As I bring my feelings and desires, will and actions, to you by faith, a right order emerges within my soul. And by faith, when I accept all others as your sons and daughters, I come into right relationship with them as well. Truly, we are justified by faith.

MORNING
God of everlasting love, I pray for all those who will face
a crisis of faith today. Help their unbelief.
(Prayers of Intercession)

EVENING
God of everlasting love, I pray for all those who do not yet
believe in you. Grant them the gift of faith.
(Prayers of Intercession)

GOD, I PRAY TO YOU IN CONFIDENT FAITH.
(Pray the Prayer of Our Savior.)

MORNING
Today, O God, increase my faith,
and let my every thought, word, and
deed be an expression of my faith
in you. In Jesus' name. Amen.

EVENING
O God, forgive me for all the times
today that I did not act in accordance
with your gift of faith. In Jesus' name.
Amen.

Saturday, June 5

(Read Romans 5:3–5)

MORNING

Loving God, help me to love you today,
not merely in word, but in deed.

EVENING

Loving God, thank you for the signs of your love today,
those I saw and those I did not see.

We willingly sacrifice for those who love us and whom we love in return. Faith enables us to experience divine love. Out of love, we become willing to endure any affliction for you, the God who first loved us. May this willingness give rise, not to isolated acts, but to a way of life. Your love, Loving God, will form our entire character. And our hope for final union with you will not be disappointed, since it has already begun through the indwelling of the Holy Spirit in our hearts.

MORNING

God, I rejoice in your love and pray for all those I will meet today.
May they experience your love through me.
(Prayers of Intercession)

EVENING

God, I rejoice in your love and pray for all those
who do not know your love. May I help them to do so.
(Prayers of Intercession)

GOD, I PRAY TO YOU, TRUSTING IN YOUR LOVE.
(Pray the Prayer of Our Savior.)

MORNING

O God, may I remain confident
of your love in whatever trials I face
today. In Jesus' name.
Amen.

EVENING

O God, forgive my failings
in love today and help me love you as
you have loved me. In Jesus' name.
Amen.

Sunday, June 6 · Trinity Sunday

(Read John 16:12–15)

MORNING
Christ, Revelation of God, today, send your
Spirit of truth to guide me in all of my ways.

EVENING
Christ, Revelation of God, I have grown another day in age.
Let me grow in wisdom and understanding too.

Christ, you are the final and definitive revelation of God. There can be no further revelation beyond you. Yet, after twenty centuries, we have not exhausted the mystery of God as revealed in you. We need the Spirit to guide us into all truth. An important part of that truth, however, concerns not only the nature of God and you, the Christ, but the coming of God's realm on earth as it is in heaven. In order that we, the people of God, may embody your truth, we need the guidance of the Spirit who announces the things to come.

MORNING
God, may your Spirit of truth descend upon me
and all those who are seeking the truth.
(Prayers of Intercession)

EVENING
God, send your Spirit of truth to free me and
all those entrapped in ignorance and fear.
(Prayers of Intercession)

GOD, LET YOUR SPIRIT TEACH ME HOW TO PRAY

AS YOU TAUGHT YOUR DISCIPLES TO PRAY.

(Pray the Prayer of Our Savior.)

MORNING	EVENING
O God, may I see your truth today in ways I have not seen it before. In Jesus' name. Amen.	O God, thank you for the insights of this day. May they deepen as I meditate on them tonight. In Jesus' name. Amen.

Monday, June 7

(Read 1 Kings 21:1–10, (11–14), 15–21a)

MORNING
O God of Love, help me to use this day
in ways that bring honor to your name.

EVENING
O God of Love, when I have wronged you
or another person and seek your forgiveness, remind me
that your mercy is wider than the measure of human minds.

Awakening God, in all my comings and goings, may I look beyond my own desires and consider the effect of what I do and say on other people and situations. Let me never forget that I am responsible for the consequences of my daily decisions, but that just as I cannot escape your judgment, I cannot escape your love.

MORNING
For all those who have been hurt by cruel hearts and selfish acts,
may today bring a sense of peace and healing.
(Prayers of Intercession)

EVENING
May those who have come across my path today
rest well this night.
(Prayers of Intercession)

THROUGH PRAYER AND CAREFUL PLANNING,
KEEP ME FROM APPEASING EARTHLY IDOLS OR GOING AFTER
THOSE THINGS THAT DETRACT ME FROM BEING MY BEST.
(Pray the Prayer of Our Savior.)

MORNING
Abide with me, O God,
and keep me safe this night.
In Jesus' name. Amen.

EVENING
Thanks be, in Jesus' name,
for blessings brought to me this day
through the goodness of others.
In Jesus' name. Amen.

Tuesday, June 8

(Read Psalm 5:1–8)

MORNING

God of all beauty and delight, attune my ear and eyes
that I too, like the psalmist, may read the lessons of life
we learn through nature.

EVENING

God of all beauty and delight, never let me assume
that evil done in this world is ever a part of your plan,
O God of justice and peace.

You are always with me, before me, behind me, above me, and below me. Even when I cannot feel your presence, or when I forget to look for it, you are there. Write on my eyes and my ears, my lips and my hands, this assurance; and when my heart is heavy, speak your still, small voice of calm.

MORNING

For those who have never heard the good news
of your spiritual bounty, may this prayer move some
in their lives to speak up and out for you.
(Prayers of Intercession)

EVENING

Convince all who carry heavy burdens that they can
indeed lay them at your feet.
(Prayers of Intercession)

I OPEN MY HEART TO YOU, DEAR FRIEND.
(Pray the Prayer of Our Savior.)

MORNING

Hear my voice this morning,
Great Listener. I bring to you the
things that worry me.
In Jesus' name. Amen.

EVENING

Knowing you abide in me forever,
no matter what happens this night, or
in the darkest night of my soul,
I close my eyes and rest.
In Jesus' name. Amen.

Wednesday, June 9

(Read 2 Samuel 11:26–12:10, 13–15)

MORNING
Maker of all beautiful and holy moments, thank you
for the freshness of a new day, stretched out like a new canvas,
inviting my mark upon it.

EVENING
Maker of all beautiful and holy moments, the comforts of evensong
get overpowered by off-key regrets and unfinished business from the day.
Touch my spirit, O God of Calm, for I know tomorrow I can do better.

Hold me wise to my own behavior. Never let complacency or greed
make me forget what I know is right.

MORNING
You have given me a fresh new day, Creator God. Now it is my
turn to use it creatively. Through you, may I bring beauty into the
lives around me, especially those in the shadows, those for whom
sunlight and a new start are not possible unless they are led to you.
(Prayers of Intercession)

EVENING
Dear God, it is easy to see when others are wrong,
to be wise in the ways of their shortcomings and sins. Let me hear
the story of my life as it is unfolding, to see myself not only
as others see me, but most of all, as you see me.
(Prayers of Intercession)

GOD OF LIGHT, YOU CALL ME TO BE MY SISTERS' AND BROTHERS' KEEPERS,
AND TEACH WHAT THAT MEANS, IN THE NAME OF MY SAVIOR.
(Pray the Prayer of Our Savior.)

MORNING
Keep me faithful to what is on
your mind for me to do this day.
In Jesus' name. Amen.

EVENING
Like mothers listening to bedtime
prayers, and fathers watching over a
sleeping baby, you, Loving Parent, are
with me through this and every night.
In Jesus' name. Amen.

Thursday, June 10

(Read Psalm 32)

MORNING
Loving Creator, everything ahead in this day is already
under your watch and keep. Attune my will to yours that I may see
my world and the people in it through your eyes.

EVENING
Sometimes I forget, O God, that the same spirit that moved
across the world at the dawn of creation moves in me. My life, too,
can bloom and spread light, plant seeds and nourish deserts.
Thank you for being with me this day, and all days.

Teach me, God, not only to stand in awe of roaring seas and wild
winds, but to recognize the same power in the rainbow that follows.

MORNING
For all whose sins are ever before them, who fear their story
can have no happy ending, may they be assured by the miracle
of personal witness that your divine grace is both sufficient and free.
(Prayers of Intercession)

EVENING
For all small mercies and tender moments within each day,
I give you thanks. May these blessings come into the lives of those who seem
to have neither the heart nor the time to appreciate such quiet pleasures.
(Prayers of Intercession)

O GOD OF LOVE, I PRAY IN THE NAME OF ALL WHO LOVE YOU,
IN ALL AGES AND PLACES.
(Pray the Prayer of Our Savior.)

MORNING
Take away any bitterness I have
for past wrongs and set me free from
the fear of failing you today.
In Jesus' name. Amen.

EVENING
Bless me this night with the
courage to make peace with myself
and with you, for even more than any
earthly parent, you are on my side.
In Jesus' name. Amen.

Friday, June 11

(Read Galatians 2:15–21)

MORNING
God of the Morning Light, Keeper of the Day,
walk with me as I go about my routines and responsibilities.

EVENING
God of the Evening Light, Keeper of the Night, bring rest to me
this night as all your world settles close and quiet around me.

God of the Sunrise, Painter of the Sunset, may I be led into sleep by lullabies and postcards from the natural world, knowing that just as you care for the sparrows of the air and the lilies of the field, you will care for me.

MORNING
God of my life, may I not be tempted this day to substitute lofty rules
or impressive words to carry your message. May your Church not be weighted
down in rules and regulations, but, instead, reflect deeds of kindness. May it
act as a loving body so that others may "read" through it a living statement of
who you are and how you wish for us to act towards each other.
(Prayers of Intercession)

EVENING
For all the love I have been shown from you this day,
O God, I give thanks. I pray for all who seek your guidance.
(Prayers of Intercession)

WHEN MY DOUBTS MAKE ME AFRAID,

HELP ME BUILD A BRIDGE OF FAITH UNDER THEM.

(Pray the Prayer of Our Savior.)

MORNING
Author and Creator of all things,
walk alongside me this day.
In Jesus' name. Amen.

EVENING
Even in my sleep, O God,
I trust in your watchful care.
In Jesus' name. Amen.

Saturday, June 12

(Read Luke 7:36–50)

MORNING
God of All, remind me this day that no one is too far gone
for your grace. In your eyes, no one lives "on the other side of the tracks."

EVENING
God of All, if I have been haughty with your mercy or stingy
with your kindness this day, forgive me.

Let me never think of myself more highly that I ought. May I understand from experience that more valuable than all the high rules or elegant speeches is one, single act of kindness. It doesn't have to be noticed or lauded or rewarded, and the joy it brings is better than any paycheck or payback.

MORNING
May I not fail to see the woman at the well, the widow with her mite,
the lost sheep, and the leper at my gate—this day and every day.
Let the world have eyes to see them and ears to hear their need.
(Prayers of Intercession)

EVENING
Thank you for those who, today, gave me the gift of kindness.
May they know how much it meant to me.
(Prayers of Intercession)

GOD OF ALL HOPE AND COURAGE, HELP THE WORLD SEE HOW MUCH MORE
EFFECTIVE LOVE IS THAN HATE; COMPASSION THAN CONTROL; AND PEACE THAN THE
PRICE THAT MUST BE PAID FOR POLITICAL DOMINATION.
(Pray the Prayer of Our Savior.)

MORNING
Challenge me, God, to use this day
to promote peace and justice with
some specific deed. In Jesus' name.
Amen.

EVENING
May your Spirit move over the earth
this night, bringing hope and joy
for the future. In Jesus' name.
Amen.

Sunday, June 13

(Read Luke 8:1–3)

MORNING
God of the Seasons, you paint the colors of morning,
adorn the woods in holy dress. You score the music of sunrises
and carve from clay and stone the mountains, hills, shorelines,
and continents. Keep me from the busyness of the day
so that I can notice your masterpieces.

EVENING
God of the Seasons, the night comes in splendor,
making a safe and quiet place for my prayers.

So much depends, O God, on whom I choose to love and the friends I select as companions. Help me to be wise enough to choose those who will enable me to be my best and those who support me in seeking your plan for my life.

MORNING
Bless all who travel today. Keep them from danger
and may their destinations be worthy.
(Prayers of Intercession)

EVENING
For those to whom sleep will not come,
send the comfort or forgiveness they seek.
(Prayers of Intercession)

THERE IS NO PAIN OR JOY IN MY LIFE THAT YOU DO NOT KNOW OR FEEL MORE DEEPLY THAN I. IN SHARING THAT PAIN, IT WILL LESSEN. IN SHARING THE JOY, IT EXPANDS.
(Pray the Prayer of Our Savior.)

MORNING
Open my eyes to all the possibilities
to receive joy this day. In Jesus' name.
Amen.

EVENING
May the places I have been
and the person I have been this day
bring glory to you. In Jesus' name.
Amen.

Monday, June 14

(Read Galatians 3:23–29)

MORNING

Gracious God, bless me this day. Renew my spirit of hope
as Abraham's offspring, heir to the promise of salvation;
and strengthen my confidence that Christ has made us free.

EVENING

Gracious God, bless me this evening. Reassure me
that we are all one in Christ Jesus.

We live in a society established upon law and order. We value justice, democracy, civility, and discipline. Yet, God, we are called to believe in you based upon faith. We are reminded that, before faith came, we existed under the law. But now that faith has come—through the life, death, and resurrection of Jesus Christ—we are no longer subject to a disciplinarian. It is not easy to exist within and between this chasm of freedom and faithfulness. It is difficult to accept that we as believers are descendents of Abraham, heirs to the promise. We sometimes forget the promise.

MORNING

Grant me the strength, O God, to celebrate the oneness
of all humanity within all persons that I will encounter today.
(Prayers of Intercession)

EVENING

Grant me the courage, O God, to accept the oneness
of all humanity within all persons I encountered today.
(Prayers of Intercession)

"ALL YOU OFFSPRING OF JACOB, GLORIFY HIM;

STAND IN AWE OF HIM, ALL YOU OFFSPRING OF ISRAEL!"
(Pray the Prayer of Our Savior.)

MORNING

Strengthen me, O God, to believe
that we are all equal, and to live this
day beyond prejudices. In the spirit of
Christ, I pray. Amen.

EVENING

Comfort me, O God, to rest this evening,
far from the fears of prejudice, secure
with my gender and sexual orientation.
In the spirit of Christ, I pray. Amen.

Tuesday, June 15

(Read 1 Kings 19:1–7)

MORNING
O Holy One, bless me this day. May it be an awesome journey into
the wilderness—an opportunity to experience anew your grace.

EVENING
O Holy One, my thanks to you for a wonderful day. It was an
awesome journey into the wilderness; and now it has ended.

We have all thought, at one time or another, "It is enough; now, O
[God], take away my life, for I am no better than my ancestors." At
some point, we have all feared for our reputation, if not our lives. We
have all experienced disappointment and failure. We have all known deceit and betrayal, and share apprehension about the future. We all fall
short of perfection, of others' expectations of us, and even of our own
expectations of ourselves. Yet, you call us to "get up and eat, otherwise
the journey will be too much for you." We each have more work to do.

MORNING
I pray today for those who have betrayed me,
for my enemies, and for those whom I have harmed.
(Prayers of Intercession)

EVENING
I pray this evening for those who have betrayed me,
for my enemies, and for those whom I have harmed.
(Prayers of Intercession)

"THE POOR SHALL EAT AND BE SATISFIED; THOSE WHO SEEK HIM
SHALL PRAISE [GOD]. MAY YOUR HEARTS LIVE FOREVER!"
(Pray the Prayer of Our Savior.)

MORNING
Grant me, O God, the blessing
of food and water needed to nourish
me physically, mentally, and spiritually
for today's journey. In the spirit
of Christ, I pray. Amen.

EVENING
Smile on me this evening, Angel
of God, that I may rest in the assurance of God's grace, mercy, and peace.
In the spirit of Christ, I pray. Amen.

Wednesday, June 16

(Read 1 Kings 19:8–15a)

MORNING

O Divine Redeemer, bless me this day. I have been very zealous
for God. Come into my cave and calm my fears.

EVENING

O Divine Redeemer, bless me this evening.
I have tried to live this day as a tribute to your will.

God, at some point in our lives, we all feel the need for closeness with
you. We want to take a spiritual journey to a place of refuge and solitude
for conversation and reconciliation with you. Like Elijah, often we need
to retreat to a cave. Often, we feel that we alone have been faithful to the
covenant, while others have defamed your altar and killed your prophets.
Often, we feel alone in our journey of life and in our struggle to maintain integrity and honesty as we make our contribution to the common
good. Often, we anguish that others are out to get us. Sometimes, they
are! Sometimes it is for good reason, and sometimes for naught.

MORNING

I pray for discernment of the work you have called me to do
and the lives I am to touch today.
(Prayers of Intercession)

EVENING

Thank you, O God, for allowing me to make a difference
in the world today. Bless those whom I touched.
(Prayers of Intercession)

"BUT YOU, O [GOD], DO NOT BE FAR AWAY! O MY HELP, COME QUICKLY TO MY AID!"
(Pray the Prayer of Our Savior.)

MORNING	EVENING
I seek you, O God, in the mighty winds that split mountains, or in the earthquakes and fires. But speak to my heart today in a sheer silence. In the spirit of Christ, I pray. Amen.	Calm my fears, O God, as I sleep tonight; and forgive me when I hid from others, from myself, and from you. In the spirit of Christ, I pray. Amen.

Thursday, June 17

(Read Psalm 42)

MORNING

Merciful Savior, bless me this day. "As a deer longs
for flowing streams, so my soul longs for you, O God."

EVENING

Merciful Savior, bless me this evening. "My soul thirsts for God,
for the living God. When shall I come and behold the face of God?"

Merciful God, we all experience events that disturb our peace or the stability of our lives, homes, communities, nation, and world. We all know doubt, confusion, and longing. We all experience grief, sadness, pain, and suffering. Tragedies and terror occur. Loved ones depart and leave a void. Jobs end or are just unfulfilling. Like David, I lament today, "Why are you cast down, O my soul, and why are you disquieted within me?" In times like these, Comforting God, we are reminded to praise you and to find our refuge and hope in your promise of peace.

MORNING

I pray today for those who are lost and abandoned, for those who
have lost loved ones, and for those who long for love in their lives.
(Prayers of Intercession)

EVENING

I pray this evening for those who are hungry and homeless,
for those who suffer the tragedy and stigma of HIV infection and AIDS,
and for those who are dying of cancer and other illnesses.
(Prayers of Intercession)

"FOR HE DID NOT DESPISE OR ABHOR THE AFFLICTION OF THE AFFLICTED;
HE DID NOT HIDE HIS FACE FROM ME, BUT HEARD WHEN I CRIED TO HIM."
(Pray the Prayer of Our Savior.)

MORNING

Walk with me today, O God.
Feed me; nourish me. Your steadfast
love commands me. Hear my prayer.
In the spirit of Christ, I pray. Amen.

EVENING

Grant peace, O God, to all who
are in distress. May your song be with
me this night. Hear my prayer. In the
spirit of Christ, I pray. Amen.

Friday, June 18

(Read Luke 8:26–33)

MORNING

Gracious God, cleanse my heart, purify my thoughts
with wisdom, and heal my body. Use me today.

EVENING

O Mighty Healer, command any unclean spirits to leave
my body, mind, heart, and soul this night.

Caring Savior, we all have demons in our lives. Some are real; others are irrational fears. Some are skeletons of sins we committed in the past; others represent our daily denials or our sins of omission. We often find ourselves in chains and shackles, or homeless, or lost in a wilderness of despair. Like Legion, we sometimes ask, "What have you to do with me, Jesus?" Like the demons, we fear the abyss, that bottomless pit of chaos in our lives. Like the swine, we often rush blindly into a lake, or into relationships that drown us. I beg you, Jesus, hear my prayer.

MORNING

Today, O God, I remember the homeless, the mentally ill,
the imprisoned, and the families of these victims of circumstance.
(Prayers of Intercession)

EVENING

Tonight, O God, I pray for all of those who find themselves
in relationships that are abusive and destructive; for those who are
victims of injustice; and for those who live in despair.
(Prayers of Intercession)

**"DELIVER MY SOUL FROM THE SWORD, MY LIFE FROM THE POWER OF THE DOG!
SAVE ME FROM THE MOUTH OF THE LION!"**
(Pray the Prayer of Our Savior.)

MORNING	EVENING
Bless me this day, O God. Dispel my anguish and fears. Chase my demons away. In the spirit of Christ, I pray. Amen.	Bless me this evening, O God. Forgive my sins. Be ever near me. In the spirit of Christ, I pray. Amen.

Saturday, June 19 · Juneteenth Day

(Read Luke 8:34–39)

MORNING

O Great Emancipator, free the captives of injustice in our community
and me from my bondage that I might serve you more faithfully this day.

EVENING

O Great Emancipator, free the captives of injustice in our community
and clothe me in my right mind that I might faithfully serve your will.

Giving God, we often take for granted and forget to give you thanks for life and health, daily bread, peace of mind, prosperity, and peace on earth. We often forget the demons in our lives and society, those that have gone away and those that still haunt us. Like the people of the surrounding country of Gerasenes, we often doubt those who have been restored to health. We often fear your miraculous power to heal and to reconcile communities. Like the man who was healed, we too sometimes find renewed faith and beg to be with Jesus. But the response is, "Return to your home, and declare how much God has done for you."

MORNING

I remember today the victims of injustice in our community,
and those persons whom I often take for granted and forget to thank.
(Prayers of Intercession)

EVENING

I remember this evening the victims of injustice in our community,
and those persons whom I often take for granted and forget to thank.
(Prayers of Intercession)

**"I WILL TELL OF YOUR NAME TO MY BROTHERS AND SISTERS;
IN THE MIDST OF THE CONGREGATION I WILL PRAISE YOU!"**
(Pray the Prayer of Our Savior.)

MORNING

Thank you, O God! Bless, keep,
and sustain me this day. In the spirit
of Christ, I pray. Amen.

EVENING

Thank you, O God! Bless, keep,
and sustain me as I rest this evening.
In the spirit of Christ, I pray. Amen.

Sunday, June 20

Father's Day—U.S.A., Canada, U.K. · Summer begins

(Read Psalm 43)

MORNING

Strong Deliverer, bless me this day. Judge me,
plead my cause, and defend me against my enemies.

EVENING

Strong Deliverer, bless me this evening.
You know my weaknesses. I pray for your deliverance.

We know that life sometimes is unfair and that humans are often unjust, deceitful, hateful, and vengeful. War, hunger, abuse, disease, and poverty are all part of the human experience. Like David, we sometimes complain about our enemies and about inhumanity and sin in the world. But in times of trouble, our strength, refuge, and salvation are in you, O God. Judge me, O Righteous One, and deliver me from those who would oppress me, from evil, from sin, and from myself.

MORNING

I pray for those who oppress me, for those who misunderstand me and wrongly
judge me, and for those whom I misunderstand and judge wrongly.
(Prayers of Intercession)

EVENING

I pray for those who would harm me and for those whom
I have harmed and judged wrongly.
(Prayers of Intercession)

"TO HIM, INDEED, SHALL ALL WHO SLEEP IN THE EARTH BOW DOWN."
(Pray the Prayer of Our Savior.)

MORNING

My Shepherd, "O send out your light and your truth; let them bring me to your holy hill and to your dwelling." In the spirit of Christ, I pray. Amen.

EVENING

Loving and Forgiving God, "I will praise you with the harp, O God, my God." In the spirit of Christ, I pray. Amen.

Monday, June 21

(Read 2 Kings 2:1–2, 6–14)

MORNING

Giver of Life, cause me to never leave you
as I face this day and all that it will bring.

EVENING

Giver of Life, thank you for being with me
and getting me through this day.

Loving God, you lead me and you protect me and yet I act as if I am alone. You set your plan before me, yet I go my own way. I follow my own will, even as I say that I seek yours in my life. But thank you, God, that your plan will not be deterred by my stubbornness! Not even I can get in the way of your fulfilling your purpose for me and through me. I submit to you—again.

MORNING

I begin this day worry free and filled with hope
because I can kneel at your throne of grace.
(Prayers of Intercession)

EVENING

I end this day by releasing all things to you in prayer.
(Prayers of Intercession)

GIVER OF LIFE, THY KINGDOM COME, THY WILL BE DONE—ALL DAY, EVERY DAY.

MORNING

Giver of Life, all that I am
and all that I ever hope to be,
I surrender to you on this day.
In the mighty name of Jesus, I pray.
Amen.

EVENING

Giver of Life, for the love
I shared, thank you. For the pain I
caused, please forgive me. Grant me
rest now, in your promise of a new
beginning. In the mighty name
of Jesus, I pray. Amen.

Tuesday, June 22

(Read Psalm 77:1–2, 11–20)

MORNING

God of Comfort, I awake with gratitude,
remembering how you brought me through yesterday
and how wonderful are your works.

EVENING

God of Comfort, thank you for being
my source of courage, strength, and hope on this day.

When life gets difficult I am tempted to cry out and complain to those that feed into my despair. Misery indeed loves the miserable! I am learning to trust in you, O God. Each moment when I realize that you are the source of all comfort and peace, you seek to dry every tear from my eyes. Thank you for your tender mercy and unending love.

MORNING

I begin this day with joy because you know
what is in my heart.
(Prayers of Intercession)

EVENING

I end this day knowing that you protect me
from all that seeks to destroy my soul.
(Prayers of Intercession)

GOD OF COMFORT, WHO ART IN HEAVEN — YET HOLD ME CLOSE EACH MOMENT.

MORNING

God of Comfort, thank you
for the understanding that I face
nothing alone and I will endure nothing that your love cannot heal.
In the mighty name of Jesus, I pray.
Amen.

EVENING

God of Comfort, for your grace
that sheltered me from the storms of
life, thank you. For the moments I
cried out in fear, please forgive me.
Grant me rest now, knowing I sleep
at your breast. In the mighty name
of Jesus, I pray. Amen.

Wednesday, June 23

(Read 1 Kings 19:15–16, 19–21)

MORNING
Purposeful God, help me to live this day
faithful to each moment.

EVENING
Purposeful God, thank you for the many ways
in which this day helped me to realize the true meaning of my life.

I go from job to job. I rush from role to role. My calendar is full and my soul is empty. I know I should listen for your voice—but I'm too busy! Thank you, God, for divine messengers. Thank you, God, for not giving up on me. Thank you for placing people in my life who lovingly and persistently remind me of your purpose for my life. Help me to clearly see what it is you want me to do and be.

MORNING
As I begin this day, and before I slip into myself, let me hear a
word from you, O God.
(Prayers of Intercession)

EVENING
As I end this day, I take off my mask and let down my guard and I
seek you, O God.
(Prayers of Intercession)

PURPOSEFUL GOD, LEAD ME NOT INTO TEMPTATION—AND SAVE ME FROM MYSELF.

MORNING
Purposeful God, I face this day
humbled in knowing nothing I attempt alone can compare to the greatness you can and will accomplish
in me. In the mighty name of Jesus,
I pray. Amen.

EVENING
Purposeful God, for a day
without aimlessness, thank you. For
the many ways I hid among the busy-
ness, please forgive me. Grant me rest
now, assured that the work you have
begun in me you will complete. In the
mighty name of Jesus, I pray.
Amen.

Thursday, June 24

(Read Psalm 16:1–6)

MORNING

My Chosen Portion, I face the world affirming that in you
I have all I need—sustenance, love, courage, peace of mind, and joy.

EVENING

My Chosen Portion, I rest assured in your provision for tomorrow,
for your abundance has carried me this day.

I spend. I buy. I seek. I consume. And yet it is not enough to fill the void in my soul. God, help me to know that if I seek you first, all other things will be given to me. You fill my cup and cause it to run over. Your power and presence fill my heart to bursting. Thank you for your provision and your abounding grace, love, and mercy towards me, day after day, time after time.

MORNING

I begin this day filled with your Holy Spirit.
I will work to humbly share this gift with others.
(Prayers of Intercession)

EVENING

I end this day convinced and trusting that you are Jehovah Jira.
(Prayers of Intercession)

**MY CHOSEN PORTION, GIVE ME THIS DAY MY DAILY BREAD—
THAT I MIGHT FIND NEW ENERGY IN SERVING YOU.**

MORNING

My Chosen Portion, cause me to be aware of your many gifts and to live this day with an attitude of gratitude. In the mighty name of Jesus, I pray. Amen.

EVENING

My Chosen Portion, for the many ways in which you answer my needs, thank you. For my spirit of lack and selfishness, please forgive me. Grant me rest now, satisfied in all you have made possible this day. In the mighty name of Jesus, I pray. Amen.

Friday, June 25

(Read Psalm 16:7–11)

MORNING
Mighty Counselor, direct my thoughts, my actions and my deeds
in this moment and throughout this day.

EVENING
Mighty Counselor, guide me in letting go of all I did not accomplish
and in offering thanks for what you have done through me today.

You plant seeds of wisdom within me. I do not take heed to them because my ego gets in the way. You send counsel in the form of friends, colleagues, even children. I cannot hear above the noise of my own unsettled spirit. Cause me to desire and to recognize your infinite wisdom, O God. In this discovery, I pray that I may uncover the joys of being in one mind with you and with my brothers and sisters in Christ.

MORNING
I begin this day surrounded by a great cloud of witnesses.
(Prayers of Intercession)

EVENING
I end this day trusting and grateful that you are God alone.
(Prayers of Intercession)

MIGHTY COUNSELOR, DELIVER ME FROM EVIL—
AND HELP ME TO MODEL YOUR GOODNESS.

MORNING
Mighty Counselor, I offer myself
as a living witness to your wisdom in
action this day. In the mighty name
of Jesus, I pray. Amen.

EVENING
Mighty Counselor, for your
providence displayed in creative ways
on this day, thank you. For moments
of foolishness and ignorance, please
forgive me. Grant me rest now, secure
that you are an all-knowing,
all-powerful and ever-loving God.
In the mighty name of Jesus,
I pray. Amen.

Saturday, June 26

(Read Galatians 5:1, 13–25)

MORNING

God of Freedom, help me to remember each moment
that with this gift comes responsibility.

EVENING

God of Freedom, I am grateful that even in the shadows
of night I am not free from your presence.

Freedom! I craved it as a child, a teenager in rebellion, and a member of
a colonized people in America. Freedom! I boast it as a Christian and
womanist and proclaim it to others. Yet, freedom is not cheap and it carries a cost that I must be willing to pay. Freedom and irresponsibility are
not synonymous. Freedom and injustice are not parallel. Freedom requires discipline and demands accountability. Affirming this, O God, I
submit to your Spirit for the purpose of glorifying your name.

MORNING

I begin this day bound in my conviction to serve God.
(Prayers of Intercession)

EVENING

I end this day offering you my burdens
with a sincere and humble heart.
(Prayers of Intercession)

**GOD OF FREEDOM, THINE IS THE KINGDOM, THE POWER AND THE GLORY,
NOW AND FOREVER—MAY MY LIVING BRING YOU HONOR.**

MORNING	**EVENING**
God of Freedom, in the name of Jesus, enable the gifts that you have deposited within me to bear fruit. In the mighty name of Jesus, I pray. Amen.	God of Freedom, in the name of Jesus, I thank you for the ability to freely express my faith and values. For the many ways I have abused my freedom, please forgive me. Grant me rest. In the mighty name of Jesus, I pray. Amen.

Sunday, June 27

(Read Luke 9:51–62)

MORNING

Reconciling God, help me to see this day as a new beginning in
my relationship with you and others.

EVENING

Reconciling God, thank you for the healing that will take place as I sleep,
within my body, mind, and spirit, for you neither sleep nor slumber.

God, everywhere Jesus went he spoke of your realm. But this was not
about some future destination or far away place and time. Jesus was teaching his followers how to live in right relationship with you and with others—every day and right now. Jesus was attempting to reconcile you with
all creation. Thank you, Creator God, for loving me so much that you
sent Jesus to be an example of how I am to live in you and with others.

MORNING

As I begin this day, help me to follow the example
of Jesus and walk in the light of the Christ.
(Prayers of Intercession)

EVENING

As I end this day, I pray for all of the brokenness
I have witnessed and experienced today.
(Prayers of Intercession)

**RECONCILING GOD, ON EARTH AS IT IS IN HEAVEN—
IS MY LIFELONG MANTRA AS A SEEKER OF SHALOM.**

MORNING

Reconciling God, I claim my
wholeness today because I have been
wondrously created in your image.
In the mighty name of Jesus,
I pray. Amen.

EVENING

Reconciling God, thank you for the
gift of the ability to offer forgiveness.
Grant me rest now, so I might be
renewed to work towards a day when
we shall "all be one." In the mighty
name of Jesus, I pray. Amen.

Monday, June 28

(Read 2 Kings 5:1–14)

MORNING

God of all beginnings, today, let me find you
both in large visions and small duties.

EVENING

God of all endings, may my life of faith—begun in baptism—
end in communion with you and all the saints in glory.

Blessed God, when my parents presented me for baptism, you claimed and named me. You pronounced me clean before I had ever sinned, healed before I was ever sick, and alive forever in Christ even though I am all too mortal. But that was long ago; and I have no memory of the event. Like Naaman, I hanker for a personal word, for a sign, a touch. Could you perhaps take away my allergies? Banish my neurosis? Straighten my back? Make me look young again? Better yet, send me a spiritual healer, who could lay hands on me and make me whole! But no, I was born again of water and the word. Help me to receive that gift of wholeness.

MORNING

God, I know many who are in need of healing.
Hear me as I name them, one by one:
(Prayers of Intercession)

EVENING

Let sleep, with all its healing powers,
be granted to those for whom I now pray:
(Prayers of Intercession)

"LET HIM COME TO ME, THAT HE MAY LEARN THAT THERE IS A PROPHET IN ISRAEL."

MORNING

God of the unloved and unlovely,
do not turn away from our infirmities
and deformities. Accept us as we are,
warts and all. In the Savior's name.
Amen.

EVENING

O God, do not let the day's
frustrations and failures fret us.
Give us the sleep of those who know
themselves cleansed, forgiven,
and redeemed. In the Savior's name.
Amen.

Tuesday, June 29

(Read Isaiah 66:10–14)

MORNING

O God, as a child looks to its parents for food,
so I turn to you, trusting that my soul will be fed.

EVENING

O God, may this coming night's sleep be for me a foretaste
of the rest you have promised to your faithful ones.

You give us food and drink for our journey. From the broken bread of the table and the promises of the gospel, we receive nourishment and strength. Still, there is a longing that even these gifts cannot satisfy. We seek the city that you are building and making for us, the New Jerusalem. There, at last, we shall find rest. There we will know a comfort we have not known since we were taken from our mother's breasts. There we shall find peace at last, like travelers who have reached their destination, like children who have returned home.

MORNING

I would pray for those who hunger and thirst after righteousness.
Feed their hunger and slake their thirst, O God.
(Prayers of Intercession)

EVENING

For those who have grown weary in building the New Jerusalem,
I pray. Grant them restorative rest.
(Prayers of Intercession)

**"AS A MOTHER COMFORTS HER CHILD, SO I WILL COMFORT YOU;
YOU SHALL BE COMFORTED IN JERUSALEM."**

MORNING

For bread in mercy broken,
for blood in mercy shed, for heavenly
food so freely given, I give you thanks,
O God. In the Savior's name. Amen.

EVENING

Spare us, O God, from the grief of
those who have no hope, who sigh and
sorrow for what is past, for whom tomorrow looms as dark and foreboding.
Banish our nightmares. Refresh us for
our labors. In the Savior's name. Amen.

Wednesday, June 30

(Read Psalm 66:1–9)

MORNING

Gracious God, enable me to find my way this day.

EVENING

Gracious God, thank you for this day
and the blessings that I have received.

Giver of Life, give me energy and enthusiasm commensurate with the work that waits for me. If we are walking unshod through the sea, you will guard our feet. You who led your people safely through the Jordan will not let us slip! We remember your great deeds of deliverance, and our feeble knees are strengthened. We remember your care for Israel in their wanderings, and the burdens we carry become light.

MORNING

I know many, Gracious God, who have lost their way.
Hear my prayers for them.
(Prayers of Intercession)

EVENING

I know some who are so very close to the end of their journeys.
Now I pray for them in their final days and hours.
(Prayers of Intercession)

**"COME AND SEE WHAT GOD HAS DONE:
[GOD] IS AWESOME IN [GOD'S] DEEDS AMONG MORTALS."**

MORNING

Dear God! I want to finish the race
a winner! I don't want to give in to
weariness or despair. I want my
crown! I want to hear my Savior say,
"Well done!" In the Savior's name.
Amen.

EVENING

O God, at the hour of my death,
I want to say with the apostle—
and with joy—I have finished the
race! I have kept the faith! I faltered
and stumbled, but I did not fall.
To that end, guard my feet, O God.
In the name of the Savior. Amen.

Thursday, July 1 · Canada Day

(Read Galatians 6:1–16)

MORNING

Merciful God, I thank you that I do not pray alone.
I am one of that great company of the faithful who turn to you at the
beginning of day. Our prayers rise like smoke from thousands of fires.

EVENING

Merciful God, thank you for health and strength and daily food.
I looked to you for sustenance and I was not disappointed.

Ours is not a solitary journey, O God. You have joined us to a great company of pilgrims. And you have bid us to share one another's burdens. Give us strength to do just that. We confess that the hardest burden to bear is the other's freedom! Why can't the others all be like us?! It would be so much easier if we marched in lock step, to the same drummer, to the same beat. But that is not your will; it is not Christ's way. For freedom Christ has set us free. Let it be so.

MORNING

God, I pray for those who will carry my burdens today: My family,
my friends, and my coworkers, my brothers and sisters in Christ.
(Prayers of Intercession)

EVENING

God of the weary, the oppressed, the careworn, the unloved: Hear
my prayers for those who are ground down and laid low.
(Prayers of Intercession)

**"BEAR ONE ANOTHER'S BURDENS, AND IN THIS WAY
YOU WILL FULFILL THE LAW OF CHRIST."**

MORNING

O God, your yoke is easy; your
burden is light. I approach this new
day in trust and confidence that my
strength will be equal to my tasks.
In the name of the Savior. Amen.

EVENING

For all the saints who rest
from their labors, whose work is done,
whose good works live on in me and
many others, I thank you, God.
In the name of the Savior. Amen.

Friday, July 2

(Read Luke 10:1–11)

MORNING
O God, I have heard your call; I have pledged my loyalty; I have taken
the yoke of Christ. I would be a faithful steward of the good news.

EVENING
O God, we, your servants, plow and sow and water but you give
the increase. And you guarantee a fine harvest. Yours is the praise and glory.

You have called us to be ambassadors of your realm—to preach peace,
to show good will, and to bind up the hurts of others. But some are not
ready to believe that we come in peace. Many are indifferent, if not resentful. Prepare our hearts for disappointment, rejection, and outright
hostility. Guard us against bitterness when we are not well received or
when our good intentions are misunderstood. Grant us gentle spirits
and peaceful speech.

MORNING
For those disappointed, distressed, and despairing in their ministries,
I pray, O God. Give them a new birth of hope. Give them the mind
of Christ, who was humble and lowly of heart.
(Prayers of Intercession)

EVENING
Forgive those, merciful God, who treated me this day with indifference,
coldness, or hostility. I name them now before you and ask that you bless them.
(Prayers of Intercession)

"THE HARVEST IS PLENTIFUL, BUT THE LABORERS ARE FEW; THEREFORE ASK THE
[GOD] OF THE HARVEST TO SEND OUT LABORERS INTO [GOD'S] HARVEST."

MORNING
Though we sow in tears, we know
that we will reap in joy. Your Word
cannot and will not fail. May we stay
faithful to our calling. In the name
of the Savior. Amen.

EVENING
We are but sowers of seed. Even while
we sleep, your Word is working in the
hearts and minds of women and men.
In that confidence we persevere.
In the name of the Savior. Amen.

Saturday, July 3

(Read Luke 10:16–20)

MORNING
O God, you have not only called me; you have called me by name.
And so I begin this day by calling on your name.

EVENING
O God, it is enough that you have enrolled me in the
Book of the Living. No earthly honors can compare with that!

We rejoice that our names are written in the Book of the Living. Here on earth we may not attain prizes, nor see our names in headlines, nor have even fifteen minutes of fame. We remember that Christ Jesus made himself of no reputation. Let it be enough for us that you know our names. We give thanks that you have hidden us in your heart, O God. We give thanks that we are named, blessed, enrolled in the heavenly places.

MORNING
I acknowledge with sorrow, most merciful God, that there are
many in my city who are homeless, forgotten, friendless.
They are often numbered, but never named. For these I pray:
(Prayers of Intercession)

EVENING
I bless you, O God, that I may name before you—for your
blessing—the members of my family, my friends,
and my brothers and sisters in Christ.
(Prayers of Intercession)

"WHENEVER YOU ENTER A TOWN AND ITS PEOPLE WELCOME YOU,
EAT WHAT IS SET BEFORE YOU; CURE THE SICK WHO ARE THERE, AND SAY TO THEM,
'THE [REALM] OF GOD HAS COME NEAR TO YOU.'"

MORNING
How grateful I am, O God, that
I may venture forth this day in the
confidence that you have called me by
name. In the name of the Savior.
Amen.

EVENING
Hallowed be your name, O God.
May your name be blessed in all corners
of the world, by people of every land.
In the name of the Savior. Amen.

Sunday, July 4 · Independence Day—U.S.A.

(Read 2 Kings 5:7–10)

MORNING

O God, I have heard your call; I have pledged my loyalty;
I have taken the yoke of Christ. I would be a faithful steward
of the good news.

EVENING

Gracious God, thank you for this day and the blessings
that I have received.

God of new beginnings, through Elisha you enable Naaman to see the
power of your blessings. Wash and cleanse us so that we can have a new
flesh in which to worship you.

MORNING

Merciful God, thank you for health and strength and daily food.
I looked to you for sustenance and I was not disappointed.
(Prayers of Intercession)

EVENING

God of all endings, may my life of faith—begun in baptism—
end in communion with you and all the saints in glory.
(Prayers of Intercession)

**"WHY HAVE YOU TORN YOUR CLOTHES?
LET HIM COME TO ME, THAT HE MAY LEARN
THAT THERE IS A PROPHET IN ISRAEL."**

MORNING

God of the unloved and unlovely,
do not turn away from our infirmities
and deformities. Accept us as we are,
warts and all. In the Savior's name.
Amen.

EVENING

O God, do not let the day's
frustrations and failures fret us.
Give us the sleep of those who know
themselves cleansed, forgiven,
and redeemed. In the Savior's name.
Amen.

Monday, July 5

(Read Colossians 1:1–14)

MORNING
O living God, I rise to meet your Spirit
and thank you for your gift of sleep.

EVENING
O living God, I give thanks for your grace and appreciate
those who labor in the summer heat to prepare the bounty that
graced my table tonight. Remember them as evening comes.

Our gracious God, I am reminded how dependent I am on you for my
daily existence. Your love provides all that I need, making this life of
privilege possible. I am also thankful for the challenges you bring to my
life each day. Help me fulfill them.

MORNING
Eternal Creator, I have often failed to bear fruits
of justice, equality, and hope. Lead me in paths that build
and do not destroy human dignity within our communities.
(Prayers of Intercession)

EVENING
O God, just as grass cannot survive without water,
I cannot live without your Spirit, which created me from the clay
of the earth. Remind me to be thankful for this gift today.
(Prayers of Intercession)

**"MAY YOU BE MADE STRONG WITH ALL THE STRENGTH
THAT COMES FROM GOD'S GLORIOUS POWER."**

MORNING
Thank you, O God, for rescuing me
from evil and bringing me into the
community of Jesus' forgiveness and
grace. Help me live a life that reflects
this reality and love. Because of my
Savior, I pray. Amen.

EVENING
Today has been another joyful gift of
life. Help me be thankful and appre-
ciative when I awaken to tomorrow's
new promise of life. Because of my
Savior, I pray. Amen.

Tuesday, July 6

(Read Amos 7:7–9)

MORNING
O God, by your grace I was spared.
Open my heart to understand all that this means.

EVENING
O God, truly my heart is glad for the moments of joy
I experienced today. Continue to make me a believer
of your truth through love.

By all measures of what I should be doing with my life, I fall short of your glory and requirements, O God. Spare me and judge me not for those things I have left undone, but move me to be a true witness of your grace, peace, and truth wherever I go today. Only your truth, O living God, is the final measure of faithfulness; let me not be satisfied with anything less in life.

MORNING
Loving God, I need your Spirit to help me distinguish
the untruths of this world from your truth, and I pray
you will give me the courage to act appropriately.
(Prayers of Intercession)

EVENING
O God, I thank you that you have not judged my life harshly
for what I have undone this day. Forgive my shortcomings
with your Spirit of love.
(Prayers of Intercession)

"SEE, I AM SETTING A PLUMB LINE IN THE MIDST OF MY PEOPLE ISRAEL."

MORNING
It is easy to be a judge if I see things only from my point of view. It is more difficult when I consider our world through your eyes and your judgment, which is infallible. Because of my Savior, I pray. Amen.

EVENING
I am thankful after this long day. Thank you, God, for sparing me your judgment. Because of my Savior, I pray. Amen.

Wednesday, July 7

(Read Amos 7:10–17)

MORNING
O God, thank you for this amazing morning.
May your goodness be with me all the day long.

EVENING
O God, it is a joy to be part of the human community
that supports our life, and we give you thanks. We remember
it was Jesus who said, "I am the way, the truth, and the life."

O God, you are the maker of heaven and earth, yet you allow us freedom and choice. We cannot fathom the trust you have in us, but we can appreciate it when we realize how quickly we grab power for ourselves. Never forsake us, God, for we are an unfaithful generation.

MORNING
Restore a right spirit within me, O God, that my life
might be saved. Restore a right relationship between my heart
and your heart, that I might be wise.
(Prayers of Intercession)

EVENING
It is within your power to take everything I own and
strip me of my possessions, yet you have given me so much.
Make me responsive to your generous Spirit of acceptance this night.
(Prayers of Intercession)

"THEREFORE THUS SAYS GOD: 'YOU YOURSELF WILL DIE IN AN UNCLEAN LAND.'"

MORNING
To accept our life of ease
without concern can be our downfall.
Our God wants a clean and contrite
heart. God, may you be merciful unto
us this day. Because of my Savior,
I pray. Amen.

EVENING
Today the world moved closer
to being more humane because I took
a moment to hear another person's
troubles. Thank you, Jesus, for giving
me the patience to listen. Because of
my Savior, I pray. Amen.

Thursday, July 8

(Read Psalm 25:1–10)

MORNING
Merciful God, what a joy it is to awaken to a world
you have given us today. It is, indeed, an Easter morning again.

EVENING
Merciful God, it is good to come home to a clean home
and running water, yet I remember many places where these
basic needs are not being met. Be mindful of them this night.

When I see the stars in the sky, I am reminded of your promise to
Abraham. Renew that sense of hope within me, for in the vastness of
space my life seems so small. Thank you, God, for the promise of your
presence to even the least of those in your creation.

MORNING
Lift my spirits to a level of compassion for others this day,
O God. Do not let me be put to shame, nor let my enemies exult
over me. Then, lead me in paths of your light and truth.
(Prayers of Intercession)

EVENING
Forgive me for those I have ignored today. In my rush
to accomplish my tasks, I did not hear your cries for understanding.
"Whoever welcomes me, welcomes the one who sent me."
(Prayers of Intercession)

"LEAD ME IN YOUR TRUTH, AND TEACH ME, FOR YOU ARE THE GOD OF MY SALVATION."

MORNING
O God, I am committed to
making this day have meaning for me.
Teach me the pathways that lead to
your righteousness and joy, as I seek
your face. Because of my Savior,
I pray. Amen.

EVENING
The news on television sounds
bleak tonight. It is good to know
there are also many acts of kindness
done in your name, O God, renewing
my faith in humankind. Because of
my Savior, I pray. Amen.

Friday, July 9

(Read Deuteronomy 30:9–14)

MORNING

O God, "Choose life" is a powerful commandment for me today.
May I choose to bring down barriers so I can learn to live by this
commandment and enjoy its many benefits.

EVENING

O God, the promised land for Moses was never realized
in his lifetime. If it pleases you, allow me to enjoy this life
of promise and hope for many more years.

I understand little of how I became the person I am. I am learning that I am more than just a mind with a body. I also have a spirit where your compassion and feelings abide. Teach me to coordinate my life through mind, body, and spirit as I follow Jesus who teaches me.

MORNING

Moses was right: Your commandments are not beyond our
understanding or beyond our doing. It is our spirit that is weak.
Let us turn our hearts toward you, God, today.
(Prayers of Intercession)

EVENING

O God, our God, when I am blinded by anger and hate,
calm my spirit and bring your focus to my life again.
In the name of Jesus, our redeemer.
(Prayers of Intercession)

"I HAVE SET BEFORE YOU LIFE AND DEATH, BLESSING AND CURSES. CHOOSE LIFE."

MORNING

The admonitions of Moses are clear,
yet I so often choose evil over good.
May the spirit of the Christ be my
guide for making ethical decisions
that are best for all concerned.
Because of my Savior, I pray. Amen.

EVENING

For Asians, harmony is the highest
community value. May the American
spirit soon begin to appreciate Jesus'
call to peace, which comes from this
ancient Eastern teaching. Because of
my Savior, I pray. Amen.

Saturday, July 10

(Read Luke 10:25–2)

MORNING
Our gracious God, remind me to work toward eternal life
by loving you with all my heart, and soul, and strength, and mind.

EVENING
Our gracious God, it is hard to consider Jesus' question:
"Who is your neighbor?" I pray for honest answers.

In a busy life, it is hard to take time to consider the costs of that lifestyle. O God, your Child Jesus is asking all of us to consider a larger question about eternal life. Is that a priority for me, or do I choose to ignore it and miss an excellent opportunity for growth? Help me choose wisely.

MORNING
It is a hard thing to consider Jesus' call to "Love your neighbor
as yourself." It is easier to isolate myself and not take time to know others.
Open my heart and make me generous.
(Prayers of Intercession)

EVENING
How have I injured another? Forgive my shortsightedness,
which made me act in haste. I am sorry. Give me your peace
that will empower me.
(Prayers of Intercession)

"WHAT MUST I DO TO INHERIT ETERNAL LIFE?"
HE SAID TO HIM, "WHAT IS WRITTEN IN THE LAW?"

MORNING
It is becoming more evident that I
need to deal with my isolationism.
What can I do to change this today?
God, you call me to be in community,
but I find myself too weak. Why?
Because of my Savior, I pray. Amen.

EVENING
Do not let this night fall before I
deal with my anger. Perhaps some of
my anger is justified; let it become an
avenue for needed changes. Help me
be honest about this. Because of
my Savior, I pray. Amen.

Sunday, July 11

(Read Luke 10:29–37)

MORNING

God, as I go about my daily routines today, how will this story
of the good Samaritan make me think differently?
Let it sink in and challenge me anew.

EVENING

God, I did not find time enough to stop; but I wish I had,
because my life is not getting better. I need to reach out more
to those who are suffering with me on the roadside of life.

"Too busy!" "Too much to do." These are excuses I have used to keep
from getting involved in the lives of other persons who have needed my
help. Renew your Spirit of love within me, O God, and put a right
spirit within me.

MORNING

God, I did not mean for it to begin this way,
but it was almost beyond my control.
(Prayers of Intercession)

EVENING

God, tonight we both ended up being upset. It is important
that we take time to bind up each other's wounds and heal
our broken spirits, so the spirit of cooperation can live again.
(Prayers of Intercession)

**"Which one of these three do you think was a neighbor to the man who
fell among robbers? Go and do likewise."**

MORNING

It is dangerous to get involved in
other people's lives on the side of the
road. Is there an easier way? Perhaps
Jesus was right. The gate is narrow
and not many will pass through it.
Because of my Savior, I pray. Amen.

EVENING

It felt good to be a neighbor. Perhaps
those who have been helped will remember it and not be so hesitant to help
someone if the opportunity arises in
their lives. I live in that hope this night.
Because of my Savior, I pray. Amen.

Monday, July 12

(Read Amos 8:1–12)

MORNING

Holy and Just God, grant me a renewed sense
of your justice as this day begins.

EVENING

Holy and Just God, for your presence with me
throughout this day, I thank you.

It was the way of life—and death—in Amos' day. "Come, let us worship [God!]" exclaimed the temple goers. Silently during the sacrifices, they pondered, "How can we tighten the thumbscrews on a few more widows and orphans?" It was the way of life for those with power, and the way of death for the poor in the village. God, you, the searcher of hearts, knew and Amos spoke, "The sun is going to darken and the earth is going to shake!" Caring God, could this still be a way of life—and death—for people in our world? Are there ways that I harm or heal the least of your people? Help me to answer honestly.

MORNING

Give me eyes to see, a heart to feel,
and hands to help the poor and needy.
(Prayers of Intercession)

EVENING

For those who still suffer as the skies grow dark
on another day, I pray.
(Prayers of Intercession)

HELP ME TO LIFT UP THE POOR AND NEEDY!

MORNING

As your sun brings light
to this new day, help me to bring
light to someone's life before darkness
returns. Through Christ, Amen.

EVENING

Grant me rest and a renewed sense
of your justice while the stars shine
this evening. Through Christ,
Amen.

Tuesday, July 13

(Read Psalm 52)

MORNING
Thank you, God, for your steadfast love,
that guides me through each day.

EVENING
Thank you, God, for sticking with me today,
even when others doubted me.

Words are serious business. Like the thin hair that suspended the sword over Damocles' head, words hold the power of life or death. Just ask any young teen who has come home from school in tears after being been called too fat or too skinny, stupid or a nerd, pretty or ugly, or any of the thousands of other missiles that are in the arsenal of cruelty. Plotting, scheming, and deceitful and lying words are weapons of the first degree. Now I remember the power of words! I remember how they have brought me joy, or inflicted pain. God, the psalmist was right. You take our speech seriously. Help me to use honest, healing, and serious speech.

MORNING
Loving God, you are my source of life.
For those who take confidence in other sources, I pray.
(Prayers of Intercession)

EVENING
For the blessing of sweet rest, I thank you, God.
For those who are still searching for rest, I pray.
(Prayers of Intercession)

KEEP MY TONGUE FROM HARMING OTHERS!

MORNING
Steadfast God, help me
to cling to you today as I go
about life. Through Christ,
Amen.

EVENING
God, with the psalmist of old,
"I will thank you forever, because
of what you have done for me."
Through Christ, Amen.

Wednesday, July 14

(Read Genesis 18:1–10a)

MORNING

God of new possibilities, I look forward
to what the new day holds for me.

EVENING

God of new possibilities, for the exciting discoveries
of this day just lived, I give you thanks.

Uncle Charlie and Aunt Margie only made it back home to Kentucky once a year. I had never traveled more than fifty miles from the small farm that we tended; and I didn't have a telephone. I knew the world through the three channels on our black and white TV. So, when relatives arrived from Florida, a brand new world opened up. Stories of large fish that lived in the ocean and oranges and grapefruit that grew on backyard trees kindled the imagination. God, you create so many possibilities in life! Like your visit to Abraham and Sarah; you promised a child to a hopeful old couple. You certainly keep the life of faith exciting!

MORNING

God, you visit us with new possibilities daily.
For those who see only bleakness, I pray.
(Prayers of Intercession)

EVENING

For the hospitality that I have known today, I thank you.
For people who have known only misery, I pray.
(Prayers of Intercession)

MAKE ME QUICK TO SERVE YOU!

MORNING	EVENING
God, keep my eyes open for you in all the faces that I meet today. Through Christ, Amen.	God, as I close my eyes this evening, fill my dreams with bright hopes for tomorrow. Through Christ, Amen.

Thursday, July 15

(Read Psalm 15)

MORNING
Holy God, on this new day that you give,
assist me to do what is right and to speak the truth.

EVENING
Holy God, in this new evening that you give,
I continue to remember your expectations of me.

I tripped over sacred space memorably when I was a young pastor. I thought coffee and doughnuts would create an informal learning setting in our church school class. Most approved, until one woman quickly said that church school was the place to study and pray, not the place to eat and drink. Although I could think of arguments to the contrary, I realized that I had unwittingly transgressed her sense of sacred space. Even now, God, I remember the lesson. To stand before you calls for certain actions—inside and outside the church school. Thank you for Psalm 15.

MORNING
I sense the joy, Dear God, of doing what is right.
I pray for those who have suffered for wrong I might have done.
(Prayers of Intercession)

EVENING
As the stars begin to shine, I think of those who do not know
the joy of your presence and pray for them.
(Prayers of Intercession)

REMIND ME HOW TO ENTER YOUR SACRED SPACE.

MORNING
As this new day begins,
remind me to let my worship shape
the way I live. Through Christ,
Amen.

EVENING
This evening, God,
I sleep confidently as you surround
me with your sacred presence.
Through Christ, Amen.

Friday, July 16

(Read Colossians 1:15–23)

MORNING

Loving and Considerate Christ, as the concerns
of the day approach, help me to stay focused on you.

EVENING

Loving and Considerate Christ, as the memories of the day
flood my mind yet again, I thank you for the peace you bring.

There were students' papers to grade, writing deadlines to meet, my daughter's financial aid forms to complete, and my lawn was starting to look more and more like the Kentucky hayfields that I worked in as a kid. There are so many important things that scream for attention and demand time. The danger of becoming lost in this jungle of worries looms large. God, thank you for the epistle that reminds us of the sacred center that holds all things together. When we feel stretched to the breaking point, you are there with your healing, nourishment, love, and redemption. That is good news indeed!

MORNING

For the nurture of the church, over which you stand, I thank you.
For those who have not known the love of your church I pray.
(Prayers of Intercession)

EVENING

For those who do know the joy of reconciliation, I pray.
(Prayers of Intercession)

HELP ME BEAR THE IMAGE OF GOD BETTER THAN IN THE PAST.

MORNING

As this day passes, remind me
in trying moments that you are the
sacred center of life.
Through Christ, Amen.

EVENING

God, as the dust settles
and the dew falls, I am grateful for
your reconciling love.
Through Christ, Amen.

Saturday, July 17

(Read Colossians 1:24–28)

MORNING

God, show me how to make your Word known,
in this new day you've given me.

EVENING

God, as I sleep this evening, fill me with dreams
of how to be a faithful servant of the Church.

Last Sunday our youngest daughter, Lindsey, returned from a soup kitchen where she has worked with her church youth group. It's her idea, not one that we forced on her. She told us that one of the women who came to the soup kitchen had a small baby that she held and played with while the mother ate. It was a moment of sanctuary in a place where your love is proclaimed. Later the woman and her baby left hesitantly— to where, no one was sure. O God, there are ways, and then there are ways, to make your Word fully known. Help me to choose the wise way.

MORNING

For those who have not felt the gentle touch
of your loving hand, I pray, O God.
(Prayers of Intercession)

EVENING

The whisper of the evening breeze reminds me
of those still in need. I pray for them, dear Christ.
(Prayers of Intercession)

WHEN WAS THE LAST TIME THAT I SUFFERED FOR YOUR SAKE?

MORNING

Help me to proclaim you
in word and deed today, and in every
tomorrow that lies ahead.
Through Christ, Amen.

EVENING

Tonight, you are my life
and you are my hope.
Though Christ, Amen.

Sunday, July 18

(Read Luke 10:38–42)

MORNING
God, don't let my business get in the way
of important things today.

EVENING
God, as the darkness approaches, comfort me in the knowledge
that I have made the right choices today.

Parent God, when Jesus stood up for Mary, he went against the grain of conventional wisdom. Proverbs 6, for example, offers the busy ant as a model for human work. Martha probably had the words hanging over her fireplace: "A little sleep, a little slumber, a little folding of the hands to rest, and poverty will come upon you like a robber . . ." But your son, Jesus, knew that life consisted of more than endless work and he understood that sometimes conversation is more important than consumption. God, I keep forgetting this. Thank you for reminding me; and you can remind me again tomorrow if you want to!

MORNING
My neighbor has to work two jobs to make ends meet.
For her and others like her who have no time to listen, I pray.
(Prayers of Intercession)

EVENING
For people still struggling to sort out
what is really important in life, I pray.
(Prayers of Intercession)

DO I REALLY HAVE THE TIME TO SIT AND LISTEN FOR GOD'S VOICE?

MORNING
God, you know that I love to talk.
Help me spend today listening for
your voice in others.
Through Christ, Amen.

EVENING
The day's end is near and I have heard
you, God, in new and amazing ways.
Thank you, Compassionate Friend.
Through Christ, Amen.

Monday, July 19

(Read Psalm 85)

MORNING

Omniscient God, you know my need to start the day
in quiet time with you. Speak to me now.

EVENING

Omniscient God, in the quiet time of evening,
I come once more to you. Speak to me again.

The writer of today's psalm has shared words that surely came from your
mouth, Most Holy God. They are wise words, convincing and inspiring
words. He remembers how in the past you forgave your people's sins and
restored their fortunes to them. He knows that you are the giver of peace
and salvation. I feel assured that you will do the same for me and for the
people of this generation. But I am also reminded that those gifts come
in response to actions on my part. Your people must turn to you in their
hearts, be faithful to you, and strive for righteousness. Help me to take
those words seriously and to know your steadfast love and goodness.

MORNING

Hear the prayers of those who seek a closer relationship
with you, gracious God.
(Prayers of Intercession)

EVENING

Hear the unspoken prayers of hearts that are seeking you,
Kindly God.
(Prayers of Intercession)

MEMORIZE THE POETIC LINES OF PSALM 85:10. REPEAT THEM OFTEN.

MORNING

Help me, God, to listen for your voice
coming through words of the people I
meet this day. In Jesus' name. Amen.

EVENING

O God, your words coming through
the psalmist comfort me tonight.
I pray for peaceful, restful sleep.
In Jesus' name. Amen.

Tuesday, July 20

(Read Hosea 1:2–10)

MORNING

God, many mornings I pray for an easy day, free of troubles
and problems. Forgive me for my self-centeredness.

EVENING

God, as I expected, today was not free of problems
but you were in every moment. Thank you for helping me.

It must have been hard for Hosea to obey you, God, and marry a wife who then turned to harlotry. It was also hard for Hosea to give their children names that would constantly remind him of the infidelity of Gomer and of Israel. Still harder it must be for you to see the unfaithfulness of your people. I stand in awe of your steadfast love and promises of hope and restoration in spite of all our misdoing.

MORNING

Within my circle of family and friends are people struggling
with hardships of many kinds. I pray that you will comfort,
help, and guide them.

(Prayers of Intercession)

EVENING

Outside my circle of family and friends, are many whom
I do not know. I ask that you respond to prayers prayed on their
behalf as they face difficulties in their lives.

(Prayers of Intercession)

READ MORE CHAPTERS OF HOSEA FOR MESSAGES OF HOPE.

MORNING

God, open my mind and my heart
to your thoughts and your love
throughout this day. In Jesus' name.
Amen.

EVENING

God, thank you for your loving
presence in my life. Keep me safe
throughout the night. In Jesus' name.
Amen.

Wednesday, July 21

(Read Luke 11:9–13)

MORNING

Thank you, Creator God, for the glorious rising sun,
bringing light and warmth to a waiting world.

EVENING

Thank you, Creator God, for the beauty of sunsets,
bringing peace and hope for another tomorrow.

Another chance? You said to ask. I feared to speak And so no answer came. You said to seek. I had my doubts. You could not help me find. You said to knock. Why did I stop before I reached the door? I beg now, God, for another chance to ask forgiveness, to seek your will, to boldly knock upon your door and hear you say, "Come in."

MORNING

God of light and brightness, I pray for those
in sick rooms and confining cells.
(Prayers of Intercession)

EVENING

God of life and death, I pray for those
who may not see another sunrise.
(Prayers of Intercession)

GOD'S INVITATIONS ARE OPEN TO ALL.

MORNING

Today, Benevolent God, enable me
to receive the opportunities you will
give me to serve you and those whom
you will choose to send my way.
In Jesus' name. Amen.

EVENING

Accept my prayer of gratitude
for all the wonderful gifts you have
given me today. In Jesus' name.
Amen.

Thursday, July 22

(Read Psalm 138)

MORNING
Heavenly God, you have given me another day of life.
I will rejoice, be glad in it, and sing your praise.

EVENING
Heavenly God, as this day comes to a close, I reflect upon the joys
it brought through your grace. You are truly praiseworthy.

As I read and reread today's portion of your Holy Scriptures, so many thoughts and impressions come crowding into my mind. Like the psalmist, I can feel your timelessness, your constant love and your past, present, and future concern for me. Like the psalmist, I can say, "On the day I called you, you answered me." Like him, I know that though I may walk in the midst of trouble, you preserve me and stretch out your right hand to deliver me. I can also look to the future knowing that you will fulfill your purpose for me and your steadfast love will endure forever.

MORNING
For those who have not felt your saving love,
I pray today.
(Prayers of Intercession)

EVENING
For those who fail to ask for your favor and grace, I pray.
(Prayers of Intercession)

LOOK IN YOUR BIBLE FOR OTHER PSALMS THAT SPEAK TO YOUR HEART.

MORNING
Dear God, you have filled another
day of my life with health and
strength and joy. I thank you.
In Jesus' name. Amen.

EVENING
I shall lie down to sleep this night,
Dear God, comforted by the
knowledge of your presence.
I thank you. In Jesus' name.
Amen.

Friday, July 23

(Read Luke 11:1–8)

MORNING
Giving and Forgiving God, teach me to pray
as your Son taught his disciples.

EVENING
Giving and Forgiving God, forgive me when I have missed
moments to pray and live in the spirit of Jesus the Christ.

When the disciples asked Jesus to teach them to pray, he wasted no words or time explaining when, where, or how to proceed. Heavenly God, he immediately gave them a model putting your name and your realm first. Then without preamble, he told a parable. How long should we continue praying what seems like an unanswered prayer? What parent enjoys dealing with an overtired child who keeps pleading to stay up long past bedtime? How weary you must get hearing our prayers over and over when we act like a whining child! It is reassuring to learn from your Son's teaching that you care about our genuine needs and respond when we take them to you in persistent prayers.

MORNING
God, who art in heaven, listen to prayers
for those of us who seek your forgiveness.
(Prayers of Intercession)

EVENING
Loving Parent, listen to our persistent prayers
when we fail to understand your answers.
(Prayers of Intercession)

PRAY WITHOUT CEASING.

(1 Thessalonians 5:17)

MORNING
Your scriptures tell me how to pray. Help me apply those teachings in the hours ahead. In Jesus' name. Amen.

EVENING
May I go to sleep confident that you will listen to my prayers tomorrow as you did today? In Jesus' name. Amen.

Saturday, July 24

(Read Genesis 18:20–32)

MORNING
God, help me put aside worries about this day.
Let me focus on you instead.

EVENING
God, despite its problems, today was good
with you at my side. For this I am grateful.

Righteous God, I have questions about Abraham that lead directly to questions about me. How did he feel when he learned that you chose him to be the father of a great and mighty nation? Honored or disbelieving? Empowered or inadequate? Have you called me for a special part in your plans and how will I respond? Where did Abraham find courage to address you, Immortal God, when he himself said he was "but dust and ashes?" Why am I reluctant to talk freely to you? Was he frightened when he dared to challenge the severity of your threatened punishment of the people of Sodom? How can I overcome my fear of speaking out against injustices that I see in the world around me? Please, God, help me find answers to my questions.

MORNING
Let prayers arise for those who find it easy
to yield to temptations in an evil society.
(Prayers of Intercession)

EVENING
Let prayers arise for those who tend to weary in well-doing.
(Prayers of Intercession)

PRAY FOR SOMEONE WHOM YOU ADMIRE AS A MODEL OF A RIGHTEOUS PERSON.

MORNING
Righteous God, keep me alert
to your calls to follow in your
righteous ways. In Jesus' name.
Amen.

EVENING
Thank you, Savior God,
for sending answers to my questions
and opportunities to serve you.
In Jesus' name. Amen.

Sunday, July 25

(Read Colossians 2:6–15)

MORNING
Dear God, you are good, for I have seen your flowers grow.

EVENING
Dear God, the sun, the moon, and the starry night
assure me that you are Light.

Paul's remarks to the Colossians remind me of flowers in midwestern gardens during late July days. Some, Creator God, are straggly with blossoms fading and falling while others have withstood extremely dry, hot weather and stand straight and tall, in colorful full bloom. They have continued to thrive because they are deeply rooted in good soil. Nurtured by caring gardeners, they have developed into well-established plants. In similar fashion, Paul urges us to continue lives rooted in Jesus Christ, built up in faith and nurtured by his teachings. Thanks abound for your Son, in whom there is fullness of life.

MORNING
I ask divine guidance in the rooting and nurturing of little ones
who are just beginning their faith journeys. Lead them to Christ.
(Prayers of Intercession)

EVENING
Youth, mature and elderly adults, all of us need help
in our lifetime search for fullness of life. Stay with us, Jesus.
(Prayers of Intercession)

STUDY PSALM 1:1–3.

MORNING
Thank you for flowers and trees,
for the enjoyment they give us and for
the lessons about life that we can learn
from them. In the name of Jesus.
Amen.

EVENING
Thank you for bright summer days
and quiet summer evenings. Thank you
for Christ our Savior in whom we can
find fullness of life. In the name
of Jesus. Amen.

Monday, July 26

(Read Hosea 11:1–5)

MORNING
Eternal and Faithful God, I see this new day you have given;
help me by faith to see what is unseen.

EVENING
Eternal and Faithful God, I have been challenged
to see the substance of hope in the randomness of this day.

Eternal and Faithful God, you are always doing a new thing. You call my earthly eyes to see heavenly substance and hope. Grant me vision to see possibility in the impossible, to see the substance of hope. I am thankful for the new things available to faithful seeing each day.

MORNING
Faithful God, I am grateful for this day
and for the evident promise you have placed in it.
(Prayers of Intercession)

EVENING
Faithful God, thank you for the new thing
I have seen today. I pray that others might also see
and experience the new things you do.
(Prayers of Intercession)

**MAY THE FAITH OF ABEL AND ENOCH,
WHICH PLEASED GOD AND PLEASES GOD,
PUT FLESH ON OUR WORDS AND WITNESS.**
(Pray the Prayer of Our Savior.)

MORNING
May the new thing of God's doing be
seen by those who seek it in all things.
Through Jesus Christ. Amen.

EVENING
God of faith, I pray that my living
this day was an activity of your will.
Through Jesus Christ. Amen.

Tuesday, July 27

(Read Hosea 11:6–11)

MORNING
Eternal and Faithful God, help my believing
to see rather than my seeing to believe.

EVENING
Eternal and Faithful God, my believing has found
great challenge in seeing what you continue to show me.

Eternal and Faithful God, you have called me to believe before I see. I know that to do otherwise makes pleasing you impossible. I thank you, Eternal God, for your patience with eyes that still want to see before believing.

MORNING
Faithful God, I am thankful for the promise
of knowing that your call on this day will exceed my plans
and the expectations of those close to me.
(Prayers of Intercession)

EVENING
Faithful God, thank you for the knowledge
that your call beckons beyond my areas of comfort.
Help me move beyond the tendency to be tentative.
(Prayers of Intercession)

MAY THE FAITH OF NOAH, ABRAHAM, SARAH, ISAAC, AND JACOB
BE REMEMBERED IN OUR WORDS, WAYS, AND OUR WITNESS.
(Pray the Prayer of Our Savior.)

MORNING
May we all be found believing
you to be faithful in all that you
promise. Through Jesus Christ.
Amen.

EVENING
God of revelation and promise,
I pray that my believing has seen
more of your promise today than
yesterday. Through Jesus Christ.
Amen.

Wednesday, July 28

(Read Psalm 107:1–9, 43)

MORNING
Steadfast Creator, let me remember
your enduring and watchful power this day.

EVENING
Steadfast Creator, the challenges of this day
have not exhausted the infiniteness of your enduring love.

Steadfast Creator, your power is indeed the same today as it was yesterday, the same now as it was then and will be forevermore. Create in me a remembrance of redemption. Do not let me refrain from rejoicing when doubting eyes stare and mocking mouths persist. Remind me that their ridicule cannot destroy or deny your redeeming power. Strengthen me with the unwavering knowledge, O God, that I may be found focused, faithful, and unwavering in thankfulness.

MORNING
Steadfast Creator, I give you thanks for this day
and the steadfastness of your love.
(Prayers of Intercession)

EVENING
Steadfast God, thank you for the provisions of this day
that have assured me of your love and protection.
(Prayers of Intercession)

MAY THOSE WHO LISTEN WITH HEARING EARS
KNOW THE STEADFAST AND ENDURING LOVE OF GOD.
(Pray the Prayer of Our Savior.)

MORNING
May all things we see and do
be reminded of your steadfast love.
Through Jesus Christ.
Amen.

EVENING
God of rescue, promise and provision,
may the blessings of this day allow me
to rest in perfect peace.
Through Jesus Christ. Amen.

Thursday, July 29

(Read Colossians 3:1–11)

MORNING

God of Renewal and Possibility, I am reminded
often of where I was and what I did. Help me to hold
to where I am and what I can do now.

EVENING

God of Renewal and Possibility, the drag of my past has been
overcome by the power of promise and change.

God of Renewal, the new walk in you is refreshing. I hold to new threads of hope while mindful of the thick ropes of former ways. You stand with patience and power as I realize that some old ways still die hard. Your grace reminds me that the power to overcome comes from you.

MORNING

Renewing God, I get up knowing that strength to change
will be gained through the struggle with change this day.
(Prayers of Intercession)

EVENING

God of new change, I am reminded of the importance
to refrain from doing that which is hurtful but to seek
that which is helpful and hopeful.
(Prayers of Intercession)

**MAY THE NEW SELF, THOUGHTS, AND WAYS PRESS ON
TOWARDS THE IMAGE OF OUR RENEWING GOD.**
(Pray the Prayer of Our Savior.)

MORNING	EVENING
May the newness of renewal remind all that Christ makes the difference in all differences. Through Jesus Christ. Amen.	God of Renewal and Change, I pray that my being in process will continue to resemble what you had in mind. Through Jesus Christ. Amen.

Friday, July 30

(Read Luke 12:13–21)

MORNING
Gracious and Giving God, let not my spirit become resentful
or covetous of the gifts of others. Help me to appreciate
and be generous with what I have to give.

EVENING
Gracious and Giving God, there is always a tendency to tug at and
want the gifts of others. I am thankful for the grace of restraint.

Gracious, merciful, and giving God, I am mindful of tugs of envy and
greed. You call me to consider my own gifts and possessions. Grant that
I may know what it is to freely give to others without strings, that I
might not become possessed by possessions.

MORNING
Giving God, I am thankful for what I have today
and grateful that you are the supplier of all my needs.
(Prayers of Intercession)

EVENING
Giving God, thank you for freedom of knowing
that I am not defined by my possessions.
May others also know this freedom.
(Prayers of Intercession)

MAY THE DESIRE TO ACQUIRE MORE STUFF
BE OVERCOME BY A MIND TO ACQUIRE A BIGGER AND GIVING HEART.
(Pray the Prayer of Our Savior.)

MORNING
May the demand to get
be tempered by the desire to give.
Through Jesus Christ. Amen.

EVENING
God of Giving, I pray that
my understanding of receiving and
giving has become pleasing
in your sight. Through Jesus Christ.
Amen.

Saturday, July 31

(Read Luke 12:19–21)

MORNING

Gracious and Giving God, I am reminded of what I have this day;
help me to not allow what I have to have me.

EVENING

Gracious and Giving God, I have pondered the value
of my things deeply. In doing so their value has distracted me.

Merciful God, I know that material things can shift from being blessings to possessions. Keep me ever mindful of the power of things to create thirst and lust. Let my thirst be first for you so that things become secondary.

MORNING

Giving God, I am thankful for the riches I have,
but am aware of the seduction of riches. I pray for richness
in you instead of richness in things.
(Prayers of Intercession)

EVENING

Giving God, thank you for the hard lessons on riches
in your word. I pray that familiarity with your word
will not numb me to the teachings in them.
(Prayers of Intercession)

MAY THE SEDUCTION OF RICHES BE OVERCOME
BY A MIND RICH IN LOVING YOU, O GOD.
(Pray the Prayer of Our Savior.)

MORNING

May the thoughts about things
this day be bathed in thankfulness to
our giving God. Through Jesus Christ.
Amen.

EVENING

Giving God, I pray that the life
you require of me will be worthy
of your riches. Through Jesus Christ.
Amen.

Sunday, August 1

(Read Ecclesiastes 1:2, 12–14, 2:18–23)

MORNING

Vainless God, I wake this morning
thankful of all with which I have been blessed.
Keep me mindful of these blessing as I live in a land of plenty
yet where many go seeking.

EVENING

Vainless God, I, like so many others, sought your wisdom this day.
Forgive me if vanity reared its foolish head.

Wisdom God, the thirst for your wisdom and knowledge is enticing. Quench my thrist so that I may not labor in vain and fall prey to the sin of vanity.

MORNING

I pray with an unselfish heart
for those who are in need of your guidance.
(Prayers of Intercession)

EVENING

Guiding Teacher, help me to learn your truths
through the petitions that I pray on behalf
of myself and others.
(Prayers of Intercession)

"VANITY OF VANITIES, SAYS THE TEACHER, VANITY OF VANITIES! ALL IS VANITY."
(Pray the Prayer of Our Savior.)

MORNING

Guide me, Savior God,
as I seek to do your will throughout
the day. Through Jesus Christ.
Amen.

EVENING

Bless me now as sleep
and the night blanket me.
Through Jesus Christ.
Amen.

Monday, August 2

(Read Isaiah 1:1, 10–20)

MORNING
O Holy One, with some trepidation I bow before you this morning.
I come before you to pray and to worship. Prod me today to honor you in all I do.

EVENING
O Holy One, as I scan the day's horizon, I confess my failure to do good
and seek justice. I celebrate the ways you have worked through me
to rescue those who have depended on me.

You have spoken, O God, and so often I have refused to listen. I want to be safe. I ache for comfort and reassurance. Time and again, with all my sisters and brothers, I have betrayed you by seeking security and safety and forgetting that I am responsible for my neighbor. Each day I encounter someone in need—recently widowed, perhaps, or without a home, or grieved or abandoned—someone who could use my presence, my word, my resources, my love. Grant me the wisdom and the fortitude to be a gift to others.

MORNING
God, help me to begin this day by remembering someone
who struggles or aches. May I be a blessing to that person today.
(Prayers of Intercession)

EVENING
Forgive me for the ways in which I have failed to do good and seek justice.
Hold in your arms those whom I have not reached.
(Prayers of Intercession)

HELP ME TO CONQUER MY VARIOUS IDOLATRIES AND TO PUT YOUR WORK AT THE CENTER.

MORNING
Today I give myself to you to be
a person for justice and righteousness
and peace. In the name of him who is
also known as the Rose of Sharon,
I pray. Amen.

EVENING
Forgive me my shortcomings, O God,
and inspire me this night, that your
great work of justice might begin
again in me tomorrow. In the name of
him who is also known as the Rose of
Sharon, I pray. Amen.

Tuesday, August 3

(Read Psalm 50:1–8, 22–23)

MORNING

O Most High. you have given me this day. I could not have
created it myself. Both its joys and its sorrows will find your hand
in them. You shine forth in it all. Thank you.

EVENING

O Most High, from the rising of the sun to its setting,
this entire day has come to be at your behest. Heaven and earth declare
your righteousness. I thank you for your dominion and presence.

How hard it sometimes is, O God, to confess that my faith has missed the
mark. I am often convinced that I need little correction. Where I have
neglected you and put my own needs and desires at the forefront, gently
correct me. Where I have been too sure of what is right, set me straight.
Plant within me this day a seed of gratitude that will flower into a con-
stancy of praise. Show me again that I am utterly dependent on you.

MORNING

This morning I thank you for the abundance of the gifts
that have come from you, and I name them now.
(Prayers of Intercession)

EVENING

As day recedes, I give thanks for the many wonders this day
has brought me. Hear now my recital of them.
(Prayers of Intercession)

THOUGH LIFE MAY NOT BE EVERYTHING THAT I HAD HOPED IT WOULD BE,
THANK YOU FOR THE MANY MARVELS YOU HAVE GIVEN TO ME.

MORNING

Today, O God, keep me from taking
for granted the marvelous world that
surrounds me and the extraordinary life
you have given me. In the name of him
who is also known as the Rose
of Sharon, I pray. Amen.

EVENING

You have shone forth in countless
ways today, O God. As I give thanks,
show me your salvation. In the name
of him who is also known as the
Rose of Sharon, I pray. Amen.

Wednesday, August 4

(Read Isaiah 1:1, 10–20; Psalm 50:1–8, 22–23)

MORNING
O God, teach me and let me attend to you. Sometimes I am proud,
sometimes haughty. All too often, for whatever reason, I dismiss you. Envelop
me. Let me not escape you. Speak, and I will hear. Command, and I will obey.

EVENING
O God, it is tempting as I pray to think that it is in this alone that I do
my duty to you. Hear my prayers, I ask, but remind me, as well, that my
faithfulness is lived out in my love.

Too often I have taught, O God, that faith is a matter of intellect and feelings, of proper prayers and suitable sacrifices. I may say the right words
and do the appropriate ritual, but if I "do not have love, I am a noisy gong
or a clanging cymbal." Lead me today and tomorrow to do something for
someone else's sake, to stand by the side of someone for whom sorrow or
injustice or loneliness is crushing. May I devote myself to you.

MORNING
As I begin this day, instill in me a sense of justice, O God.
(Prayers of Intercession)

EVENING
Take me back over this day, O Holy One. Where I have been just,
I offer my gratitude. Where I have failed to be just, I confess.
Forgive me and strengthen me for tomorrow.
(Prayers of Intercession)

I KNOW THAT YOU REQUIRE MERCY AND NOT SACRIFICE,
O MOST HIGH. MAKE ME MORE MERCIFUL.

MORNING
Awaken me from slumbers of
self-centeredness, O God. Make me
alive and responsive to aches and
pains all around me. In the name of
him who is also known as the Rose
of Sharon, I pray. Amen.

EVENING
As I rest from my labors, strengthen
me to be ever more faithful tomorrow.
In the name of him who is also
known as the Rose of Sharon, I pray.
Amen.

Thursday, August 5

(Read Hebrews 11:1–3, 8–16)

MORNING

O God, where will you lead me today? Will I dare to follow?
May I trust you in all your ways.

EVENING

O God, guide and protector, you have led me on a journey today
and will lead me again tomorrow. You have promised much.
Give me the wisdom and persistence to follow.

Throughout all of history, you have led your children. It is not always easy to follow you, O God. The territory into which you call us is scary and unknown. In this moment, may I trust you. Make me wise enough to live toward what you promise, even when I cannot see the end. Give me a sense of adventure unbowed by fear. And let me not be dependent on having to reach the goal, but rather let me be satisfied with the pilgrimage itself.

MORNING

In all that I do today, may I trust and obey, O Holy One. If you lead me
on new paths, let me not resist, but give me the wisdom to respond and follow.
(Prayers of Intercession)

EVENING

Today in some ways I followed you, O God. I give thanks for your leading,
and I rejoice in my following. In other ways, I said no to your leading.
In my sleep, build my trust.
(Prayers of Intercession)

O GOD, MAKE ME BOLD IN FAITH, A SERVANT OF TRUST AND NOT OF FEAR.

MORNING

Lead me today, O God. I promise
to try to follow. Reassure me in my
fear. Bring me to the true home you
promise. In the name of him who is
also known as the Rose of Sharon,
I pray. Amen.

EVENING

Lead me in my sleeping as in my
waking, O Holy One. Bring me ever
closer to you. Make me a persistent
dogged follower of you. In the name
of him who is also known as the
Rose of Sharon, I pray. Amen.

Friday, August 6

(Read Luke 12:32–40)

MORNING

O God, how startling it can sometimes be to hear your reassurance: "Do not be afraid." I have known my share of fears, and I rejoice in the comfort of those embracing words. Let me live fearlessly today.

EVENING

O God, may my whole life be a gift to you. You have given me life and energy. Without my having to earn anything, you have received me as I am. Let me live boldly, gratefully rejoicing in your unfailing presence.

As much as I wish it weren't so. I sometimes live as though "whoever has the most toys at the end wins." I hoard or crave this or that, and I value worldly possessions. Meister Eckhart once said, "Do what you would do if you felt most secure." Let me celebrate my security today, O God. Give me grace to remember that I live not by bread alone but by every word that comes from you. Let me bury my treasure in your heart alone.

MORNING

Release me from my clinging ways. At every opportunity, guide me to give rather than to get. Let me be your gift to those whom I meet today.
(Prayers of Intercession)

EVENING

Where I cling tightly to lesser things, free my grip. Let me live in the light of your promises rather than in the prison of my fears.
(Prayers of Intercession)

MAY I LIVE GENEROUSLY TODAY, CONFIDENT IN YOUR PROMISES.

MORNING

Turn me back toward you today with your never-failing promises. In the name of him who is also known as the Rose of Sharon, I pray. Amen.

EVENING

As day closes and light fades, remind me that my treasure and my heart belong to you. In the name of him who is also known as the Rose of Sharon, I pray. Amen.

Saturday, August 7

(Read Luke 12:32–40)

MORNING

O Holy One, as I embark on this day, remind me
that everything I do or say makes a difference.
Let me live not casually but passionately and intensely.

EVENING

O Holy One, guide me in my living to an alertness
that expects to encounter you at every moment.
Keep me from being bored and uninvolved. Make me ready.

How easily I fall into ruts, O God. I forget that my life is brief, that you have made each moment holy, and that you have charged me to pay attention. Let me not pretend that what I do has no meaning or that my ethical shortcuts will be greeted with impunity. Remind me that my slightest action is charged with meaning. Make me ready to convey your love in all I do today.

MORNING

As I live through this day, O God,
make me attentive to you in everything that happens.
(Prayers of Intercession)

EVENING

Let me be as alert for you, O God,
as I would be for a thief prowling outside my door.
(Prayers of Intercession)

MAY EVERYTHING I DO BE ATTENTIVE TO YOU, O HOLY ONE.

MORNING

I promise today to look for you,
and to find you, again and again and
again. In the name of him who is also
known as the Rose of Sharon,
I pray. Amen.

EVENING

Make me vigilant in my faith,
O God, that I might not miss you
when you come. In the name of him
who is also known as the
Rose of Sharon, I pray. Amen.

Sunday, August 8

(Read Hebrews 11:1–3, 8–16; Isaiah 1:1, 10–20; Psalm 50:1–8, 22–23; Luke 12:32–40)

MORNING

O God, how awesome you are. How great the faith you offer me.
I cannot help but be intimidated yet enthralled and nourished
by the challenge you put before me.

EVENING

O God, I have not lived up to your hopes for me today. But I trust
that you forgive me and that you will start me again fresh tomorrow.

You ask much of me, O Holy One, that I live justly and righteously, that I hold my neighbor's welfare as dear as my own, and that I stop worrying about my own security. You ask that I give with abandon. It is hard, O God. I find myself coming up short. So remind me again of your promises: that you bless and keep me and shine forth in my life, and make me thankful.

MORNING

I give thanks this day for all that is special in my life,
and I remember that all of it comes from you.
(Prayers of Intercession)

EVENING

Let me live this day not by sight but by trusting in you.
Let me relinquish my hold on false treasures and cling tightly to you.
(Prayers of Intercession)

LET ME LIVE THIS DAY, AND ALWAYS, BY THE LIGHT OF YOUR PROMISE.

MORNING

Though aware of my failings today,
O God, let me not be weighed down
by them. Let me rejoice in all that you
have given me. In the name of him who
is also known as the Rose of Sharon,
I pray. Amen.

EVENING

Hear me as I recite my blessings.
Reassure me again of the certainty
of your grace. In the name of him
who is also known as the
Rose of Sharon, I pray.
Amen.

Monday, August 9

(Read Isaiah 5:1–7)

MORNING
God of the vineyard, touch me today like a vintner
touching roots, vines and branches, so that I may thrive
and bear good fruit for you and your people.

EVENING
God of the vineyard, touch me tonight that I
may be more fruitful tomorrow.

God of the vineyard, I confess that I did not produce all fruit you were looking for. I became busy and disconnected. When you and your people came looking for great grapes, they found sour grapes. I turn to you, connecting like a branch to a vine, letting your new life flow into me.

MORNING
God, I pray for those whom you have made part of your vineyard
and those whom you long to see flourish in your vineyard.
(Prayers of Intercession)

EVENING
God, I give thanks for each moment today that I
remained in you, and your life, vitality, and energy flowed into me.
I pray for those who seek to be connected to you.
(Prayers of Intercession)

GOD OF THE VINEYARD, I PRAY IN YOUR NAME.
(Pray the Prayer of Our Savior.)

MORNING
May I be rooted and grounded
in your love today, God.
In Jesus' name. Amen.

EVENING
Goodnight, God of the vineyard.
Keep me growing in your love
even as I sleep the sleep of peace.
In Jesus' name. Amen.

Tuesday, August 10

(Read Jeremiah 23:23–29)

MORNING

God of near and far, may I live today like you are at my side,
a step ahead of me, and on the far side of my life.

EVENING

God of far and near, I live not according to my dreams
but according to your word. I awake and my dreams pass,
but your word is as solid as a hammer chipping at a rock.

Your word has the power, light, and passion of fire. In those moments when I am tempted to think that truth is as pliable as straw, help me to remember that straw is dead and so are lies. God, I thank you for each time your truth touched me like a hammer today. Wham!

MORNING

God, thank you for those close to me today.
I pray for those far and near who need the hard edge of truth
to keep them safe in you.

(Prayers of Intercession)

EVENING

God, I give thanks for each moment today that you showed me
the word of truth and gave me the inner strength to choose your word.
I pray for those far and near in need of you.

(Prayers of Intercession)

GOD OF THE VINEYARD, I PRAY IN YOUR NAME.
(Pray the Prayer of Our Savior.)

MORNING

May the word of truth
bring me close to you today.
In Jesus' name. Amen.

EVENING

Goodnight, God.
Slip your truth into my dreams
tonight. In Jesus' name.
Amen.

Wednesday, August 11

(Read Psalm 82)

MORNING
President of the Great Assembly, thank you
for making just decisions for the poor and needy.

EVENING
President of the Great Assembly, thank you
for a day of blessings for those in need.

Sovereign God, I look around and I see people making minimum wage in a land of plenty. I see a land of more big houses, and fewer houses that your poor and needy can afford. Your people with minimum wage struggle to rent because of all the deposits required to enrich contractors, mayors, and governors. Just Judge, defend the weak and give them affordable housing.

MORNING
God of justice, thank you for my dwelling place.
I pray for those who long for affordable housing and those who are
crying out for justice.
(Prayers of Intercession)

EVENING
God, thank you for being the God of justice.
I pray for each person needing justice today.
(Prayers of Intercession)

GOD, I THANK YOU FOR THE JUSTICE I RECEIVED TODAY
AND I PRAY FOR THOSE WHO CONTINUE TO WAIT.
(Pray the Prayer of Our Savior.)

MORNING
May justice ring, God,
for all who are part of your inheritance.
In Jesus' name. Amen.

EVENING
Goodnight, God. Thank you
for another day of justice.
In Jesus' name. Amen.

Thursday, August 12

(Read Hebrews 11:29–38)

MORNING
God of Rahab, thank you for opening the door
to the despised among us through faith.

EVENING
God of Rahab, when your people show up at our workplace,
help us to recognize them and provide a place of safety for them.

Rahab had the faith to take in two foreigners who had come to spy on her country. Accepting God, help us to see your people in whatever surprising shapes or colors they show up. Help us, too, when we are pursued by need and threat to accept your help from the most unlikely source. Help us to have the faith of Rahab and of Joshua's two spies.

MORNING
God of safety, thank you for protection even when this world
is not safe. Give faith to those who face threat, loss, and need.
(Prayers of Intercession)

EVENING
God, thank you for being the God of Rahab today. I pray for
each person making the journey from their people to your people.
(Prayers of Intercession)

GOD, THANK YOU FOR YOUR PROTECTION TODAY. I PRAY FOR REFUGEES
AROUND THE WORLD WHO ARE IN TROUBLE AND FLEEING THEIR OPPRESSORS.
TAKE THEM INTO YOUR PEOPLE LIKE YOU TOOK IN RAHAB.
(Pray the Prayer of Our Savior.)

MORNING
God, by faith may your people
pass all the tests of this day.
In Jesus' name.
Amen.

EVENING
Goodnight, God.
I put my faith in you as I sleep and
prepare for tomorrow's journey.
Amen.

Friday, August 13

(Read Hebrews 11:39–12:2)

MORNING

God, thank you for opening the door to life.
Through you, Jesus, I shake off shame so that I am free
to run a race of faith in your footsteps today.

EVENING

God, thank you for the blessings of your grace throughout the day.

God, thank you for placing me and my local church into a long line of people of faith. Moses, David, and Elijah were great men of faith who listened to you, obeyed your voice, and did amazing things for your people. Still, you had an even better plan. Through your son Jesus you have added many into the people you are perfecting.

MORNING

God of safety, thank you for going through the shame
of the cross so that you might gather a shame-free people of faith.
I pray for those needing to be set free.
(Prayers of Intercession)

EVENING

God, thank you for the freedom to race with you today.
I pray for each person who, in faith, is willing to run this race
with you.
(Prayers of Intercession)

GOD, THANK YOU FOR THE CLOUD OF WITNESSES

WHO HAVE CHEERED US ON TODAY.

I PRAY FOR ALL THOSE NEEDING ENCOURAGEMENT.

(Pray the Prayer of Our Savior.)

MORNING	**EVENING**
Jesus, I will fix my eyes on you	Goodnight, God. In faith,
and run the race with joy today.	I rest in you and trust you for strength
In Jesus' name. Amen.	for tomorrow's race. In Jesus' name.
	Amen.

Saturday, August 14

(Read Luke 12:49–56)

MORNING
Passionate God, thank you for sending your son Jesus
to redeem those willing to follow him.

EVENING
Passionate God, thank you for blessing those
who are considered outcasts in your world.

Passionate God, you know that sometimes I choose peace without conflict even though the only path to true peace is through conflict. In those moments when you lead through fiery times, like you, may I be willing to be an outcast so that I may be close to those in need of your love, healing, and forgiveness.

MORNING
God of conflict, thank you for dying on the cross for me.
You were abandoned by those closest to you, distressed by pain and
ignominy, and divided from freedom. You went through the fire so that
we might be free people of faith. I pray for those facing conflict.
(Prayers of Intercession)

EVENING
God, thank you for each sign of your faithfulness that we see in
the midst of conflict. I pray for each person who walks in faith in
the midst of conflict.
(Prayers of Intercession)

O PASSIONATE GOD, I PRAY IN YOUR NAME.
(Pray the Prayer of Our Savior.)

MORNING
May I be faithful in the fire
and test of this day. In Jesus' name.
Amen.

EVENING
Goodnight, God. I rest,
knowing that you are the God who,
out of conflict, brings peace.
In Jesus' name. Amen.

Sunday, August 15

(Read Psalm 80:1–2, 8–19)

MORNING
Loving God, thank you for all that you will do
on this Sabbath day. I rejoice in the blessings to come.

EVENING
Loving God, thank you for the time to rest
and to savor the beauty of your day.

God, you who are maker of heaven and earth, forgive me if I have not heeded your Word. Plant in me a vine that will spread to all whom I meet. Restore in me a clean heart so that I might be saved.

MORNING
God, I pray for those who may turn their backs on you.
Forgive them. Do not turn from them.
(Prayers of Intercession)

EVENING
Bless us, O God, and forgive us
when we fall short of your glory.
(Prayers of Intercession)

**"BUT LET YOUR HAND BE UPON THE ONE
AT YOUR RIGHT HAND, THE ONE WHOM YOU MADE STRONG
FOR YOURSELF."**
(Pray the Prayer of Our Savior.)

MORNING
During this day, O God,
restore me so that I may be
in your favor. In Jesus' name.
Amen.

EVENING
I will call on your name
for strength and renewal as I rest
and prepare for a new day.
In Jesus' name. Amen.

Monday, August 16

(Read Psalm 103:1–12)

MORNING

Creator God, I know that storms come in life and that the rain of trial and temptation will fall, even on me. But as I meet the new day, I do so with great faith that you will walk with me, not letting me drown in the midst of the storm.

EVENING

Creator God, thank you for being with me today.
No matter where I went, you were there and I felt strong.

Creator God, sometimes I feel as though I am in the midst of a quiet storm. Nevertheless, I know that I must hold on because help is on the way. God, when you forgive my iniquities, I am forgiven. When you heal me from all my diseases and transgressions, I am healed. When you redeem me from the pit of problems, I am crowned with love and mercy. No matter what storm is raging in my life, you forgive me. Your anger will cease and you will be merciful to me. Thank you for calming the quiet storms.

MORNING

O God, help me to start this new and wonderful day, assured that if I hold my peace and let you fight the battle, you will say to my storms. "Peace, be still!"
(Prayers of Intercession)

EVENING

Loving God, thank you for being with me today. Forgive me if I, at any time today, doubted your ability to protect me from the storm.
Let me sleep the sleep of renewal in you.
(Prayers of Intercession)

THANK YOU FOR YOUR WORK OF VINDICATION AND JUSTICE FOR ALL.

MORNING

I pledge to develop a great faith in you and in your mighty power. In the name of the Mighty Counselor. Amen.

EVENING

O God, let me awaken tomorrow with a strong conviction to meet whatever and whomever knowing that you are with me and in me. In the name of the Mighty Counselor. Amen.

Tuesday, August 17

(Read Psalm 103:13–22)

MORNING

O God, I need you today more than I ever have needed you.
I come to you because there are situations in my life that are raging.
I need strength for this day. Thank you, God, for being God all by yourself.

EVENING

O God, thank you for always reminding me that you are in charge
of everyone and everything and that you are in complete control.
I rest easier because your throne is everlasting.

God, as a child I would exclaim, "Just wait until I become an adult, then I will be in charge!" However, one of the most interesting things about being an adult is that when storms rage I often wish I could run to my parents for protection and comfort. But while I cannot run to my parents, you are the Great Parent who always has compassion for me. You know me and love me. God, help me always to remember that I can run to you for shelter from the storm.

MORNING

O God, may I start this new day with the blessed assurance of knowing
that if I need to run to you for comfort, you will be there.
(Prayers of Intercession)

EVENING

Thank you, God, for continuing to prove yourself to me. Every time I get weak,
you are there to comfort me. Every time I doubt your love, your love lifts me.
Let me sleep assured that you will never leave me or forsake me.
(Prayers of Intercession)

THANK YOU FOR YOUR ANGELS WHO WATCH OVER ME. BLESS GOD, O MY SOUL.

MORNING

I pledge to witness to the world
your love for me, as a parent loves
a child. In the name of the
Mighty Counselor. Amen.

EVENING

O God, let me awaken tomorrow
assured that while I am frail like the
flowers and the grass, you make
me strong. In the name of the
Mighty Counselor. Amen.

Wednesday, August 18

(Read Jeremiah 1:4–10)

MORNING

O God, you have richly blessed me. You have seen me
through many storms, but today I face a problem that I am not sure
I'm strong enough or seasoned enough to handle. Be my guide today.

EVENING

O God, thank you for calming my fears of inadequacy.
I did not believe that I would be able to meet the challenge, but you
are the one who promoted me and set me in such a high place. I should have
known that you would not lift me up just to let me down.

God, I can remember the first time I was in charge of something, and
while at first all was going well, problems developed. I felt that I was
not good enough to meet the challenge. But then I remembered that I
was chosen by you for such a time as this. What you did for me yesterday, you will do again for me today. God, thank you for reminding me
that you are with me to deliver me.

MORNING

O God, touch my mouth with your hand of guidance
and wisdom, so that your words and will might be spoken through me.
(Prayers of Intercession)

EVENING

Thank you, God, for speaking to and through me today.
May I submit my will to yours so you might be glorified. Grant me a rest
that will refresh and encourage me to serve you even more.
(Prayers of Intercession)

THANK YOU FOR CHOOSING ME TO BUILD AND TO PLANT.
THANK YOU FOR YOUR DIVINE GUIDANCE.

MORNING

I pledge today to do the very best I
can for others and to use wisely the
gifts that you have given me. In the
name of the Mighty Counselor. Amen.

EVENING

O God, let me awaken tomorrow
determined to make a difference
where I live. In the name of the
Mighty Counselor. Amen.

Thursday, August 19

(Read Isaiah 58:9b–14)

MORNING

O God, I continue holding on in the midst of this storm in my life.
Help me to move away from my problems, so that I might minister to someone else
who is in greater need. Help me to minister to others even in the midst of my pain.

EVENING

O God, thank you for helping me to move away from my problem
and help another find joy and meaning in life. I am encouraged that,
despite my state of affairs I am still worthy to be used by you to help others
repair what the storms in their lives have wrecked.

God, there have been times when I have felt totally immobilized. All was very bleak. But during those times, a knock on the door or a call on the telephone broke through my despair. It was a cry for help from someone else. I disregarded my troubles and went to assist another. God, you remind me that if I make myself available to others, you will guide me and make me strong. You will enable me to endure and overcome.

MORNING

God, help me to be determined to get the most
out of my worship experience this week at church.
(Prayers of Intercession)

EVENING

Thank you, God, for helping me take my mind off my troubles by giving
me the opportunity to serve others in their hour of need. As I go to sleep
tonight, anoint me so I am able to discern when another is in need.
(Prayers of Intercession)

THANK YOU, GOD, FOR YOUR GIFT OF WORSHIP. I WILL STRIVE EVER TO DELIGHT IN
YOU AND YOUR GLORY. O GOD, REPAIR THE BREACHES IN MY LIFE.

MORNING

Today, I pledge to be open to your
Spirit. In the name of the Mighty
Counselor. Amen.

EVENING

O God, should I awaken tomorrow,
give me the yearning to worship you
and to give you the honor and glory.
In the name of the Mighty Counselor.
Amen.

Friday, August 20

(Read Psalm 71:1–6)

MORNING

O God, I'm stepping out on your promise of deliverance.
Today I leave my home trusting in you, because I know that if I
run into trouble, you will be there to protect me.

EVENING

O God, thank you for looking out for me today. When I had to take
time out and regroup, you made it possible for me to take shelter in you.
I regained my balance, despite the storm winds blowing upon me. You became
for me a rock of refuge. I survived the day and was victorious.

Storms in life come, and storms in life go. But you, O God, remain
constant during the time of trauma and trial. Even from our birth, we
have depended upon you. God, you delivered us at birth, and you will
continue to deliver us from the storms in our lives.

MORNING

O God, as I face a new day, deliver me from anyone
or anything desiring to do me harm. Be my fortress and my rescue
from the storm. Give me the strength to meet this day.
(Prayers of Intercession)

EVENING

Thank you, God. I was not sure how the day would turn out,
but you let me lean upon you. In you I placed my trust, and because
of this I was delivered. As I leaned upon you today, let me sleep
in you tonight and rest assured that you are with me.
(Prayers of Intercession)

THANK YOU, GOD, FOR PROTECTING ME TODAY. MY PRAISE IS CONTINUALLY OF YOU.

MORNING

I pledge today to put my trust
in you. Be my strength and my guide;
let me ever lean on you. In the name
of the Mighty Counselor. Amen.

EVENING

O God, as I prepare to retire for the
night, thank you for protecting me.
Keep me as I sleep and encourage me to
do better tomorrow. In the name of the
Mighty Counselor. Amen.

Saturday, August 21

(Read Hebrews 12:18–29)

MORNING

O God, I realize that without you I would be lost. Thank you for
your Child, Jesus Christ. In Jesus I find my direction and am coming to know my purpose in life. In Jesus I am steady and focused.

EVENING

O God, thank you for your precious grace. Without your grace
I could not have accomplished all that I did today. I embrace you
and look forward to one day being with you in your heavenly realm.

God, sometimes in this life I am called upon to sacrifice something of
great importance to me. Your Child Jesus, through the shedding of his
blood, brought into being a new covenant between you and humankind. Because of Jesus' sacrifice, I have the opportunity for eternal
life. Jesus experienced a storm that cost his life. But because Jesus sacrificed his life, I gained mine. When I sacrifice myself, I actually gain
more than I have lost.

MORNING

Dear God, if I am faced with the opportunity to make a sacrifice for
someone else, help me to do so cheerfully so that my gift will be from my heart.
(Prayers of Intercession)

EVENING

O God, today you called upon me to make a sacrifice. Thank you for
helping me work through my difficulty in making it. Help me to rest in you
and learn from you, so that I might better serve and love you.
(Prayers of Intercession)

GOD, YOU ARE WORTHY, AND YOUR REALM IS FOREVER. LET ME BE WORTHY OF IT.
IN YOU I STAND STRONG AND FIRM, NO MATTER WHAT IS ASKED OF ME.

MORNING	EVENING
Jesus, I thank you for your sacrifice.	Now God, as I lie down to sleep, help
Let me hear your voice today. In the	me to be worthy of your promise. I will
name of the Mighty Counselor.	trust in you to face tomorrow. In the
Amen.	name of the Mighty Counselor. Amen.

Sunday, August 22

(Read Luke 13:10–17)

MORNING

O God, I was in the midst of a terrible storm last week. My life was in trouble, and I sought you. You heard my cry. I trusted in you, and you healed me. I awaken to stand tall and strong again because of you.

EVENING

O God, thank you for your concern. I rest tonight assured that because I claim Jesus as my Sovereign Savior, no matter what might happen, you will deliver me.

God, your work cannot be confined to one specific time or place. When I must stop what I am doing because of a greater demand placed on me, I cannot worry that what I am called to do appears to some to be strange or different. I cannot let ceremony get in the way of healing. However, I must be Spirit-led. When I operate under your power, my service becomes anointed and healing occurs.

MORNING

Dear God, give me the ability today to discern when you need me to do something for another. Help me to place in proper perspective what I should do and when I should do it.

(Prayers of Intercession)

EVENING

Thank you, God, when you made an opportunity for me to assist someone today in their healing. As I go to sleep, be with me. Should I awake to see the morning sun, help me to be a blessing to someone else.

(Prayers of Intercession)

GOD, YOU ARE MY HEALER, MY SUSTAINER, AND MY LIFE. I SUBMIT MY DREAMS TO YOU. NEVER CEASE FROM CALMING THE STORMS IN MY LIFE.

MORNING

Jesus, you have been my salvation from the beginning of my life. Help me to do good. In the name of the Mighty Counselor. Amen.

EVENING

O God, as another day ends, thank you for being with me. Even when I fell short, you were still there. In the name of the Mighty Counselor. Amen.

Monday, August 23

(Read Jeremiah 2:4–5, 13)

MORNING
God of those who stray and stay, I am thankful
for this day in which to draw closer to you.

EVENING
God of those who stray and stay, thank you
for not forsaking me when I wander. And thank you for inviting
me out of holes I dig for myself and back to living water.

God, it is no surprise that we prefer our exchanges with you to be nurturing. We balk at the suggestion of criticism. But that is exactly what Jeremiah discusses. The words, we might defensively voice, written for people a long time ago, fit our times and people today. Whatever the distance we may have strayed from fully living as your people, we are invited to return.

MORNING
As the new day awakens my heart and soul, I bring you my concerns.
(Prayers of Intercession)

EVENING
As I move toward day's end, I bring you new concerns
and seek to be refreshed today.
(Prayers of Intercession)

**BELOVED, KEEP US WILLING TO HEAR THE WORD,
WHICH CHALLENGES OUR COMPLACENCY.**
(Pray the Prayer of Our Savior.)

MORNING
Be present, Faithful God, as I approach this day. Knowing I disappoint you with my unfocused wandering, help me find my way closer to you. In the name of the Christ. Amen.

EVENING
Evening is here, Faithful God.
My hours of trying to put purpose to my journey are drawing to a close. I have sensed your presence as my pathway has intersected with those of others. In the name of the Christ. Amen.

Tuesday, August 24

(Read Hebrews 13:1–2)

MORNING

God of gracious hospitality, thank you for inviting me to this special
day in your creation, and for the possibility of entertaining angels.

EVENING

God of gracious hospitality, thank you for your gifts of grace,
for your tender yet challenging love, and for strangers met
on my pathway this day.

Caring and Concerned God, a slight man, dressed in serviceable but
ragged and smoke-saturated clothing, exhausted and troubled, was in need
of someone who might honor his humanity. As our relationship developed
his once better status in life surfaced, showing his wisdom, wit, and professional education. Soon I recognized him as my resident theologian.
Hardly the customary image of an angel, but an angel none the less.

MORNING

As day begins, I am aware of strangers who have entered my life.
I pray for them and for those issues that weigh heavily.
(Prayers of Intercession)

EVENING

As evening falls, I am alive with fresh awareness of angels
crossing my pathway. Hear my prayers of joy and concern.
(Prayers of Intercession)

BELOVED, HEAL ANY FEAR AND ANXIETY THAT COMES WHEN I AM CONFRONTED WITH
SOMEONE WHO DIFFERS FROM MY EXPECTATIONS.
(Pray the Prayer of Our Savior.)

MORNING

My antennae are up,
God of Surprises. This day I will be
alert to the strange ones with whom
I come in contact, knowing that each
is one of your beloved. In the name
of the Christ. Amen.

EVENING

This day provided gifts galore,
God of Surprises. As long as I
remained focused on the genius of
your human creation, the angels
were manifest. In the name
of the Christ. Amen.

Wednesday, August 25

(Read Hebrews 13:1, 5)

MORNING

Creator God, as I greet the morning, focus my love and energy on what
is important, not on layers of material obsessions that come between us.

EVENING

Creator God, this day has exhibited conflict between spiritual and secular values.
Your promise not to leave me has helped me through.

God of the changing seasons, it's back-to-school time at the mall. We
see signs trumpeting sales, weary parents and children weaving through
minefields of point-of-purchase displays and the lure of name brand
clothing. Conflict, cheerlessness, a daily spectacle—perhaps we do love
money. Yet here in this mall there is still a relentless reminder that we
should be content with what we have.

MORNING

God of Variety, you provide opportunities to be aware of the needs
of others rather than ourselves. Hear my prayers for others.
(Prayers of Intercession)

EVENING

God of Variety, with senses aware, I have experienced
your presence in human life, in nature around me this day.
Hear my thanks, and my continuing concerns.
(Prayers of Intercession)

BELOVED, YOU HAVE KEPT YOUR PROMISE ONCE AGAIN,
THAT YOU WILL NEITHER LEAVE NOR FORSAKE ME.
(Pray the Prayer of Our Savior.)

MORNING	**EVENING**
A day lies before me, Gracious Spirit,	Gracious Spirit, this day concludes
to experience being content with what	and a night of rest awaits me. Grant
I have received from you and to	me peace that I may use this night as
recognize your love. In the name	preparation for tomorrow. In the
of the Christ. Amen.	name of the Christ. Amen.

Thursday, August 26 · Women's Equality (Suffrage) Day

(Read Hebrews 13:1, 16)

MORNING
Gentle Spirit, sacrifice is not a word with which I am very familiar.
But I am thankful to begin life anew this morning. I ask you to walk with me
as I learn to share more fully of the blessings I have received.

EVENING
Gentle Spirit, what a day this has been!
Your presence has buoyed me up as I walked through
the experience of sharing in some significant ways.

God of Mystery and Surprises, the interim minister found herself between assignments, without a place to carry on her specialized ministry for months. Keeping up with insurance costs, rent, and normal living expenses had become a formidable task. Seemingly out of nowhere, a check for one thousand dollars appeared in the mail, marked "It's our turn." Someone knew. Someone shared!

MORNING
Just as I will share what I have this day, O God,
let me share my prayer concerns with you.
(Prayers of Intercession)

EVENING
I have given and received today, O God,
and as the day ends, I wish to share my concerns again.
(Prayers of Intercession)

BELOVED, PLEASE PROVIDE EACH DAY WITH SIMPLE REMINDERS
OF THE GRACE OF GIVING AND RECEIVING.
(Pray the Prayer of Our Savior.)

MORNING
O God of Grace, on this day
and every day, may I manifest the
good that is sharing what I have received from you. In the name
of the Christ. Amen.

EVENING
O God of Grace, if I have pleased
you this day, surround me with the
blessing of a good night of restoration
and repose. In the name
of the Christ. Amen.

Friday, August 27

(Read Luke 14:10–11)

MORNING

Good Morning, Wakan Tanka, and thank you for the gift
of new dawn. We are met with another word challenging our usual
ways. Humble is not in our vocabulary, so keep us company this
day as that word enters our being.

EVENING

Good evening, Great God; once again we give you thanks
for the learnings of this day.

O God of Sharing, as we waited to sail aboard the Amistad, we over-heard conversation among crew members. One young, seemingly wise man, who had been a cook on a number of boats, acknowledged that while he was very good at cooking, he had learned it was best not to boast about it. For, he said, when one claims to be good, the expectations of the remaining crew only increase.

MORNING

Given a new morning, O God, I ask you also for the means
to not take myself too seriously.
(Prayers of Intercession)

EVENING

Given the gifts and lessons of this day, O God,
I humbly ask that you hear my prayers for others.
(Prayers of Intercession)

**BELOVED, HELP US TO STRUGGLE WITH WORDS
THAT ARE NOT COMMON TO OUR VOCABULARY.**
(Pray the Prayer of Our Savior.)

MORNING	EVENING
Patient God, today may I learn as I live; challenge my nature, that I will not fall into the trap of exalting myself. In the name of the Christ. Amen.	Patient God, today you have reminded me just how patient you are, as I struggled with the notion of being humble. In the name of the Christ. Amen.

Saturday, August 28

(Read Luke 14:12–14)

MORNING

Beloved One, as I rush about today, stewing in my own
urgencies, awaken my spirit to those who are near and those with
whom you would have me share my table.

EVENING

Beloved One, I hope that, in addition to family and friends,
I have touched the lives of some without the expectation of repayment.

God who provides all that we have, an affluent, retired executive was invited to visit a large soup kitchen in a nearby major city. His expectation was that they wanted his money. He arrived. They handed him a
paper hat and plastic gloves and put him to work on the serving line. It
was to be a life-changing experience. They didn't need to ask for his
money; his heart told him sharing his bounty was essential.

MORNING

Your affection for the have-nots, O God,
reminds me of how I must pray for others.
(Prayers of Intercession)

EVENING

As a full day ends, O God, my eyes have seen anew
those with whom I need to share your love.
(Prayers of Intercession)

BELOVED, IN MY SPIRITUAL POVERTY YOU SHARE YOUR TABLE,
THAT I WILL COMMUNE WITH OTHERS WHO ARE DEPRIVED.
(Pray the Prayer of Our Savior.)

MORNING	**EVENING**
I enter a day of new possibilities, Bountiful God, ready to be enriched, just as I hope to nurture the lives of others. In the name of the Christ. Amen.	As my day concludes, Bountiful God, I have been nurtured as I sought to nurture, blessed as I sought to bless. In the name of the Christ. Amen.

Sunday, August 29

(Read Psalm 81:1, 10–16)

MORNING

Yahweh God, on this Sabbath morning as I sing, shout,
or even whisper in praise of you, I am reminded of the many blessings
I have received in these past and wonder-filled days.

EVENING

Yahweh God, as our Sabbath draws to a close, I pause to give you
thanks for filling me with the nurture of journey, food, and spirit.

God, you promise that if we open our mouths in songs of praise, we
will be filled with the appealing, sweet nourishment of honey from the
rock, not the bitter sustenance of a turnip. You promise to provide the
faithful with an unlikely product from a more unlikely source. Like
those who sat around ancient campfires telling stories, let us proclaim,
"What a wonderful God have we!"

MORNING

Hear my Sabbath prayers of worry and fret,
Gracious God, as I come to you in praise.
(Prayers of Intercession)

EVENING

My Sabbath day has been full and rich,
Gracious God, and I still have concerns for others.
(Prayers of Intercession)

BELOVED, I COME TO YOU WITH THE SWEET TASTE OF HONEY
RECEIVED AND YET TO BE RECEIVED.
(Pray the Prayer of Our Savior.)

MORNING

Singing and shouting your praises,
coming to you in prayer and worship,
I look forward, Faithful God, to this
day of fulfilled promise. In the name
of the Christ. Amen.

EVENING

O what a glorious day,
Faithful God! From my mouth have
come words in response to your felt
presence. In the name
of the Christ. Amen.

Monday, August 30

(Read Deuteronomy 30:15–20)

MORNING

God, enable me to make the right choices. Guide me
in your ways so that I may choose life over death. If I stumble
and fall, pick me up and hold me in your loving embrace.

EVENING

God, thank you for giving me the power of choice
so that I may choose life, not death, choose love, not hate.
Keep me as I keep you close to my heart.

Every day I am fated with an abundance of choices. These choices affect my life, as well as the lives of others. Continue to create in me a clean heart, O God, so that the choices I make lead to life.

MORNING

As I step out into the world today, I will make good use
of the gift of choice you have given me.
(Prayers of Intercession)

EVENING

Everlasting and omnipotent God, I have felt your presence today.
You enabled me to choose life. For this, I am so thankful.
Guide me through the dream world, so that I may return to you anew.
(Prayers of Intercession)

I TRULY DO POSSESS THE POWER OF CHOICE. THANK YOU, GOD.

MORNING

I am responsible for the choices I
make in life. Therefore, I will make
choices that support and enable life.
In Jesus' name, I pray. Amen.

EVENING

I will search for you in my dreams,
O God. I know that your omnipotence
will enable me to choose life, even
while I sleep. In Jesus' name,
I pray. Amen.

Tuesday, August 31

(Read Psalm 139:1–6)

MORNING

O God, as I watch the pearl drops of dew
in the morning sun, myriad little rainbows appear.
I am reminded of your covenant with humankind.

EVENING

O God, your name should be "Awesome."
For when I think of you I stand in awe.
Thank you for bringing me to this place.

I have no desire to walk on hot coals; neither do I have a desire to stretch my body upon a bed of nails. Just knowing that you love me, O God, is good enough for me. What a wonderful thing your love is! I sifted through the many layers of self to experience the joy of finding you there. You are the essence of my being.

MORNING

I am in awe of your magnificence, Great Spirit!
(Prayers of Intercession)

EVENING

Wonderful One! Everlasting and ever-present God,
whose great Spirit is all-knowing, thank you for granting me
another day to experience your creation.
(Prayers of Intercession)

THANK YOU FOR INSTILLING IN ME THE WILLPOWER TO ATTAIN HIGHER HEIGHTS.

MORNING

I will continue to be amazed and
awestruck by your perfect knowledge.
In Jesus' name, I pray. Amen.

EVENING

I will try to attain higher heights,
knowing that such knowledge and
heights are not easily attained.
But it is comforting to know that you
know me. In Jesus' name, I pray.
Amen.

Wednesday, September 1

(Read Jeremiah 18:1–11)

MORNING

God of all creation, whose power is fathomless, you are indeed
the most skillful potter! Keep bringing me to the place where I
hear your words. Your creation is a marvelous work of art.

EVENING

God of all creation, thank you for reminding me I am but a piece
of clay on your potter's wheel. Shape me to your liking.

It has been said that in art there are no mistakes. As I look around me
at your work of art, I can attest to this truth. Not only are you the potter who takes me to your potter's wheel, you are also the painter who
paints the sunshine in my sky. Enable us, O God, to be potters and
painters. Help us to shape our lives in a way that is pleasing to you.

MORNING

As I journey into this day, I will be open to the many places
and spaces where I may hear your Word.
(Prayers of Intercession)

EVENING

O God, thank you for this day. Your Word came to me
as I watched the children play. So much joy, hope, and laughter.
Thank you for allowing me to be an apprentice potter
in their lives, for you are their most skillful potter.
(Prayers of Intercession)

YOU ARE THE CHANGER, O GOD, AND I AM THE CHANGED.

MORNING

I commit myself to your potter's
wheel, O God. In Jesus' name,
I pray. Amen.

EVENING

When tomorrow comes,
continue to work on me, O God,
so that I may be a vessel for your
goodness. In Jesus' name,
I pray. Amen.

Thursday, September 2

(Read Psalm 139:13–18)

MORNING
Great Spirit, whose breath I first breathed as an infant,
your works are indeed wonderful! And your thoughts are deeper
than the deepest waters. Enable me to be more present to my body, mind,
and spirit, so that I may become more balanced and whole.

EVENING
Great Spirit, lead me to the still waters,
so I may drink of your life-sustaining thoughts.

Modern science enables us to see, in living color, just what our inner bodies look like. While the psalmist would surely be mesmerized by the microcameras that can gain access to our inward parts, the wisdom the psalmist brings to us remains timeless: "I praise you, for I am fearfully and wonderfully made." Thank you, Great Spirit, for the breath of life.

MORNING
I want to begin this day by acknowledging the intricate details
of my body, mind, and spirit, which you have formed
into one body, mind, and spirit.
(Prayers of Intercession)

EVENING
You have brought me through one more day, O God.
Walk with me through the dream world.
(Prayers of Intercession)

THANK YOU FOR CREATING THE HUMAN FAMILY
WITH SUCH INTRICATE DETAILS SO WELL PLANNED. I SING WITH THE PSALMIST,
"HOW WEIGHTY TO ME ARE YOUR THOUGHTS, O GOD!"

MORNING
I will respect my body,
which you have made wonderful.
In Jesus' name, I pray. Amen.

EVENING
May I awake with a new readiness
to be all that you have created me.
In Jesus' name, I pray. Amen.

Friday, September 3

(Read Philemon 1–21)

MORNING

Most compassionate and loving God, teach me the
"ways of the heart." Enable me to use the tools of love, not force.
Thank you, O God, for another day to practice love.

EVENING

Most compassionate and loving God, you are my everything.
Enable me to quench the thirst of the thirsty, with your everflowing love.

God, the letter Paul wrote to Philemon should be of keen interest to all Christians. It reminds us of how Christians ought to be. Jesus teaches us in Mark 10:42–44, "You know that among the Gentiles, those whom they recognize as their rulers lord it over them, and their great ones are tyrants over them. But it is not so among you; but whoever wishes to be great among you must be your servant, and whoever wishes to be first among you must be slave of all." As Dr. Martin Luther King Jr. said, "We all can be great, because we all can serve." Help me, O God, to keep my self-importance in balance.

MORNING

O loving God, help me to become a better servant to your people.
Allow me to sow seeds of love in your garden of creation.
(Prayers of Intercession)

EVENING

O God of my salvation, strengthen me, so that I may be
impeccable in the struggle for a more just world order.
(Prayers of Intercession)

ENABLE ME TO FORGIVE THOSE WHO HAVE WRONGED ME, O GOD.

MORNING

I will commit myself to being a faithful servant. Your will be done, not mine. In Jesus' name, I pray. Amen.

EVENING

O God, continue to instruct me in your ways. Enable me to break down the barriers that keep me from being a loving and forgiving human being. In Jesus' name, I pray. Amen.

Saturday, September 4

(Read Psalm 1)

M O R N I N G

Everlasting and loving God, I can feel you this morning.
Enable me to face this day with a new determination, a determination
to do what is pleasing in your sight.

E V E N I N G

Everlasting and loving God, everything about you is good.
There is no injustice in your law. Let me not stand with the wicked,
for there is no justice in the ways of the wicked.

Thank you, God, for being my shepherd. When the wicked come to devour me, you will protect me. The wicked cannot claim me. I belong to you, O God. I will profess my faith in you, God Almighty, and send the wicked running for cover. I will delight in the way of the righteous, so that I may choose life. You are the life.

M O R N I N G

Loving God, lead me to your will, so that I may
quench my thirst with your living water. Grant me clarity,
so that I may recognize the wicked in all their disguises.
(Prayers of Intercession)

E V E N I N G

"And do not bring us to the time of trial,
but rescue us from the evil one."
(Prayers of Intercession)

FOR THE SAKE OF RIGHTEOUSNESS, USE ME AS YOU WILL, GOD.

M O R N I N G

Enable me to be discerning,
for the ways of the wicked are devious
and misleading. I will rejoice in your
justice. In Jesus' name, I pray.
Amen.

E V E N I N G

As sleep beckons me, O God,
I am thankful for your guidance.
Guide me through the dream world to
that place by the streams of water
where the righteous are planted.
In Jesus' name, I pray. Amen.

Sunday, September 5

(Read Luke 14:25–33)

MORNING
God of all creation, you are the Alpha and the Omega.
Strip me of all that is superficial in my life. And when my ears
become dull from the noises of this world, whisper into them,
so that I may listen and await your instruction.

EVENING
God of all creation, help me as I seek ways to rid my life
of the superfluous. Take my life, for only you can restore the saltiness.

Asleep or awake, the body rests, but not the mind. And God, why does
the mind not rest? It is our unwillingness to let go. Seek the power of
silence, and the mind will rest. By letting go, we begin to trust in the
natural order of your creation. We begin to trust our own natural order.
When the ways of the world attempt to interrupt my loving you,
Creator God, shore up my shoulders so that I may carry my cross.

MORNING
Eternal and loving God, when the burdens of this world rest heavy
on my shoulders, lift my burdens as only you can do.
(Prayers of Intercession)

EVENING
God of all creation, show me the middle way.
Your children are living in a world full of avarice. Guide me so that
I may be greedy for spiritual wealth and not material wealth.
(Prayers of Intercession)

"HAVE SALT IN YOURSELVES, AND BE AT PEACE WITH ONE ANOTHER."

MORNING
Grant me the wisdom, O God,
to think before I act, so that the consequences of my actions build upon
your foundation. In Jesus' name,
I pray. Amen.

EVENING
As I come to the close of this week, it is
comforting to know that in "your house
there are many dwelling places." Thank
you for Jesus, who prepared a place for
me. In Jesus' name, I pray. Amen.

Monday, September 6 · Labor Day—U.S.A., Canada

(Read Exodus 32:7–10)

MORNING

God of new beginnings, on this day when many relax,
bless those who labor so that others may enjoy.

EVENING

God of new endings, for the events of this day
and the blessings of my life, I give you my thanks.

When you look down today, God, you still see people whom you have richly blessed, people like me. I am here, God. For these moments, you have my attention. But blessed as I am, is my life pleasing to you? I have erected so many golden calves, worshiped so many false idols, launched into glad pursuits that you could not enjoy. I have been hard of heart and stiff of neck and have caused you grief and pain. Grant me the grace to find you and cling to you.

MORNING

I offer my prayers, God, for all who will forget you today.
Forget not them.
(Prayers of Intercession)

EVENING

I offer my prayers, God, for all who took today
and its blessings for granted.
(Prayers of Intercession)

BLESSING AND BETRAYAL CAN EXIST SIDE BY SIDE.

MORNING	**EVENING**
Into your hands, God,	For all that has blessed me
I commit my life this day.	this day, God, I am grateful.
Thanks be to God.	Thanks be to God.
Amen.	Amen.

Tuesday, September 7

(Read Exodus 32:11–14)

MORNING
God, give me the vision to see clearly today
and to act with compassion.

EVENING
God, I offer you my day. I am grateful for everything
I have done well—and I pray forgiveness for my failures.

Understanding God, how do I react to the things that horrify or distress me? It is so easy to condemn, so easy to say "Serves them right!" when someone gets into difficulty. But Moses acted differently. He must have been absolutely dismayed when he heard what his people had done. But instead of being mad, God, he got busy—busy in prayer, busy pleading for mercy, forgiveness, and a new start—not for himself, but for those who had betrayed his and your trust. When I am deceived and let down, please don't let it fester in my soul. Give me the grace to react with faith and nobility. I will pray for understanding and forgiveness—for your love to descend and enwrap those who betrayed me.

MORNING
Guide those who today will make great decisions that affect many.
(Prayers of Intercession)

EVENING
Hear my prayer for those who have grieved you today.
(Prayers of Intercession)

"GOD, DO NOT HOLD THIS SIN AGAINST THEM."

MORNING	**EVENING**
Into your hands, O God,	You have held the world
I commit my life and my living	in your hands today, God. I commit
throughout this day. Thanks be	this night to your loving care.
to God. Amen.	Thanks be to God. Amen.

Wednesday, September 8

(Read Psalm 51:1–10)

MORNING

Wondrous God, you see everything with a clear eye
and yet you forgive. You are truly a wondrous God.

EVENING

Wondrous God, you have seen everything I have done today
and known every thought. Grant me forgiveness.

I am quite content with my life, God. I am not a rascal. I try to live my life with quality. Is that how you see me, Parent God? Or am I looking through rose-colored spectacles? "You desire truth in the inward being." Give me the same desire. Give me the desire to see myself as you see me—loved, but imperfect. Even as I pray that prayer, God, I wince. I want to think well of myself. I do not want to see all the things that are wrong in my life. Sadly, the real truth is that I already see too many of them, and do not want to have to change. "Wash me thoroughly from my iniquity, and cleanse me from my sin."

MORNING

May your people believe your promise,
and turn to you for wholeness.
(Prayers of Intercession)

EVENING

I pray for everyone I have encountered today.
(Prayers of Intercession)

"ALL HAVE SINNED AND FALL SHORT OF THE GLORY OF GOD."

MORNING

Create in me a clean heart,
O God. Thanks be to God.
Amen.

EVENING

Let me sleep well
and arise to live with a new
and right spirit. Thanks be
to God. Amen.

Thursday, September 9

(Read 1 Timothy 1:12–14)

MORNING
Wondrous Love, let my day begin with gratitude.

EVENING
Wondrous Love, let my day end with gratitude.

God, Paul knew that he was forgiven. He knew because of the way his life had been turned around. Every day he shook himself and marveled at what you had done in him, and how different life was now. He had been changed from a blasphemer, persecutor, and man of violence into a man of faith and champion of the gospel, enduring persecution instead of meting it out. I can't compete with Paul, God. I hadn't sunk so low. I was never such a fierce opponent of the faith. So please, God, give me the courage to know with certainty, as he did. Every day keep me grateful that your love surrounds me, your life strengthens me, and your grace and forgiveness flow in my life too. And may I too be judged to be faithful and trustworthy enough to serve you.

MORNING
I pray for everyone I will talk to today, treating each with grace.
(Prayers of Intercession)

EVENING
I pray for my loved ones, and all who treat me with grace.
(Prayers of Intercession)

GOD'S RIVER OF GRACE OVERFLOWS ITS BANKS.

MORNING
May I live today as a forgiven person who is a forgiving person. Thanks be to God. Amen.

EVENING
At day's end, I cast myself on your mercy. Thanks be to God. Amen.

Friday, September 10

(Read 1 Timothy 1:15–17)

MORNING

Praiseworthy God, I rise to a new day and a fresh start.
Guide me.

EVENING

Praiseworthy God, for your known and unknown presence
with me today, I praise you.

Paul knew that he was forgiven and believed it was because he had acted "ignorantly in unbelief." Forgiving God, do you only forgive those who have made honest mistakes—those who didn't really know what they were doing? If so, there is little hope for me. Yes, God, I have done lots of things without thought. I have done things that I should have realized were wrong, but didn't—until the consequences hit me hard. But there are too many things that I have done willfully, knowing they were stupid, risky, and wrong. Do you forgive people like me too? Give me grace to claim your forgiveness as one truly determined to change, holding fast to the sure saying that even "the greatest of sinners can be forgiven."

MORNING

I pray this morning for all who are lured
by false delights and deceitful ideas.
(Prayers of Intercession)

EVENING

I pray tonight for all those I have wronged
and for all who have wronged me.
(Prayers of Intercession)

"FORGIVE US OUR SINS, FOR WE OURSELVES FORGIVE."

MORNING

May your loving wisdom guide
my every act and decision today.
Thanks be to God. Amen.

EVENING

To the ruler of the ages,
immortal, invisible, the only God,
be honor and glory forever and ever.
Thanks be to God. Amen.

Saturday, September 11

(Read Luke 15:1–10)

MORNING
God, keep me close to you today.

EVENING
God, draw my wandering soul back to your throne of grace and
welcome.

Some people are like sheep—they get lost because they wander foolishly.
Some people are like coins—they get lost because others treat them
without sufficient care. You love the lost, God. I know, because you
found me. You were longing for me before I even knew that you existed.
O God, how grateful I am! But I am also amazed that there is so much
rejoicing in heaven. How do I treat the lost, God? Usually, I leave them
to their own devices, vaguely hoping that they will come to their senses.
Sometimes in righteous anger, I condemn them. Is it righteous, God?
Or are there those who are lost because I did not care enough to reach
out with love and thoughtfulness? Make me an effective channel of your
grace, so that the bells of heaven can peal again and again with joy.

MORNING
I pray for those who have lost direction, lost faith, and lost hope.
(Prayers of Intercession)

EVENING
I pray for those who, drawn to your light,
are finding their way home.
(Prayers of Intercession)

JESUS' PRESENCE COULD ENRICH THE WORST OF COMPANY THEN—AND EVEN NOW.

MORNING
May my life this day extend light
and love to those who need it.
Thanks be to God. Amen.

EVENING
Hold me in the arms of faith tonight,
God, that I may sleep secure.
Thanks be to God. Amen.

Sunday, September 12 · National Grandparents Day

(Read Jeremiah 4:11–12, 22–28)

MORNING

Parent God, I pray that I will not shame
nor forsake you this day.

EVENING

Parent God, as a child seeking direction,
I pray that I brought honor to your name.

God, through your Word, you have made it clear how you want your children to live in relation to your universe. Regretfully, we continue to rape the land of its resources while destroying our own temples through stupidity, foolishness, and lack of understanding. Teach me, O God, to be a good steward of your earth and of my own body, that I may turn your wrath away from me. Use me as your instrument for change—a change that will heal your land.

MORNING

I pray for those who continue to waste the riches of your earth.
(Prayers of Intercession)

EVENING

I pray for the healing of your people and of your land.
(Prayers of Intercession)

"I HAVE NOT RELENTED NOR WILL I TURN BACK."

MORNING

May my life this day
be an example to those who continue
to make ruins of your creation.
Thanks be to God. Amen.

EVENING

Make me accountable
for any wrongs I have done this day.
Bless me as I sleep to do better
tomorrow. Thanks be to God.
Amen.

Monday, September 13

(Read Jeremiah 9:1)

MORNING
Source of comfort, grant me peace of mind
in the midst of difficulty and turmoil. May I always sense your
nearness, and may your presence lighten my burdens.

EVENING
Source of comfort, thank you for watching over me.
I give to you the stresses and trials of this day,
and I rest secure in your love.

From time to time, the challenges of life threaten to overwhelm me. Alone I am inadequate to meet the seemingly insurmountable obstacles. God, sometimes it even begins to feel as if you have ceased to watch over me. It is during these times that I question your presence. Help me always to remember that your hand is guiding me through the difficult passages. Thank you for the security of your presence and strength, and thank you for the opportunity to use these challenges to grow stronger in you.

MORNING
Make me aware of your presence throughout this day.
(Prayers of Intercession)

EVENING
I commit to you, all-knowing God, the tensions and worries
of this day. Grant me rest and peace of mind.
(Prayers of Intercession)

STRENGTHEN ME AS I PRAY.
(Pray the Prayer of Our Savior.)

MORNING	EVENING
May I meet today's challenges with renewed confidence, knowing that you, loving God, are my strength and comfort. In Christ's name, I pray. Amen.	Eternal and everlasting God, who is without beginning or end, thank you for your guidance and protection throughout this day. In Christ's name, I pray. Amen.

Tuesday, September 14

(Read Jeremiah 8:18–9:1)

MORNING
Compassionate God, let my mind be turned from my own
troubles to the distress of my neighbors. Keep my worries from
blinding me to the needs of others.

EVENING
Compassionate God, thank you for Christ's example of compassion
and selflessness. Make me, like him, sensitive to the needs of others.

Merciful God, you care even for the tiny sparrow, and you alone know
what every man, woman, and child is going through. It is easy to insulate myself and to become immune from the sorrow and suffering in
the world. You created us to care for one another. Grant me the strength
to seek the hurting and the helpless, and grant me the courage to minister to them as Christ would—selflessly and tirelessly.

MORNING
May I be mindful throughout this day of the needs of others. Grant me
patience and humility, that I may serve others without thought of reward.
(Prayers of Intercession)

EVENING
Loving God, whose gentle Spirit encompasses all people, grant me a night
of peaceful rest, that tomorrow I may be refreshed and renewed to serve you.
(Prayers of Intercession)

IN YOUR SPIRIT, I PRAY.
(Pray the Prayer of Our Savior.)

MORNING	EVENING
It is so easy to become immune or insensitive to the pain of my neighbors. Help me, O God, to be compassionate. In Christ's name, I pray. Amen.	Compassionate God, thank you for loving us enough to send Christ Jesus. With your guidance, I will strive to be Christlike in my dealings with my neighbors. In Christ's name, I pray. Amen.

Wednesday, September 15

(Read Psalm 79:1–9)

MORNING
Merciful God, I pray this morning for the nations of the earth.
Deliver us from our willfulness and hard-heartedness, and grant us your peace.

EVENING
Merciful God, whose loving Spirit enfolds the earth,
tonight I lay at your feet all the troubles and conflicts in this world.
Have mercy on us, and grant us peace.

Loving God, it is impossible to watch the news or pick up a newspaper without seeing the destruction that people all over the world are wreaking on one another. King David cried out to you as my heart cries out now: How can you allow such things to happen to innocent people? Where are you in all of this? As you revealed to Elijah, you are not in the fire, in the wind, or in the earthquake; you are in the absolute silence. You are sorrowful at the injustice and cruelty, but you know and understand the pain.

MORNING
O God, to the leaders of nations grant wisdom and the ability
to reconcile differences. To the casualties of conflicts too numerous
for any except you to know, grant eternal rest.
(Prayers of Intercession)

EVENING
Hear my prayer this night for peace. Quiet the rage of those who are angry,
reconcile those who are in conflict, and comfort the innocent victims of violence.
(Prayers of Intercession)

PEACEFULLY I PRAY.
(Pray the Prayer of Our Savior.)

MORNING	**EVENING**
You alone, O God, comprehend the extent of the suffering in the world. Forgive us for our pettiness, stubbornness, and selfishness. In Christ's name, I pray. Amen.	God, have mercy upon the people of this world. In Christ's name, I pray. Amen.

Thursday, September 16

(Read Amos 8:4–7)

MORNING
Righteous God, I am accountable to you for all of my actions.
Help me to glorify you in everything I do today.

EVENING
Righteous God, you are the final authority and the supreme justice. I tremble before
so righteous a judge. Have mercy on me, and forgive me my many, many sins.

God of Creation, you endowed humans with the will to choose right
from wrong. When Adam and Eve disobeyed you, they bequeathed to
all humanity the predisposition to sin. There are a great many people
who deliberately defy you. There are also many people who strive to do
your will and never seem to get ahead in the world. You, righteous God,
will never forget what any of us have done, and at the judgment, you
will require us to answer for our actions.

MORNING
As much as I want to do your will, my flesh is weak.
I have sinned against you time and time again, and you have forgiven me
time and time again! Thank you for being patient with me.
(Prayers of Intercession)

EVENING
Help me to recognize in myself my disobedience to you.
Make me aware of my unworthy thoughts and actions.
(Prayers of Intercession)

OBEDIENTLY I PRAY.
(Pray the Prayer of Our Savior.)

MORNING
I come before you this morning,
knowing that no matter how much
I strive to be a good person, my
attempts are inadequate. Today guide
me so that I am all you want me to
he. In Christ's name, I pray. Amen.

EVENING
Merciful God, forgive me for my
sinful deeds, both those I know of and
those of which I am not aware.
Thank you for your promise of eternal
love and eternal life. In Christ's name,
I pray. Amen.

Friday, September 17

(Read Psalm 113)

MORNING

Glorious God, I give thanks this morning for your love, mercy,
and graciousness. I will praise you with my whole heart and soul, from the
rising to the setting of the sun. Praise be to you, Sovereign God!

EVENING

Glorious God, I rest secure in your power and majesty, knowing that you
are the Alpha and Omega, eternal and everlasting, and that I am your child.

You, O God, are the Creator of all; without you, nothing was made.
Your glory is over all of heaven and earth—in the song of the birds, the
smell of mown grass, the warmth of a fire, the expanse of the starry sky.
It is in the company of family and friends and in the touch of a loved
one. Everywhere I turn, I find a new reason to praise you. I will trust
you to raise my thoughts above the tasks of everyday life, and I will seek
to glorify you in everything I do.

MORNING

Today, God, I will look around me with new eyes. In everything,
I will see your presence and your glory, and for everything I will give thanks.

(Prayers of Intercession)

EVENING

Eternal God, thank you for making me aware of your presence
in everything and everyone I saw today.

(Prayers of Intercession)

WITH PRAISE I PRAY.

(Pray the Prayer of Our Savior.)

MORNING

This day, everlasting God, make me
aware of those times when I lose sight
of you; forgive me, and grant me the
ability to see you more clearly.
In Christ's name, I pray. Amen.

EVENING

Everlasting God, may I fall asleep
feeling the presence of your Spirit,
and may my first thought upon waking be of your glory, power, and love.
In Christ's name, I pray. Amen.

Saturday, September 18

(Read 1 Timothy 2:1–7)

MORNING

Heavenly God, I pray this morning for all humankind.
Grant wisdom to those who lead, peace to those at war, comfort to
those who suffer, and healing to those who are broken.

EVENING

Heavenly God, Creator of everyone and everything,
hear my prayer for the people of this world.

O God, you sacrificed your Child, Christ Jesus, to redeem us all and to
give us a living example of your goodness and love. I choose this day to
live as Christ lived—with selflessness, kindness, patience, and generosity. Today, with your help, I will be a Christlike example of your love
for all humankind. Enable me to see people as you see them, and grant
me courtesy, kindness, and patience in my dealings with others. Today,
I will pray for everyone as the apostle Paul instructed Timothy.

MORNING

Loving God, let your love shine through all my words, thoughts, and deeds.
Grant me courage and patience in the face of confrontations.
(Prayers of Intercession)

EVENING

Loving God, may tonight's rest renew and refresh me for the new day.
Forgive me if my actions or words today did not honor you.
(Prayers of Intercession)

IN YOUR HONOR I PRAY.
(Pray the Prayer of Our Savior.)

MORNING

Creator of all humankind, help me
today to be more like Christ. May
everyone who meets me recognize your
love, and may all of my actions glorify
you. In Christ's name, I pray. Amen.

EVENING

May tomorrow and every day
bring new opportunities to glorify you
and to share your love with others.
Let your light shine through me.
In Christ's name, I pray. Amen.

Sunday, September 19

(Read Luke 16:1–13)

MORNING
Giving and forgiving God, you have entrusted me with both time and material goods. Help me manage them in such a way that you are pleased and honored.

EVENING
Giving and forgiving God, thank you for your guidance today. Forgive me if my actions had any impure or selfish motives, and grant me a night of peaceful rest.

God, you have generously blessed me, and I am thankful not only for what you have given me but for the opportunity to use these resources to serve you. Again today I commit myself to be a good steward of the things you have bestowed on me: I will manage my time and my material wealth so that you are honored and glorified. I will seek ways, both big and small, to be of service to others. Help me to manage all my resources so that you are pleased, and never let me forget that without you my belongings are hollow and unimportant.

MORNING
Grant me, O God, the clarity of insight to manage my affairs so that you are glorified. With your help, I will strive this day to turn over to you my greed, selfishness, and unkindness. Enable me to serve you humbly and completely.
(Prayers of Intercession)

EVENING
Heavenly God, you have been generous and gracious to me.
Thank you for the opportunity to serve you by wisely managing your gifts.
(Prayers of Intercession)

UNSELFISHLY I PRAY.
(Pray the Prayer of Our Savior.)

MORNING
Giving and forgiving God, with your help, I will use my possessions and resources to serve and glorify you. In Christ's name, I pray. Amen.

EVENING
Gracious God, make me a worthy steward of my worldly goods. In Christ's name, I pray. Amen.

Monday, September 20

(Read Jeremiah 32:1–3a, 6–15)

MORNING
Creative God, help me to be prepared for what I know
will happen today and for the unexpected.

EVENING
Creative God, thank you for seeing me through
the unexpected events of this day.

Creative God, for all that comes to teach me and to support me, I am most grateful. May my gratitude anticipate your direction, for I am never sure where you will lead me. But I do know that you will help me to be aware that we can always go there together.

MORNING
God, as I begin this day, help me to be aware of all needs.
(Prayers of Intercession)

EVENING
God, as I end this day, help me to remember
all we have done together.
(Prayers of Intercession)

JEREMIAH HEARS A WORD FROM GOD:
"HOUSES AND FIELDS AND VINEYARDS SHALL BE BOUGHT AGAIN
IN THIS LAND."

MORNING
God, sometimes, in the midst
of everything that is going wrong,
we are able to find strength in you—
our everlasting God—a strength that
we can not find anywhere else.
In Christ, I pray. Amen.

EVENING
Morning and night, faith in you,
Creative God, is a strength that will
sustain us. So in faith we join with
Jeremiah in recording our relationship
with you. In Christ, I pray.
Amen.

Tuesday, September 21

(Read Psalm 91:1–6)

MORNING
God almighty, all day long we will trust in you.

EVENING
God almighty, our trust has been rewarded all day long.

"In God We Trust" is the inscription on the piece of money I was looking at. I know what it is worth—and its worth is guaranteed by the government. Sovereign God, if my quarter has your name on it, is that a violation of some code of separation of church and state? Forgive us, God, when we feel we have all the answers, and we overlook your presence. In the little things of life, as well as the big, teach us your ways.

MORNING
Almighty God, help me to trust you today with all these things:
(Prayers of Intercession)

EVENING
Almighty God, at the close of day,
my trust is in you for all these things:
(Prayers of Intercession)

"MY REFUGE AND MY FORTRESS; MY GOD, IN WHOM I TRUST."

MORNING
God, if I pray to you
in the early morning, my prayer
is heard, and if I do not pray until late
in the evening, you, Glorious God,
are still listening.
In Christ, I pray.
Amen.

EVENING
Caring God, someone today
will see your psalm as a psalm of assurance. Morning, noon, or night,
I, too, can trust in God.
In Christ, I pray.
Amen.

Wednesday, September 22

(Read Psalm 91:14–16)

MORNING

Generous God, hear my prayer, and turn toward me.

EVENING

Generous God, for this day together with you,
your name is praised.

We were in a church meeting. Several mothers had put their children in the nursery. At one point, we all heard the cry of a child. Only one mother got up and went to the nursery to calm her child. Upon her return, I asked them all—how did one mother know the cry of her child? Smiling, those mothers gave me a wonderful lesson. Each recognized her particular child's cry. Because, O Generous God, you not only hear our prayer, but you know our names, and our needs, we rejoice. We are excited about our relationship together.

MORNING

Generous God, your humble servants come
to make the following request:
(Prayers of Intercession)

EVENING

Generous God, at close of day, hear our prayers
and our humble request:
(Prayers of Intercession)

"WHEN THEY CALL TO ME, I WILL ANSWER."

MORNING

Once again, in the everyday events of living I learned a valuable lesson to apply to my own prayer life. God, thank you for recognizing my voice. In Christ's name, I pray. Amen.

EVENING

Morning or night, in my care or at the dinner table, on my knees or standing, God hears my cry—and answers. My need to pray and my understanding of prayer is reaffirmed from a child's cry. In Christ's name, I pray. Amen.

Thursday, September 23 · Autumn begins

(Read Psalm 146)

MORNING
Compassionate God, help me to help others throughout this day.

EVENING
Compassionate God, bless my attempts to help throughout this day.

Caregiver God, she stood in the doorway to the office. Clinging to her were two small children. She had tears in her eyes. Life had not been good to her and she needed some financial help. It was apparent that she was uncomfortable. As she stood there, I looked down on my desk, where my Bible was open to Psalm 146. The passage was about how you executed justice for oppressed people and gave food to the hungry. We have a list of questions we often ask of those in need as a part of our cynical nature—but on that day, those questions seemed so distant from the Christian faith. From that lady, and her two precious children, the lesson of caring and helping was brought home. May I help some soul along the way and in so doing, God, share your love.

MORNING
Compassionate God, today, I pray for and promise to help in all these ways:
(Prayers of Intercession)

EVENING
Compassionate God, hear our prayers for all those less fortunate that ourselves:
(Prayers of Intercession)

A PART OF A DAILY PRAYER IN OUR FAMILY IS "LORD, KEEP US EVER MINDFUL OF THOSE LESS FORTUNATE THAN OURSELVES."

MORNING
Morning and night, Loving God, we pray for the opportunity to do your work in helping the poor. In Christ's name, I pray. Amen.

EVENING
Loving God, you care for all who are in need. Bless them this night. In Christ's name, I pray. Amen.

Friday, September 24 · Native American Day

(Read 1 Timothy 6:6–19)

MORNING

All-knowing God, for all people, like me and different, I give you thanks.

EVENING

All-knowing God, for all the events of this day, your name is praised.

Creator God, as an American Indian, I am very much aware and proud of my heritage. Reared in Southeastern Oklahoma, I am also very much aware of the poverty of my people. A number of "naholos" (white people) have traveled to South Dakota with me to work with the wonderful Lakota Sioux Indians when I visit each year. On one occasion, a little Sioux Indian girl had gone to the Pine Ridge trading post and bought some earrings and a broach for one of the young white girls who had befriended her. While it would be inexpensive to us, it was generous of her. I thought little about it, until I saw the young white girl take off her expensive sneakers and give them to the little Sioux girl. As they hugged, I thought, for those two the most important peace treaty had been signed.

MORNING

All-knowing God, teach me about those things I can do without,
and those people I dare not do without.
(Prayers of Intercession)

EVENING

All-knowing God, we thank you for sharing these events
and people with us today:
(Prayers of Intercession)

IT MAY BE THAT OUR "THINGS" WILL DESTROY US. IT'S GOOD TO KNOW
THAT IT IS NOT MONEY, BUT THE LOVE OF MONEY, THAT IS AT THE HEART OF EVIL.

MORNING

Forgive our insensitivity toward other human beings. Help us to see the worth of all humanity, All-knowing God. In Christ's name, I pray. Amen.

EVENING

Today I learned a lesson from the poor and from the affluent—God, all of your children are precious. In Christ's name, I pray. Amen.

Saturday, September 25

(Read Luke 16:19–31)

MORNING

Holy God, give me the ability to know what matters and what doesn't matter.

EVENING

Holy God, today I have learned much. Help me to be fresh for tomorrow.

Sometimes, I try to manipulate you, O Holy God. Forgive me and teach me your ways. Lazarus, poor, covered with sores, dies. The rich man, dressed in purple and full of food, dies. It is apparent that it was not just riches that punished one and poverty that rewarded the other. There must be more, and we must be careful about our conclusions. One conclusion, however, is that we will all die. The second is the importance of what we do while we are living. Five brothers had not paid attention to your message and it appears that this sixth brother did not pay attention, either. But it does make a great deal of difference, how we live. And that difference is influenced by why we live as we live.

MORNING

Holy God, take my life and consecrate it to you
and help me use my gifts, at least for these things . . .
(Prayers of Intercession)

EVENING

Holy God, my day has been busy, and I seek
your guidance in all these times . . .
(Prayers of Intercession)

**"IF THEY DO NOT LISTEN TO MOSES AND THE PROPHETS,
NEITHER WILL THEY BE CONVINCED EVEN IF SOMEONE RISES FROM THE DEAD."**

MORNING

Day and night, I seek guidance
for my generosity. In Christ's name,
I pray. Amen.

EVENING

Help me to understand the
importance of generosity in all
that I do. In Christ's name,
I pray. Amen.

Sunday, September 26

(Read Amos 6:1a, 4–7)

MORNING
Caring God, you are present morning, noon, and night.
Be with me this day in all that I say and do.

EVENING
Caring God, the night has come.
Bless me in my sleep as you did in my waking hours.

Judging God, we are forewarned of the decadence of self-indulgence, yet we continue to destroy your creation around us as well as our human temples. Do not let me become complacent and greedy by "lying on beds of ivory and eating lambs from the flock and calves from the stall." Help me to be mindful of the blessings that you have given me, both big and small.

MORNING
Loving God, I pray for those who have become
obsessed with greed.
(Prayers of Intercession)

EVENING
Loving God, I pray for those who have become
obsessed with self-indulgence.
(Prayers of Intercession)

**"THEREFORE THEY SHALL NOW BE THE FIRST TO GO INTO EXILE,
AND THE REVELRY OF THE LOUNGERS SHALL PASS AWAY."**

MORNING
Bless this day, Loving God,
so that I may continue to walk in
your light. In Christ's name,
I pray. Amen.

EVENING
Bless this night, Loving God,
so that I may continue to walk in
your light. In Christ's name,
I pray. Amen.

Monday, September 27

(Read 2 Timothy 1:1–7)

MORNING
Good morning God! I awaken this day
with the promise of life that is in Christ Jesus!

EVENING
Good evening, God! The day is spent. I am tired and weary.
Rest cannot come soon enough. My prayer is that I lived this day
in its entirety in your will. If not, please forgive me.

God, I am grateful this day for those who saw something in me years ago that I did not see in myself. Those persons believed in me and taught me how to believe. They encouraged me and never stopped praying for me. I am grateful for their continued prayers. There are days when I forget who I am and whose I am. When faced with the challenges of life and ministry, it is easy to become timid or fearful. Thank you, God, for reminding me at those times that you did not give me a spirit of timidity or fear, but a spirit of power, love, and self-discipline.

MORNING
Giver of every good and perfect gift, help me to fan into flame
the gift that you have placed in me.
(Prayers of Intercession)

EVENING
As I prepare to retire for the evening I do so remembering
those with whom I share the joy of loving relationship.
(Prayers of Intercession)

IN FAITH, I PRAY TO YOU, O GOD.

MORNING
As I enter the day, may I do so
with a sincere faith—the faith of one
who accomplished great things for
you, O God. For the sake of Jesus,
I pray. Amen.

EVENING
May the promise of life
be renewed in me as I sleep, O God.
For the sake of Jesus, I pray.
Amen.

Tuesday, September 28

(Read 2 Timothy 1:8–14)
Sing "Evening Prayer" or another familiar hymn.

MORNING
O God, renew in me this morning a sense of your purpose for my life
and for this day. I don't want to waste a minute of the life you have given me.

EVENING
O God, it was a tough day. Fulfilling your purpose for my life
and living up to your holy calling is not easy.

I'm really not ashamed of you, God. I just don't like conflict. Being places every day with persons who question whether or not you are real is a challenge for me. I want to defend you, but at times I'm not sure what to say. I suppose I should just tell them my story. It is only by your grace that I am who and what I am. You have called me with a holy calling to share with others the good news of grace found in your Child Jesus. I am ashamed. I will tell everyone I have an opportunity to tell who Jesus is even if they shun me.

MORNING
Give me the words to say this day that will bring honor and glory to you!
(Prayers of Intercession)

EVENING
What a wonderful day this was! I claimed your power to speak boldly
and to take a stand. I pray for those who may have seen my witness so that they,
too, will claim the power of a new life in Christ and will boldly witness.
(Prayers of Intercession)

I AM PRAYING TODAY WITH RENEWED CONFIDENCE IN THE POWER OF PRAYER!

MORNING
I know I believe in you, O God, and I know you will guard what I entrust to you this day. For the sake of Jesus, I pray. Amen.

EVENING
If I have wounded any soul today, if I have walked in my own willful way, if I have caused one foot to go astray, dear God, forgive me. For the sake of Jesus, I pray. Amen.

Wednesday, September 29

(Read Lamentations 3:19–26)

MORNING
God, what a joy to wake up this morning
with the assurance of your love and mercy.

EVENING
God, thank you for keeping me safe this day!

I was tempted to give up today, God. I had lost all hope. I thought about all that I have already been through, and at times it looks like things are getting worse and not better. I didn't know how much more I could take. I wasn't sure I wanted to take any more until I remembered how loving and compassionate you are. You know what I am going through. You have been faithful to keep me thus far, and I know that you will continue to be faithful. My hope has been restored. I will be delivered. All I have to do is wait for you.

MORNING
You are so good to me, God! Your Word says that you are good
to those whose hope is in you. I will live this day in anticipation
of your goodness and your love.
(Prayers of Intercession)

EVENING
I am still waiting for you, Compassionate One.
I know that you know what I need.
(Prayers of Intercession)

WAITING FOR YOU, MY STRENGTH IS RENEWED.

MORNING
Every morning, your love for me
is renewed. I feel brand new in the
fullness of your love for me.
For the sake of Jesus, I pray.
Amen.

EVENING
I can lie down and rest secure
in knowing that I am loved by you.
For the sake of Jesus, I pray.
Amen.

Thursday, September 30

(Read Habakkuk 1:1–4, 2:1–4)

MORNING

Creator God, this is the day that you have made.
I will rejoice and be glad in it.

EVENING

Creator God, rejoicing in you this day
gave me the courage to see it through.

God, I know that it seems like I am always complaining, but I have some concerns about the way things are going in the world. Violence has never been so prevalent. Young people make plans for their funerals rather than their graduations. It is not safe for children to walk the streets. Some of them are not even safe at home. How long must I cry to you about the injustices in the land? Isn't it time that we dealt with racism, sexism, classism, and ageism? Why are you tolerating these wrongs? Say something, God!

MORNING

I lift up to you this day all those who work for
and practice peace with justice. I pray for myself,
that I may be a part of the solution and not the problem.
(Prayers of Intercession)

EVENING

I bring to you all those who have been the perpetrators
and victims of violence.
(Prayers of Intercession)

I AM WAITING PATIENTLY FOR AN ANSWER FROM YOU.

MORNING	**EVENING**
Your Word makes clear to me that the righteous shall live by faith. I have faith this day that those things that concern me are of concern to you as well. For the sake of Jesus, I pray. Amen.	I don't always understand your timetable but I know that you are always on time and in time. Your timing is always perfect. I trust that! For the sake of Jesus, I pray. Amen.

Friday, October 1

(Read Psalms 37:1–9)

MORNING

Sustaining God, trusting in you I am safe.
Delighting in you I have the desires of my heart.
What can anyone do to me?

EVENING

Sustaining God, I had another day of rest in you
and your love for me. I am so blessed!

Today, I am clear that I am not to fret, even when evil persons succeed in their plans or when they carry out their wicked schemes. Their plans and schemes soon come to nothing, just like them. But the righteous flourish and your just cause will overcome the wickedness of those who are unjust. You see to that, God, in your own time and in your own way.

MORNING

One day the wicked will cease from troubling
and the weary will be at rest.
Thank you, O Giver of Rest, for this blessed promise.
(Prayers of Intercession)

EVENING

God, give me the strength not to want to seek revenge
or to get even when folks mess with me.
(Prayers of Intercession)

I WILL LIVE EACH DAY IN PEACE WITH MY NEIGHBOR.

MORNING

As I begin this new day,
I commit everything to you, God: all
my hopes, dreams, and desires.
For the sake of Jesus, I pray.
Amen.

EVENING

As I end this day. I commit to you,
God, all my hurts, disappointments,
fears, and frustrations. I will lie down
in peace. For the sake of Jesus,
I pray. Amen.

Saturday, October 2

(Read Luke 17:5–6)

MORNING
God, I have only one request of you this morning:
Increase my faith!

EVENING
God, I believe you. It is by faith that I find myself
in relationship with you. Help my unbelief.

God, you keep challenging me to trust you more, to take you at your word and step out on your promises. I keep asking myself, "What have I got to lose?" It's not like you are asking a lot of me. If I had faith the size mustard seed. . . . A mustard seed isn't very large; it is quite small, actually. It doesn't take a whole lot of faith to do great things for you. You can take nothing and make something of it. If I can conceive it, I can achieve it. Help my unbelief.

MORNING
I have faith in you to help me accomplish
the following tasks or to help me achieve victory
in the following areas of my life.
(Prayers of Intercession)

EVENING
I have faith in you to do great and small things
in the lives of the following persons.
(Prayers of Intercession)

WITH FAITH, NOTHING IS IMPOSSIBLE TO ME!

MORNING
Faith sees the invisible,
claims the unreachable, and does
the impossible. Faith can conquer
anything! For the sake of Jesus,
I pray. Amen.

EVENING
Without faith it is impossible
to please you, God. I want to please
you. For the sake of Jesus,
I pray. Amen.

Sunday, October 3

(Read Luke 17:5–10)

MORNING
God, I ask so much of you;
what is it that you would have me do for you today?

EVENING
God, I am not worthy of all that you do for me.
I give you the best of my service. I owe it to you.

God, I am so fortunate that you would even let me serve you. I know that I am not worthy. Whatever I give is my duty. I need to remember this, because sometimes I want to act like I am doing you a favor. I really don't mean to be so arrogant. Forgive me when at times I tend to think of myself and my gifts more highly than I should.

MORNING
I offer this prayer with thanksgiving
for all those who serve you faithfully.
(Prayers of Intercession)

EVENING
God, I offer this prayer with thanksgiving
for those who fulfill thankless duties for you.
(Prayers of Intercession)

THANK YOU, GOD, FOR THE GIFT OF FAITH.

MORNING
Prepare me this day, O God,
for another day of meeting the needs
of persons on your behalf and in your
name. For the sake of Jesus,
I pray. Amen.

EVENING
I want to hear you say one day,
"Well done, good and faithful
servant." For the sake of Jesus,
I pray. Amen.

Monday, October 4

(Read Psalm 66:1–7)

MORNING

O Holy One, I rise and greet a fresh new day with a song of praise on my lips,
"To God be the glory for the great things God has done!"

EVENING

O Holy One, I join a world that worships your acts of faith in
human history. Thank you for your living presence this day.

I live in a world that mocks the miraculous, a world that celebrates the
mediocre and the mundane. God, human wizardry in the form of high
technology has become a substitute for your mighty deeds. Today I will
open my heart, my mind, and my eyes to sense and see your mighty
hand at work in the world. Today my words and deeds will be a response to your miraculous presence in my life and my world. I will see
your hand in the birth of each new baby and in the tentative steps toward peace among nations too long at war. Thank you for all of creation and for my small part in your plan for the earth.

MORNING

Let me begin this day inhaling your creation
and exhaling your will for my life in your world.
(Prayers of Intercession)

EVENING

Living God, you have been faithful to me throughout this day.
You know when my actions have betrayed your presence.
Be near me now as I labor to put this day to rest.
(Prayers of Intercession)

WHERE MY VISION FAILS, GIVE ME HOPE THAT THE WORLD
SEES YOUR WONDROUS DEEDS AND MIGHTY WORKS.

MORNING

My life shall be a song and dance
in praise and worship of your name.
In the name of him who is known
as the Rose of Sharon, I pray. Amen.

EVENING

I rest from the work of the world
to find peace in the silence of your
night. In the name of him who is known
as the Rose of Sharon, I pray. Amen.

Tuesday, October 5

(Read Psalm 66:3–12)

MORNING

Loving God, so ordinary seems the new day that greets me,
yet so wondrously made. New and mysterious are the possibilities
that lie ahead. Thank you, God of creation!

EVENING

Loving God, I thank you for today and welcome the coming of night. Let me stay
near you, so that in the hours that remain, my life will reflect your truth.

Am I up to the challenge today? Am I prepared to face myself, and the world? God, I know and believe you are with me, in every breath, in each moment. Help my unbelief. This day, give me confidence to accept the reality that, in each encounter, a piece of your truth awaits me and your strength supports me. Help me to understand that my struggle is a strand in the fabric of a world seeking your mind in the affairs of humanity. Grant me your blessing.

MORNING

O God, my sure defender, give me the courage to face the trials of the day
and to trust that in my weakness your strength is made perfect.
(Prayers of Intercession)

EVENING

God of eternity, the day is not too long for you, the burden not too heavy.
You are God of all time and every situation. Grant me patience and endurance.
(Prayers of Intercession)

"WE KNOW THAT ALL THINGS WORK TOGETHER FOR THE GOOD OF THOSE
WHO LOVE GOD, WHO ARE CALLED ACCORDING TO GOD'S PURPOSE."

MORNING

When I stumble and fall, you reach out your hand to me; you bind my wounds and guide me on my way. In the name of him who is known as the Rose of Sharon, I pray. Amen.

EVENING

Watch me soar on winds of your spirit. And if I grow weary, renew me, for I am yours; you are my strength. In the name of him who is known as the Rose of Sharon, I pray. Amen.

Wednesday, October 6

(Read Jeremiah 29:1, 4–7)

MORNING
God of silence and sound, I am wholly yours
and welcome the gift of this day and the gifts this day will bring.

EVENING
God of silence and sound, today speak to me in these moments
of prayer as I reflect upon the ways you have visited me in the people
and the places I have known.

I thank you, God, that I have a place to call home, for shelter over my head, and for daily bread. I am keenly aware that shelter and daily bread are not provided for everyone. I want to help find solutions. I thank you that home is more than houses and land; it is the extended human family in your dominion. From all the lands on earth, you have called people to this land. We are all strangers to this land and to one another, and yet it belongs to us all and we belong to one another. I thank you that each of us can call this place home. Remind me, God of all, that none of us lives alone, that the welfare of any one depends upon the welfare of all.

MORNING
Let the familiar faces I see in my town today remind me that even
the faces of strangers, here and in distant lands, bear your image.
(Prayers of Intercession)

EVENING
I rejoice that the miracle of birth confirms your promises.
Our increase is your plan and delight.
(Prayers of Intercession)

CITIES AND TOWNS COME IN EVERY SIZE; THE SAVIOR CAME FOR THEM ALL.

MORNING	EVENING
I will pray for the welfare of my town as though my life depended upon it. In the name of him who is known as the Rose of Sharon, I pray. Amen.	Like Jesus, I weep, for I know what makes for peace; I know what promise it holds. In the name of him who is known as the Rose of Sharon, I pray. Amen.

Thursday, October 7

(Read 2 Kings 5:1–15c)

MORNING

Gracious God, the promise of this morning invites me to live
trusting in your grace for my life today. Even as my eyes open, the
light of day reminds me of your faithfulness to me and all creation.

EVENING

Gracious God, both the great and the small declare your presence and convey
your truth. Open my eyes, that I may not be deceived by outward dimensions.
Let me see your face in the shapes and shadows of each day and each night.

Triumph and tragedy, truth and falsehood, power and weakness belong
to all, regardless of station or status in life. I cannot demand abundance
in life by any virtue I possess or to which I aspire. Neither you, O God,
nor humanity is in my debt because of any great achievement or grand
philanthropy. Justice and mercy, healing and wholeness are your gifts of
grace, which come to us all, often in simple, surprising, and unexpected
ways. Not my way, but your will be done, O God of all.

MORNING

May I grow in strength today as I acknowledge my frailties
and weakness. May I give even as I acknowledge my need to receive.
(Prayers of Intercession)

EVENING

As evening casts a cooling shadow on this day, accept my thanks
for joys received and challenges met; forgive me for moments
I did not hear your voice and heed your Word.
(Prayers of Intercession)

THANK GOD FOR HEALING, REFRESHING, CLEANSING WATER.

MORNING

I will not let my greatness stand in the
way of your grace. In the name of him
who is known as the Rose of Sharon,
I pray. Amen.

EVENING

Thank you for your truth revealed
this day. With the night, bring rest
and renewal. In the name of him who
is known as the Rose of Sharon,
I pray. Amen.

Friday, October 8

(Read 2 Timothy 2:8–15)

MORNING

God our Creator, you spoke and there was light and life.
Today is a word you speak to humanity. I embrace it as your gift
and rise to meet the revelations that await me.

EVENING

God our Creator, "The word became flesh and dwelt among us full
of grace and truth." Thank you for that Word dwelling among us today.

Words, words, words. The Word is our salvation. Our words threaten
our very lives. God, discipline my speech. Save me from talking so much
and saying so little. Save me from the fallacy of thinking that if I could
just get the words right, get the doctrine just so, package the truth in
precise language, all would be well. All is not well. I am overwhelmed by
the aimless bantering of a noisy world and the ceaseless stream of words
that flows from my troubled conscience. Silence the noise. Let me hear,
let me know your Word. "One word frees us of all the weight and pain
of life; that word is love" (Sophocles, *Oedipus at Colonus*).

MORNING

Be still, my soul. Come to me, living God, in the deep places
within me where that peace beyond understanding resides.
(Prayers of Intercession)

EVENING

Christ is alive for me today. God, your Word is free
to transform the world. My vocation is clear.
(Prayers of Intercession)

**AS I SEEK TO WALK IN THE FOOTSTEPS OF CHRIST,
MY WORDS WILL FOLLOW, STRAIGHT AND TRUE.**

MORNING

I will stay focused on your Word.
I will not be distracted. In the name
of him who is known as the Rose
of Sharon, I pray. Amen.

EVENING

I welcome the peace evening can
bring, the rest promised by each night.
In the name of him who is known as
the Rose of Sharon, I pray. Amen.

Saturday, October 9

(Read Psalm 111)

MORNING
God of all being, I thank you for your world-creating work,
which fills this day with promise and bids me enter it with joy and hope.

EVENING
God of all being, your presence has blessed my work today. Continue to mold
and shape my witness and my work, that all I do and say will praise your name.

God, it is so easy for me to look at the world and complain, to blame and judge. I am horrified by its violence and destruction, by the pain and despair that are so commonplace, by the active practice of evil near to home and in nations far away. In the midst of disquieting realities, why is it so hard for me to be filled with gratitude when I see evidence of your wondrous and abiding presence in my life and in the world? You live above and within our history. The world is your breath of life, and from it I draw my sustenance. You were patient and faithful to the Hebrew people, and you look with kindness upon my hesitant steps. Grant me humility before your holy and awesome being. Grant me the wisdom to accept your redemption and live in covenant with you.

MORNING
Teach me wisdom as I practice living in wondrous awe
of your creation and your covenant faithfulness.
(Prayers of Intercession)

EVENING
The work of your creation sustains me when I grow weary as evening comes.
Hear my prayer for what has passed and what is yet to come.
(Prayers of Intercession)

EVERY DAY PROCLAIMS THE GREATNESS OF GOD AND INVITES OUR PRAISE.

MORNING
Today I will live fully and love freely, as if my life depended upon it. In the name of him who is known as the Rose of Sharon, I pray. Amen.

EVENING
Let me sleep comforted by peace. In the name of him who is known as the Rose of Sharon, I pray. Amen.

Sunday, October 10

(Read Luke 17:11–19)

MORNING
Loving God, come with me into the life of this day. Speak to my heart
so that my thoughts, my words, and my actions may glorify your name.

EVENING
Loving God, I thank you for every sign of your presence today:
chance encounters, meaningful work, your created world,
family and friends who know me and love me still.

O Praiseworthy God, let me confess my need for mercy. Let me be like
the one who came running and "praising God with a loud voice." Let me
be found today prostrate before Jesus, who calls me friend. Let me be like
a Samaritan who is persuaded that healing and wholeness know no
boundaries of race, clan, or creed. Let me be made whole by my faith,
trusting in the power of love that flows so freely from Jesus, who gave his
life for us all. Let me be graceful to those whose voices are silent when by
your hand they have been healed. Touch their hearts, so that their living
may be transformed. Help me to know when I am in their number.

MORNING
Come, God, visit my soul with joy and gladness.
Hear me shout, "Thank you for today!"
(Prayers of Intercession)

EVENING
O God, the night is a gift, just as is the day. Stay with me now
as darkness comes, bringing with it new promises of your faithfulness.
(Prayers of Intercession)

THERE ARE NO ALIENS IN THE HOUSEHOLD OF GOD;
WE ARE ALL BROTHERS AND SISTERS IN CHRIST.

MORNING
Today I will be alert to my needs,
and the needs of others. In the name
of him who is known as the
Rose of Sharon, I pray.
Amen.

EVENING
Let the night bring rest and
renewal, that I may greet tomorrow
with energy and thanksgiving. In the
name of him who is known as the
Rose of Sharon, I pray. Amen.

Monday, October 11

Indigenous Peoples Day · Thanksgiving—Canada

(Read Psalm 119:97–104)

MORNING

God of all life, you have called me into a direct and living relationship
with you. As I begin this day, I pray you will go ahead of me into each
new experience to prepare the next place for me.

EVENING

God of all life, your living presence has surrounded me this day,
even when I forgot or did not feel it. Now as I prepare for sleep, enfold me
in your love, breathe into me your breath of life and peace.

Great Shepherd, your love is my living law and a lamp for my feet. You
have called me directly into your presence, and your living Word is spoken directly into my heart. As I rest and quiet myself, let me hear, feel,
understand what you are saying to me and showing me. And even when
I cannot clearly sense your presence and guidance, let me rest in the
knowledge of your love, and trust that new clarity and understanding
will come to me.

MORNING

As I prepare to pray for the needs of others, let me inwardly see
them enfolded in your loving, healing light, you who have come
through the healer, Jesus Christ.
(Prayers of Intercession)

EVENING

I release those for whom I pray trustfully into your hands, for your
care and love for them is far greater than mine.
(Prayers of Intercession)

LEAD ME BEYOND WORDS AND IDEAS DIRECTLY INTO YOUR PRESENCE.

MORNING

When I feel confused, help me to
pause and wait for your inner guiding
love. In the Savior's name, I pray.
Amen.

EVENING

Eternal, unsleeping Love, into your
hands I commit my body and spirit.
In the Savior's name, I pray. Amen.

Tuesday, October 12

(Read Jeremiah 31:27–34)

MORNING

God of love, when I wake to this new day, I wake also to a
new covenant with you, a new way of loving, a new way of living
with you as the center of my heart. You are my great central sun,
shining within all that I am and do.

EVENING

God of love, sometimes I have forgotten my new freedom today
and have fallen into old traps and prisons of the spirit.
Though often I have forgotten you, you never have forgotten me.

You who shine on me through the face of Jesus Christ, this very day you
take me by the hand to lead me out of my inner prisons. You have
opened your heart to me, and you call me to open my heart to you. You
have put your arms around my mistakes and failures, and at this very
moment your deep, radical love transforms me.

MORNING

May all those for whom I pray and all whom I will meet
this day be healed and released from their past pain and inner prisons.
(Prayers of Intercession)

EVENING

Each day may I become more released into your life
than the day before, and may those for whom I pray be released
more deeply into your love.
(Prayers of Intercession)

LIBERATING GOD, WHEN WE BOND WITH YOU WE ARE RELEASED FROM ALL BONDAGE.

MORNING	EVENING
May each moment of this day be transformed and glorified by your radiance. In the Savior's name, I pray. Amen.	As I move into the depth and darkness of sleep, your shining love wraps me in radiance. In the Savior's name, I pray. Amen.

Wedneday, October 13

(Read Genesis 32:22–31)

MORNING

Faithful God, today there will be difficulties, anxieties,
challenges to face. Help me to discover your angel, your own living
presence, coming to meet and strengthen me in every conflict.

EVENING

Faithful God, even as your people so long ago were led out of captivity
by your mighty presence, so you have led me this day and will lead me
through the night by the strong light of Jesus Christ within me.

Living God, I am so often in inner conflict; so often I mistrust and resist love, seeing a threat instead of a gift. So often I strive against your
presence, resisting your help, release, and empowerment. So often I
meet my angel as my enemy, seeing only the painful shadow and not
the glowing presence. Thus I exhaust and hurt myself. But you have
never abandoned me. You hold me close during my night of inner wars.
May I recognize your offered blessing and receive your gift of healing of
my self-inflicted pain.

MORNING

May those for whom I pray feel now the majesty, faithfulness, and tenderness
of your presence, even in the midst of their conflict, fear, and pain.
(Prayers of Intercession)

EVENING

All that we suffer, all that we feel, you have shared with us.
In all our inner striving and wrestling, you are there to offer your blessing.
(Prayers of Intercession)

"IF I TAKE THE WINGS OF THE MORNING AND SETTLE AT THE FARTHEST LIMITS
OF THE SEA, EVEN THERE . . . YOUR FIRM HAND SHALL HOLD ME FAST."

MORNING	EVENING
Through the challenges of this day, may I receive your blessing and bring it to others. In the Savior's name, I pray. Amen.	Beloved God, you have embraced my hurts, pain, and resistance. Your blessing fills me. In the Savior's name, I pray. Amen.

Thursday, October 14

(Read Psalm 121)

MORNING

God, let my first thought this morning be the thought of you, the central light of my life. You are my source, my shelter, my strength, my sustenance.

EVENING

God, as a full circle joins the end and the beginning, so the end of this day joins with its beginning. As I breathed your breath of morning with all its challenge, so now I breathe your breath of evening with all its peace.

So often I have forgotten, Unsleeping Love, the mighty strength with which you surround and fill us. We need no lesser strength or source. You are the ultimate mystery. There is so much we cannot understand. But this we know, this we are told, the central life of all creation is your heart, which holds us forever. When we enter into communion with your heart, then our choices, our actions, our powers and gifts are blessed, guided, and transformed.

MORNING

May the fears and doubts of those for whom I pray be healed,
melted by your strong and limitless mercy.
(Prayers of Intercession)

EVENING

As those for whom I pray face the end of the day, help them to sleep in trust,
knowing that you keep them tenderly through the night.
(Prayers of Intercession)

LIVING CHRIST, STRONG VINE OF OUR LIFE,

HELP ME ABIDE IN YOU AS YOUR FRUITFUL BRANCH.

MORNING

Let my feet be moved by your guidance. When I go out, prepare the way for me. When I return, welcome me and restore me. In the Savior's name, I pray. Amen.

EVENING

Light of all light, you are more merciful than the sun by day and gentler than the moon by night. In the Savior's name, I pray. Amen.

Friday, October 15

MORNING

Infinite Mercy, this day I take your offered hand, leading me into wholeness
and completeness and a life drenched in love. I turn to your living Word,
shining on me through scripture and in the faces and memories of those
who have loved, helped, and guided me in your way.

EVENING

Infinite Mercy, though so often I am fragmented, not aware
of the wholeness you offer me, I know you believe in it for me and
see it in me. As I enter into sleep, I rest on your tender faith in me.

Not what we learn, but of whom we learn is our source of life, living
Christ. You have become for us the living Word, the Spirit of the scripture unfolding in our hearts. When bonded to you, when abiding in
you, Living Vine, we are transformed and made complete. It is your expanding life in us that equips us for a life of truth, strength, and love.
Unfold for me today new light and meaning from your eternal Word.

MORNING

I think of those who did not know of your love in childhood
and were not taught of your light and guidance. May special help
be given them and loving guides sent them.
(Prayers of Intercession)

EVENING

Come personally, living Christ, to those for whom I pray. Help all of us
to know that it is not a principle but a person who is our spring of life.
(Prayers of Intercession)

LIVING CHRIST, WITH YOU OUR THERE IS HERE.

MORNING

Keep my faith steadfast this day,
and keep me centered in Jesus the
Christ. In the Savior's name,
I pray. Amen.

EVENING

Living Christ, breathe on me
the healing of your peace and fire
of your Spirit. In the Savior's name,
I pray. Amen.

Saturday, October 16

(Read 2 Timothy 4:1–5)

MORNING

Beloved God, let your Holy Spirit awaken within me. This day, sometimes there will be need to witness to your love and truth—through words, compassionate silence, action, joy, and laughter, and through a look or touch of healing love.

EVENING

Beloved God, there were times today when I was absent in spirit, but you were always present. Gather up my absences, my dimness, my flickering flame into your hands and heart, and let them be transformed into new empowered life.

It is not always easy, living God, to be aflame with your love when we often feel surrounded by the indifference, doubt, and resistance of others. May the sense of your glowing presence waken me when I spiritually sleep, enflame me when I am dim and cold, strengthen me where I am weakest, heal me where I am wounded, and restore me when I am fragmented. Protect me when I feel challenged and, above all, empower me with your fire of love.

MORNING

So many feel their faith and hope crushed or chilled. Lead them into new hope, strength, and freedom, so they do not fall back into spiritual captivity.

(Prayers of Intercession)

EVENING

I pray for everyone who longs to know his or her special gifts and calling, and for the joyful strength to fulfill them.

(Prayers of Intercession)

HELP ME TO BUILD MY INNER ALTAR, SO YOUR FLAME MAY DESCEND UPON IT.

MORNING

This day may I see and understand and fulfill the special ministry to which you call me. Through the light of Jesus. In the Savior's name, I pray. Amen.

EVENING

Even in sleep I am in the presence God and Jesus Christ. Blessed be God! In the Savior's name, I pray. Amen.

Sunday, October 17

(Read Luke 18:1–8)

MORNING

Faithful God, there will be times today when I do not feel your nearness,
when my prayers seem unanswered. At these times, help me to know that your
love is forever with me and that you heard me before I even spoke to you.

EVENING

Faithful God, often today I have been like a locked and shuttered house, closed
to your loving light poured upon me. Often you knocked and I did not hear you
or open my door. As I sleep, open the deep, closed places of my heart.

When I experience the delay of my hopes, when prayer seems unanswered, when justice seems withheld, help me to trust in your unsleeping
love and justice, God of my life. You have told us that you have heard us
before we cry to you. Eternal Mercy, we do not need to plead with you.
Eternal Wisdom, we do not need to inform you. Your longing to give is
far greater than our longing to receive. The clouds that seem to block your
love are not of your making. From everlasting to everlasting, you are faithful. Enlarge me, so that I may receive all that you long to give me.

MORNING

May those who feel unloved and unheard find some sign today
that you have been with them forever.
(Prayers of Intercession)

EVENING

May those for whom I pray be led to you, where all answers are.
Your presence is our answer, our way, truth, and life.
(Prayers of Intercession)

"WE LOVE BECAUSE GOD FIRST LOVED US."

MORNING

As I awaken to this day, may I
open all the cells of my body and the
choices of my heart to your love,
which seeks and guides me. In the
Savior's name, I pray. Amen.

EVENING

Even as you welcomed me into
morning, you welcome me into sleep.
But my deep spirit is forever awake,
dancing in your joy. In the Savior's
name, I pray. Amen.

Monday, October 18

(Read Joel 2:23–32)

MORNING

Provider God, Creator of each new day, Giver of unfathomable
potential, open my eyes and intensify my sensitivity to the new ways
you may choose to work with me today.

EVENING

Provider God, I have seen your marvelous works and give thanks
for each opportunity I enjoyed to serve your will.

How aware Joel was of God's incredible gifts. Not only had God provided all the necessary means to sustain the life of his people, but the prophet had become convinced that God would do greater things in the future. A day would come when people would walk in God's ways, and justice and equity would be established upon the earth. Open my eyes to dream dreams, and to see visions of your future creation, O God. Fill my life with hope and energy to realize your dreams for me this day.

MORNING

Each morning new opportunities are extended to me by an ever-creating God.
I pray for all who are unaware and live without hope.
(Prayers of Intercession)

EVENING

As the evening falls and the shadows deepen, I pray for those
who cannot see beyond the darkness of the present to the possibilities
of your next creative acts, O God.
(Prayers of Intercession)

GOD KEEPS PROMPTING ME TO BE AWARE OF GOD'S ONGOING WORK IN CREATION!

MORNING

Provider God, Creator of each new day, Giver of unfathomable potential, open my eyes and intensify my sensitivity to the new ways you may choose to work with me today. In the spirit of Christ, I pray. Amen.

EVENING

Provider God, I have seen your marvelous works and give thanks for each opportunity I enjoyed to serve your will. In the spirit of Christ, I pray. Amen.

Tuesday, October 19

(Read Psalm 65)

MORNING

Loving God, as morning guilds the skies, I awaken to the reality that you
provide the new day and all opportunities to enjoy and enrich life.

EVENING

Loving God, as the evening shadows lengthen, I offer thanks for every
experience of your presence and every opportunity to serve you.

The psalmist gave thanks for the earth's bounty, O God, seeing you as
the One who provides for us and who listens to the prayers of our
hearts. In all things the ancient writer saw you as Merciful Provider,
kind and mindful of all creation. Teach me, this day, to make these
truths come alive for my neighbors by listening to their stories, by forgiving as I have been forgiven, and by sharing the gifts I myself have received from your hand. In all things may my joy at your goodness translate into acts of kindness toward others.

MORNING

Each new morning I awaken to the joy of your extravagant love.
O God, I pray for those who are unaware.
(Prayers of Intercession)

EVENING

In the quiet of this evening hour I thank you for the many ways
you have provided, O God. Help me to show my thanks tomorrow
and to name your gifts to others.
(Prayers of Intercession)

**GOD IS CONSTANTLY SEEKING TO SHARPEN MY CONSCIOUSNESS
TO GOD'S GREAT REDEMPTIVE WORK.**

MORNING

Loving God, as morning guilds the
skies, I awaken to the reality that you
provide the new day and all opportunities to enjoy and enrich life. In the
spirit of Christ, I pray. Amen.

EVENING

Loving God, as the evening shadows
lengthen, I offer thanks for every
experience of your presence and every
opportunity to serve you. In the spirit
of Christ, I pray. Amen.

Wednesday, October 20

(Read Jeremiah 14:7–10, 19–22)

MORNING
Loving God, open my eyes to your incredible patience with humankind,
and, in all my actions today, may I focus upon your grace.

EVENING
Loving God, I have experienced again your marvelous grace this
day. As I have received, help me to share.

Rescuing God, the ancient prophet wept as he thought of his people's and his own sinfulness and failures. He clearly saw that there was no hope for humankind other than in your loving generosity and grace. He saw that your love loved all things into being. Would your love now forsake your children? Somehow, arguing with you, he held to that love, trusting you to restore and renew life. O God, may thoughts of your never failing faithfulness and total acceptance of me, regardless of my past, inspire me to be accepting and nonjudgmental with others.

MORNING
Gracious God, I thank you that each day,
by your grace, may be a new beginning.
(Prayers of Intercession)

EVENING
Gracious Provider, I thank you for your goodness and grace
throughout this day, and I pray for others and for myself,
that we may discern and live our thanks.
(Prayers of Intercession)

GOD NEVER GIVES UP ON ME! CAN I GIVE UP ON MY NEIGHBORS?

MORNING
Loving God, open my eyes to your incredible patience with humankind, and, in all my actions today, may I focus upon your grace. In the spirit of Christ, I pray. Amen.

EVENING
Loving God, I have experienced again your marvelous grace this day. As I have received, help me to share. In the spirit of Christ, I pray. Amen.

Thursday, October 21

(Read Psalm 84:1–7)

MORNING
O God, in whom we live and have our dwelling place,
help me to discover where I belong.

EVENING
O God, our Dwelling Place, as I reflect on the day past, I thank you
for the assurance that I have a home, and that I am always with you.

It is often difficult for me to know in my heart of hearts that I have a dwelling place, O God. Enable me to see that I belong and that "home" is life lived with you. Thank you for the ancient psalmist who reminds me of this truth, and thus reaffirms my identity as your beloved child. Thank you for that calm certainty as I travel the journey of life. Even while in the darkest valleys, you provide for me and will safely lead me home.

MORNING
O God, I thank you that this day, too, may be spent with you.
I pray for all who feel lost, forsaken, and homeless.
(Prayers of Intercession)

EVENING
O God, I thank you for this day spent with you. I pray for all
who are overcome by feelings of loneliness and restlessness—that,
by your grace, they may find peace and comfort with you.
(Prayers of Intercession)

GOD ASSURES ME THAT I BELONG AND THAT UNDERNEATH ARE THE EVERLASTING ARMS.

MORNING
O God, in whom we live and
have our dwelling place, help me to
discover where I belong. In the spirit
of Christ, I pray. Amen.

EVENING
O God, our Dwelling Place, as I
reflect on the day past, I thank you for
the assurance that I have a home, and
that I am always with you. In the
spirit of Christ, I pray. Amen.

Friday, October 22

(Read 2 Timothy 4:6–8, 16–18)

MORNING

Loving God, open my eyes to see that true help,
for the living of this day, ultimately comes from you.

EVENING

Loving God, thank you for standing by me this day, and for keeping
me from danger. I pray for all who see life as a solitary journey.

When I am weak, you are strong, O God. When I feel rejected and deserted, you stand by me to rescue and restore me. When I reach the end of my journey, may I be enabled to say that I have fought "a good fight," finished the "race," and been faithful to the way of Jesus. May I firmly put my trust in you, O God; help me to be your instrument in bringing others to that blessed certainty.

MORNING

O God our help in ages past, I pray for those who see life
as a journey without your constant presence.
(Prayers of Intercession)

EVENING

Again this day you have been my helper and support,
O Loving God. I pray for all who feel helpless, weak, and forsaken.
(Prayers of Intercession)

**THROUGHOUT THE STRUGGLES OF LIFE, GOD, HELP ME TO SEE
THAT I CAN ENTRUST ALL MY TOMORROWS TO YOU.**

MORNING

Loving God, open my eyes
to see that true help, for the living of
this day, ultimately comes from you.
In the spirit of Christ, I pray.
Amen.

EVENING

Loving God, thank you for standing
by me this day and for keeping me
from danger. I pray for all who see life
as a solitary journey. In the spirit
of Christ, I pray. Amen.

Saturday, October 23

(Read Luke 18:9–14)

MORNING

O God, on this new day, keep me humble and nonjudgmental,
trusting your compassion and final judgment of me.

EVENING

O God, at the close of this day I thank you again
for your graciousness and ask that I may be humble
and live without passing judgment.

It is easy, O God, to get carried away with thoughts about my own goodness and righteous acts, to compare myself to others, and to slip into self-congratulatory thoughts. Often I judge others and I forget that you alone are judge. Teach me afresh, O God, that I cannot separate myself from my neighbors and remain united with you. Enable me to think and act in all humility and to leave the ultimate outcome of all my actions and those of my neighbors safely in your hands.

MORNING

Gracious God, remind me afresh, this day, that the outcome
of all our lives are open-ended, awaiting your new creative work.
Help me to live this day with great expectations.
(Prayers of Intercession)

EVENING

Gracious God, surprising things happen to us as we
live our lives with you. Help me to rest, this evening,
entrusting all my "finalities" to your loving care.
(Prayers of Intercession)

GOD ONLY JUDGES—AND IN SURPRISING WAYS.

MORNING

O God, on this new day, keep me humble and nonjudgmental, trusting your compassion and final judgment of me. In the spirit of Christ, I pray. Amen.

EVENING

O God, at the close of this day I thank you again for your graciousness. May I be humble and live without passing judgment. In the spirit of Christ, I pray. Amen.

Sunday, October 24 · United Nations Day

(Read Psalm 84:1–7)

MORNING

O God, in whom we live and have our dwelling place,
help me to discover where I belong.

EVENING

O God, our dwelling place, as I reflect on the day past,
I thank you for the assurance that I have a home,
and that I am always with you.

Caring and Nurturing God, thank you for a dwelling place on this Sabbath day. It is so easy to become complacent. Let me always remember your goodness and mercy.

MORNING

Loving God, open my eyes to see that true help
for the living of this day ultimately comes from you.
(Prayers of Intercession)

EVENING

Loving God, thank you for standing by me this day,
and for keeping me from danger. I pray for all who see life
as a solitary journey.
(Prayers of Intercession)

"HOW LOVELY IS YOUR DWELLING PLACE, O [GOD] OF HOSTS!"

MORNING

Loving God, as morning guilds
the skies, I awaken to the reality that
you provide the new day and all opportunities to enjoy and enrich life.
In the spirit of Christ, I pray.
Amen.

EVENING

Loving God, as the evening
shadows lengthen, I offer thanks for
every experience of your presence and
every opportunity to serve you.
In the spirit of Christ, I pray.
Amen.

Monday, October 25

(Read Luke 19: 1–10)

MORNING
Accepting and loving God, awaken in me an awareness of the joy
waiting for me this day as I encounter the people around me.

EVENING
Accepting and loving God, accepting challenges is hard, and yet when
I give my whole being to you, I find peace and strength. I give you thanks.

God of enlightenment, Spirit of peace, there is a surge of peace that
quiets my being as I reflect on the wisdom of the choices Jesus Christ
made as an example for me. There are times when I seek to reject a person like the tax collector Zacchaeus, and I judge the outside behavior.
As I grumble, I am reminded that love and acceptance change lives.
Give me the courage to reach out to those I am prone to reject. For it
is in giving love to those I find unlovable that I feel your grace and your
peace. Thanks for that gift!

MORNING
O God, help me to love the heart of each person I meet, even in disagreement
and differences, knowing that your grace holds each one of us.
(Prayers of Intercession)

EVENING
God of strength, remind me of your continual presence
and help me to prepare myself with the wisdom for looking inward
and then reaching out with your love.
(Prayers of Intercession)

ACCEPTING THE CHALLENGES AND DISAPPOINTMENTS OF RELATIONSHIPS
SEEMS TOO HARD IN OUR OWN WEAKNESS. YET WE FIND A NEW SURGE OF ENERGY
WHEN THE AWARENESS OF GOD'S SPIRIT GENTLY TOUCHES US.

MORNING
For the example of Jesus Christ's
acceptance of those he called "lost,"
I give you thanks. May I, too, find
and give acceptance. In his name,
I pray. Amen.

EVENING
I give thanks for the presence of your
Spirit as I close the day. May my wisdom
be enhanced, and my acceptance
of others expanded. In his name,
I pray. Amen.

Tuesday, October 26

(Read Habakkuk 1:1–4)

MORNING

O God, this day as I read from the prophet, I realize how close
to each other he and I seem. I thank you for the opportunity to seek
understanding, and to practice patience. Faith is at work here.

EVENING

O God, grant me patience as I close this day without answers,
without solutions, with wonderment for the future. My faith is tested.

God of all times and all places, help me to understand the mystery of your
timing. Sometimes I cry out for you, wait for an answer, give up, and try
to control the uncontrollable. I wonder why there is so much violence,
and I have to see it; why there is so much illness and death, and I have experience the pain of it; why there are so many people in positions of
power with little ethical and moral fiber, and I have to suffer the consequences of their actions. Teach me, even just for one day, to have the patience to listen for you, to let go and empty myself to be ready to receive.

MORNING

Give me strength this day to let go of what is not mine and trust that whatever is
a mystery now will become clearer to me as my faith allows it.
(Prayers of Intercession)

EVENING

Loving God, as I close my day, grant me the peace that comes with trust as I rest
and wait. Your grace, given freely, is the astonishing gift that keeps my faith alive.
(Prayers of Intercession)

**BEING OF LITTLE FAITH AND WAITING FOR AN ANSWER TO PRAYER
IS THE GREATEST STRESS WE CAN PLACE ON OURSELVES.**

MORNING

Today I will look for ways to enhance
my faith, knowing that you are with
me always. In his name, I pray. Amen.

EVENING

Give me the faith and courage to
let go of worry, relax, and move into
tomorrow, trusting your time, not
mine. In his name, I pray. Amen.

Wednesday, October 27

(Read Habakkuk 2:14)

MORNING

Creator God, thank you for another day. My faith is strong, my being is ready.
Give me courage to face the answers to the questions of a new day.

EVENING

Creator God, you are with me just as you promised. Take what you have given
to me and make me an instrument of your love in the world.

Spirit of God, after shrinking from believing, I am guided now by faith
to be reliable, confident, and trusting. Breathe into me a restlessness to
live the vision of your love, to make it plain to the world, and to be the
truth in every way. Keep me honest, tender enough to heal, and tough
enough to be healed of my own hypocrisies. Help me never to forget
that you are with me through all adversity. I have only to ask and trust.
With your love surrounding me, help me to remember the grace that
abounds with all mystery.

MORNING

Challenging God, help me as I teeter on the edge of my vulnerability
and excitement for this new day. Keep me strong and confident.
(Prayers of Intercession)

EVENING

In the silence of these few moments, God, you are my strength and my hope.
Grant me peace of mind, courage of conviction, and fruition of faith as I close
this day to all the joys and struggles of its many hours.
(Prayers of Intercession)

IF WE BUT WAIT, GOD IS HERE. IF WE BUT ASK, GOD IS HERE.
IF WE BUT TRUST, GOD IS AS FAITHFUL AS GOD EXPECTS US TO BE.

MORNING

It is easy to lose sight of your vision
and to be weak in faith. I thank you
for your patience and grace, God of
love and peace. In his name, I pray.
Amen.

EVENING

Renewal comes, great and loving God,
as I listen, trust, work, and love in
your grace. Thank you for trusting me
to be here for you. In his name,
I pray. Amen.

Thursday, October 28

(Read Psalm 119:137–44)

MORNING
Tender and compassionate God, you are the source of my life.
In this new day, form me to be a rich source of your love in all that I do.

EVENING
Tender and compassionate God, I have never known a richer gift than
your love. Slow me down to absorb your peaceful Spirit of rest and renewal.

With your love you seek me, O God. You know all about me, my imperfections, my shortcomings, my failures. Yet your love remains constant for me to embrace. I am excited and challenged to receive the outpouring of your grace, and I prepare to act out of that love today. With your love surrounding me, no matter what trouble I may encounter, you will be there. Help me to capture a new vision each day. Help me to feel your gentle guidance in the unfolding of life, that I may take the joy of wholeness to your people everywhere.

MORNING
As I accept the new challenges of the day, give me strength
to accomplish them. Bring courage to fear, faith to doubt, and
hope to the hopeless, O God of all vision.
(Prayers of Intercession)

EVENING
Be with me as I seek to understand more clearly my call to be loving,
just, and fully human. I put my faith in your words and your love, O God.
(Prayers of Intercession)

"GIVE ME UNDERSTANDING THAT I MAY LIVE."

MORNING
I seek understanding, O God,
because like a loving parent, I know
you are fair and just. Thank you
for your truth. In his name,
I pray. Amen.

EVENING
As I capture visions of the future,
help me to be reminded that I must
truly reflect your constant love.
I live fully because I have sought your
understanding. In his name,
I pray. Amen.

Friday, October 29

(Read Isaiah 1:10–18)

MORNING

All-knowing God, as I awaken to the morning, fresh from resting and at peace with the world, help me to take off the blinders and prepare myself for today.

EVENING

All-knowing God, you have filled me with love and care for the world. Help me to face another day by bringing peace and restoration to my soul.

Holy and loving God, you have touched me with your presence and filled me with love and courage. Enlighten me, so that I may enlighten others. Set before me images of what it means to be your servant, so that I may mirror those images in all that I do. If I grow apathetic and indifferent, shake me into being fully present and fully alive. Where there is desolation, help me to bring hope, where there is ignorance, knowledge. And most of all, help me to keep close to your Spirit, the source of all gifts and strength in times of trouble.

MORNING

God, help me, each day, to believe in new beginnings
and to make a new start—to be a new start.
(Prayers of Intercession)

EVENING

Spirit of the loving God, I have gone to my limits today.
Calm the chaos of my hurried mind and body so that I may rest in your love.
(Prayers of Intercession)

CREATE IN US A RESTING PLACE. KEEP RENEWING US TO MAKE OUR COMMUNITY A PLACE OF LOVE, ACCEPTANCE, UNDERSTANDING, AND AN ORDERED LIFE.

MORNING

We don't seem to be aware, yet we are,
of all that is falling apart around us.
O God, give us light to open our eyes
and courage to lead into newness of
life. In his name, I pray. Amen.

EVENING

By your grace, Sustainer God,
prod me to question what I do not
understand, to live my convictions,
and to hear with openness and love.
In his name, I pray. Amen.

Saturday, October 30

(Read Psalm 32:1–7)

MORNING
God, you know I have fallen short, yet you continue to forgive. Thank you for the grace-filled life you promise and give me. I seek to love you as you love me.

EVENING
God, your forgiveness is without a doubt the strongest aid to my rest. Thank you from the bottom of my heart.

O Ingenious God, your Spirit touches me so deeply that I am able to find a sense of myself, even in the pain of falling short of my goals. I am grateful that, in my simplicity, I can love without hesitation because I know your love will hold me. Help me to sort the essential from the trivial and grant me enthusiasm in empty and full places. I ask that you give me courage to face life as it is and to live passionately, knowing that there is a safe place with you to tell you of my imperfections. Deepen my wisdom and gift me with your healing touch to give to people struggling with the health of their souls. Thanks and praise to you, God.

MORNING
As you touch me with your wholeness, God of love, my heart overflows with gratitude. Help me to reach out constantly to touch another as I have been touched by your forgiveness and love.
(Prayers of Intercession)

EVENING
There is joy in forgiveness, God, and you have given me that joy in this hour. It is in your love that I rejoice in the freedom to be honest about myself.
(Prayers of Intercession)

TRUE ABUNDANCE COMES FROM A GIFT GIVEN BY GOD.
THANKS BE TO GOD FOR THAT GIFT.

MORNING
Remind me, God, each day I awaken, that I am forgiven and loved, forgiven and loved. In his name, I pray. Amen.

EVENING
I rejoice and give thanks for all that I am and all that I can become through your love and your care. In his name, I pray. Amen.

Sunday, October 31 ·

All Hallows Eve · Daylight Savings Time ends

(Read 2 Thessalonians 1:1–4. 11–12)

MORNING
O God, it is good to give thanks for those who work so hard
in the community of faith. May I always treat others justly and lovingly.

EVENING
O God, at the close of this day I feel enriched
by the knowledge of others who seek to follow you.

God of ancient times and of this morning, your Spirit fills my heart as I
remember the community of faith around the world. I am reminded of
your love by the saints who have gone before me, the preciousness of their
lives, and the beauty of their memory in my heart. Your love reminds me
of faithful people living the example of loving one another like hands and
hearts reaching around the world to embrace. I rejoice and give thanks for
all that the people of God around the world can be and all that we can
become because of your love and the steadfast work of your people.

MORNING
Loving God, help me to encourage those faithfully sharing themselves
with the world because you love them and they love you.
(Prayers of Intercession)

EVENING
As the day comes to a close, give me the wisdom to move out of self-centeredness;
to move toward others; to give strength in weakness, joy in celebration, peace
and quiet in chaos. Help us to know your love, so that we may love.
(Prayers of Intercession)

LOVE AND ENCOURAGEMENT ARE NEVER GIVEN AWAY IN A VACUUM. THEY GO RIGHT TO
THE HEART OF THE RECEIVER AND BRING HEALING AND PEACE.

MORNING
O God of all love, help me to
encourage those working in today's world
to pass on your love by loving one
another. In his name, I pray. Amen.

EVENING
I hear whispers of peace and fresh
breezes of promise for those feeling
loved and appreciated. I rejoice in
that love. In his name,
I pray. Amen.

Monday, November 1 · All Saints Day

(Read Haggai 1:15–2:3)

MORNING
God, your temple is here! In my very midst
I experience your love as a mighty fortress.

EVENING
God, your temple is here! You hold me, protect me, guide me.
The very place I plant my feet is holy ground.

As with the exiles who returned from Babylon, Ruler God, you have set me free. I am free to build your New Jerusalem here and now, free to set others free so they, too, may experience your transformative love. I do often feel discouraged and alone, but as with people of every generation I find myself drawn to you. Lead me to build this temple of justice, brick by brick, as in the past you led your people to rebuild the temple. You are the cornerstone, the rock of our salvation.

MORNING
Come to me God, and show me your hand of guidance.
Fill me with your truth and wisdom. God, hear my prayer.
(Prayers of Intercession)

EVENING
As I lay my head down to sleep, give me thoughts
of peace and justice. Inspire me to use my gifts for the building
of your holy temple of shalom. God hear my prayer.
(Prayers of Intercession)

AS WE ARE BOLD TO SAY, "OUR FATHER WHO ART IN HEAVEN . . ."

MORNING
May God bless me with new
challenges and new understandings.
Thanks be to God.
Amen.

EVENING
Thank you, God, for the gift
of discipleship and the formation
of your Spirit. Your presence is a
blessing to my life. Thanks be
to God. Amen.

Tuesday, November 2 · All Souls Day, Election Day—U.S.A.

(Read Haggai 2:4–9)

MORNING

Savior God, give me courage that I may have confidence in your
love!

EVENING

Savior God, thank you for the shelter of your love and affection.
Praise be to you!

There are quiet times, O God, when I wonder if you are near. I am
afraid and worried that I am alone. But you give me the courage and
strength to continue. Forgive me when I forget your promises and your
abiding care. You have brought your people out of slavery in Egypt, and
now you are leading me to that same destination. I thank you for the
gift of liberation.

MORNING

Grant me courage and forbearance, assurance and peace that I may
serve you with confidence and praise. God, hear our prayer.
(Prayers of Intercession)

EVENING

In all the times when I have doubted you, in all the times when I
have failed to turn to you, for all the times I have placed my loyalty in other authorities, God, hear my prayer.
(Prayers of Intercession)

PRAY THE PRAYER OF OUR SAVIOR.

MORNING	**EVENING**
This is the day you have made,	I make my shelter in you.
let me be glad in it. Let me rejoice	God you are a builder, a builder of
when you are near. Let me praise your	temples, a builder of inspiration.
name for your continued presence.	I am rekindled in your love.
Thanks be to God. Amen.	Thanks be to God. Amen.

Wednesday, November 3

(Read Psalm 145:1–5, 17–21)

MORNING

O God, every day I shall proclaim your praise.
Your works are many and your ways just!

EVENING

O God, another day has come and gone.
Your presence has been a great blessing to me.

From one generation to the next you have stood beside me, O God.
You reach out to me when I speak the truth, hearing my cry and my
praise. There is no greater joy to you than our cries of joy. But you hear
our pain as well. Thank you for your everlasting presence.

MORNING

Day by day you stand beside me, you protect me,
you guide me, you strengthen me. Your love is all I require.
God, hear my prayer.
(Prayers of Intercession)

EVENING

There is rest in your name and peace in your presence.
Abide with me and others as we take our rest in you.
God, hear my prayer.
(Prayers of Intercession)

PRAY THE PRAYER OF OUR SAVIOR.

MORNING	**EVENING**
What a joyous day this is!	Thanks be to God for
With you all things are possible.	the blessings I have received.
With you all things are real.	What a joy it has been to call you
Thanks be to God. Amen.	by name. Thanks be to God.
	Amen.

Thursday, November 4

(Read 2 Thessalonians 2:1–5, 13–17)

MORNING

God, I am called, named by you, and selected for service
in your realm. Let me march forward in your name
with courage and strength.

EVENING

God, having been called to speak your name
and to love your justice, I am grateful for this journey I now know
as my own. Happy am I who know your way!

Everlasting God, your ways do not change; your commandments are as
true today as they were many years ago. Keep me ever faithful to the vision
set before me by your Son. Help me to love you as my one and
only love and to reflect this love in my care for the other. I hold fast to
this with thanksgiving and praise.

MORNING

As I march for your justice and peace, I know there are those
who will be threatened by your good news. Hold me fast to the truth you
have given that sets me apart as yours. God, hear my prayer.
(Prayers of Intercession)

EVENING

As this day draws to an end, help me remain steadfast
to your promises and vision. Keep my eyes focused on you.
God, hear my prayer.
(Prayers of Intercession)

PRAY THE PRAYER OF OUR SAVIOR.

MORNING

I go forward knowing
that you love me and hold me in this
path of justice. Thanks be to God.
Amen.

EVENING

Keep my feet from stumbling,
remind me that you are at the center,
and bless all those who wish
to persecute me. Thanks be to God.
Amen.

Friday, November 5

(Read Luke 20:27–33)

MORNING

Resurrection God, whatever doubts I have, I rest my faith in you.
The resurrection of your Son makes all things new.

EVENING

Resurrection God, those things that cause me to stumble,
and those places that make my faith weak, they are nothing
compared to the new life you have promised me.

Patient God, you wait for me. When I wander off, far from your wisdom and care, you are always there. Your promise of new life lifts up even my darkest worries. This new life in your Son is more powerful than all of the criticisms and the doubts. You give us this life and the one to come.

MORNING

Doubts come and go, but your faith in me never wavers.
God, hear my prayer.
(Prayers of Intercession)

EVENING

You hold me strong when I am weak. You keep me focused
when I am astray. Remind me of your promises of eternal life.
God, hear my prayer.
(Prayers of Intercession)

PRAY THE PRAYER OF OUR SAVIOR.

MORNING

This day is new because
eternal life makes each day your day.
Thanks be to God. Amen.

EVENING

I am forever grateful
for your promises. As evening follows
day, your love surpasses our doubts.
Thanks be to God. Amen.

Saturday, November 6

(Read Luke 20:34–36)

MORNING

All-knowing God, you call me to be equal to an angel
and your child. You have named me and formed me.
You are the ground of my being.

EVENING

All-knowing God, like a chick that has flown
from the nest, I have returned to your loving care.
Hold me and remind me of who I am.

You call me an angel and you have named me as your child. Because of you I am special; because of your resurrection, I have hope. And because of my baptism, I have a new family. Remind me when I am forgetful. The world may call me worthless and forgettable but, in your divine economy, I am an angel and blessed.

MORNING

As angels we fly to you with expectation and joy.
Shape me, hold me, and lift me high. God, hear my prayer.
(Prayers of Intercession)

EVENING

As a child of your divine creation I have inherited
a heavenly realm. Make us worthy of your intentions.
God, hear my prayer.
(Prayers of Intercession)

PRAY THE PRAYER OF OUR SAVIOR.

MORNING

For the promise of resurrection
and the reality of your love, we give
you thanks and praise. Thanks be
to God. Amen.

EVENING

For another day in your realm,
another mile on your road, another
concert of your making, we rejoice
and give thanks. Thanks be
to God. Amen.

Sunday, November 7

(Read Luke 20:37–38)

MORNING

God of New Possibilities, I awake to a new day,
and I am alive to your Spirit and your new vision of resurrection.

EVENING

God of New Possibilities, you are a God of life,
not death, a God of hope, not despair. Help me to choose life,
always and in abundance.

Of all your saints there were none who sought death, except death to the old ways of living. Answering God, my faith ancestors found life in you alone, joy in surrendering to your will and guidance. The wages of sin are death, and the wages of faith is life everlasting. Thanks be to you for a life filled with joy that cannot be contained.

MORNING

A new day, a new way, a new life in you.
Help me live to your vision of Shalom and reject the powers
of the Confuser. God, hear my prayer.
(Prayers of Intercession)

EVENING

Another day of possibilities, another day of beauty and truth.
Remind me to give thanks for the joys of my present relationship
with you. God, hear my prayer.
(Prayers of Intercession)

PRAY THE PRAYER OF OUR SAVIOR.

MORNING	**EVENING**
Another day to serve you,	Your name is on my lips.
another moment in your care,	I sleep in your tender care, and
and another chance to say thank you.	I am alive to your vision. Thanks be
Thanks be to God. Amen.	to God. Amen.

Monday, November 8

(Read Luke 21:5–11)

MORNING

O Great Spirit, I see the beauty you have created and feel hope. I will not let evil frighten me, nor will I be deceived, for you are the good news. You are my defender.

EVENING

O Great Spirit, the sun sets and the heavens come alive with light. All the universe holds beauty. Thank you for the gift of life, so that I may behold all these things.

Jesus, you said the time would come when the stones of our temples would be thrown down. The signs are present today. Many of our temples are no longer adorned with beautiful stones. They have been burned by those who hate, or they have been neglected and abandoned. Yet hope prevails. The faith and hope you have given us through words and signs over centuries churn within us, and so we defy. We rebuild. I cannot think of anything more promising, more exciting, than to be a Christian and to know you. Praise the Creator!

MORNING

Creator of my life, with my mind and with my heart, I absorb the sins of the world, the sins of the people, and give them to you.
(Prayers of Intercession)

EVENING

Gracious and forgiving Spirit, thank you for what has been good and for being the keeper of my fears.
(Prayers of Intercession)

"FEAR DEFEATS PURPOSE, AND SO, WITH PURPOSE, I STRIVE FOR FAITH."

MORNING

Great Spirit, please put faith in me where remnants of fear may lie, so that my day will be filled with good. In the Savior's name, I pray. Amen.

EVENING

For the gift of life, the gift of knowledge, and the gift of forgiveness, thank you, O Great Spirit. In the Savior's name, I pray. Amen.

Tuesday, November 9

(Read Luke 21:12–19)

MORNING
Creator God, you surround me with beauty today.
My soul yearns to seek it, so that all may know you and your powers.
I will wait for your words of wisdom.

EVENING
Creator God, this day was all that you promised.
Not a hair on my head was harmed, and you kept all of my worries
so that I might do your work with a glad heart. Thank you.

Jesus, you said that not a hair on our head would perish if we followed you. What a gift to have in our lives, to know that days filled with strife need not be burdensome if we truly believe that you will protect us. We know that we will hear sad news—another child killed, or someone, somewhere, put to death because of their religious beliefs. Sadly, this has always been so. Yet when our hearts are filled with the Holy Spirit, we continue our faith journey, and we seek justice because we have to.

MORNING
As I begin this day with a clear mind, waiting to be filled
with your wisdom, be with me and those I love.
(Prayers of Intercession)

EVENING
As I end this day in contentment,
having done my best to seek your will, I ask that you
bring contentment to all others in my circle.
(Prayers of Intercession)

"THOUGH PEOPLE MAY BETRAY PEOPLE, GOD NEVER BETRAYS."

MORNING
Creator God, as the day breaks
and the sun shines warm into my
heart, help me shine warmth into my
home and my community. In the
Savior's name, I pray. Amen.

EVENING
God, my loving protector,
I cannot live without you in a world
full of strife and turmoil. This world
needs you! In the Savior's name,
I pray. Amen.

Wednesday, November 10

(Read Isaiah 65:17–25)

MORNING

Holy, holy. holy. All around me is holy. I am holy. Creator God,
there is no ugliness in your creation, only in the minds of evildoers.
Help me remember my holiness and that of those with whom I associate,
so that the New Jerusalem you have promised can begin here and now.

EVENING

Holy, holy. holy. Great Spirit of all who are spiritual in mind and heart,
the awe of the morning scripture stayed with me all day. Thank you
for lifting me and setting my mind on all that can be made new.

Living, breathing Spirit of God, your words in Isaiah bring so much
hope: a new earth, new heavens, and a New Jerusalem—a place where
there will be pure joy, long lives, and no more tears. Though I have felt
pain and sadness and cried many tears, you have always been there for
me. And because you have been there for me, I believe in you and this
promise. The longer I linger on this message, the more excited I am to
have been created just for this time.

MORNING

Eternal and Great Spirit, lift me to sacred and holy grounds,
that I might be spiritually cleansed.
(Prayers of Intercession)

EVENING

Eternal and Great Spirit, the magnitude of your work
has been manifested with the promise of a New Jerusalem.
I pray for your continuing guidance to live out this glory.
(Prayers of Intercession)

"THE SERPENT CANNOT SURVIVE ON DUST, SO FEED DUST TO THE SERPENT."

MORNING	EVENING
The New Jerusalem beckons, O God.	I take from this day what has
Make my walk pure. Keep the vision	been good and leave the rest behind.
of a New Jerusalem before me so I can	Thank you, Great Spirit, for my
do my part. In the Savior's name,	lessons today. In the Savior's name,
I pray. Amen.	I pray. Amen.

Thursday, November 11

(Read Isaiah 12)

MORNING
Praise to you, O Great Spirit, Creator of heaven and earth.
Take me to a place where I can breathe in your strength and your Spirit.

EVENING
Praise to you, O Great Spirit, Creator of heaven and earth.
With joy this evening, I receive the comfort of my Savior.

Sometimes my weaknesses overcome me. They grow like my shadow in the twilight. Confusing thoughts swirl about in my mind. I get too big. No room for you, dear God. I forget to exalt you. How can I not praise you, the One who has comforted me time and again? Scriptures like today's from Isaiah remind me to remain humble and grateful. It is you, God, who promises us a New Jerusalem. It is you who promises salvation and provides a way for us to draw water from the wells of salvation, through your Child, Jesus Christ.

MORNING
Creator God, how great is the One who can answer all prayers.
I pray for peace and serenity in a world of pain and turmoil.
(Prayers of Intercession)

EVENING
A restful sleep is necessary for the peace of mind needed
to do your work. In this world there are many who do not have a place
to rest. God bless all those who are meek and without rest.
(Prayers of Intercession)

"GOD'S ANGER IS NEVER VERY LONG, GOD'S COMFORT IS FOREVER."

MORNING
Today I will sing praises to the Most High, for glorious things have been done. Thank you, God. In the Savior's name, I pray. Amen.

EVENING
For all that has been good today, thank you, Great Spirit. For those who have helped me, I thank you. In the Savior's name, I pray. Amen.

Friday, November 12

(Read Malachi 4:1–2a)

MORNING

Dearest Jesus, some days you walk beside me, some days
you carry me, and some days you have to drag me; but you never,
never give up on me. Just knowing you are with me today is enough.

EVENING

Dearest Jesus, you were with me today, and I felt you.
I needed you. I always need you. Thank you for this very special day
and for your special presence.

Prophets like Malachi encourage our faith. God, he reminds us of your anger, wrath, and love. We leap from our idleness with conviction and begin the process of restoration when strong-willed purpose is thrust on us. Scripture reminds us that "the sun of righteousness will rise with healing in its wings," if we respond to the call. I want to respond. I want healing. Am I prepared? Am I helping you to build a New Jerusalem today?

MORNING

Holy Spirit of God, I want to respond to your call.
(Prayers of Intercession)

EVENING

My soul rests in you after a long and busy day.
(Prayers of Intercession)

"**DESPONDENCY GETS YOU NOWHERE. RESPOND, INSTEAD.**"

MORNING

Holy and Great Spirit, I welcome
this new day. May your warm winds
of heaven blow softly on me and bring
sunrise into my heart. In the Savior's
name, I pray. Amen.

(Cherokee blessing)

EVENING

Great Spirit, make me always ready to
come to you with clean hands and
straight eyes so when life fades, as the
fading sunset, my spirit may come to
you without shame. In the Savior's
name, I pray. Amen.

(American Indian prayer)

Saturday, November 13

(Read Psalm 98)

MORNING

Dear God, your mighty creation trembles. Mother Earth seems to be shrinking with fear and trauma. We are cruel. We forget the sacredness of life. Today teach me kindness and respect for all that you have made.

EVENING

Dear God, your mighty creation trembles. We forget the sacredness of life. Continue to teach me kindness and respect.

God, you are so good. Your Child, Jesus the Christ, is so good. Your Holy Spirit is so good. I give praise to the triumph over evil that I have been given through your Word. I praise you for all those blessed, tormented, committed, and loyal people who wrote down your words. I can seek justice, peace, and especially guidance from those age-old stories and words. Let us sing; let us make a joyful noise; let us bless all of Mother Earth's living creations. Let us prepare ourselves for the New Jerusalem.

MORNING

You have done marvelous things for us. Thank you, God.
I praise you today and ask you to reveal your righteousness to the nations.
(Prayers of Intercession)

EVENING

Holy Spirit, I end this day with hope and yet with some trepidation.
Salvation is needed for me, for us, here and now.
(Prayers of Intercession)

"IF WE DO NOT SING, WE MISS THE JOY OF PRAISING GOD MIGHTILY."

MORNING

God, thank you for those inspired, faithful old songs and hymns. I have a song in my heart this morning that tells me to keep "my mind stayed on Jesus." In the Savior's name, I pray. Amen.

EVENING

Great Spirit, as shadows lengthen I wait for the stars to light up the heavens, for all these things tell me how mighty you are. Thank you for another blessed day. In the Savior's name, I pray. Amen.

Sunday, November 14

(Read 2 Thessalonians 3:6–13)

MORNING
Great Spirit and Creator of all, you rested on the seventh day.
Some of us rest every day. Remove from me idleness and complacency.
Provide me with the spiritual nourishment to do your work today.

EVENING
Great Spirit and Creator of all, provide me with the
spiritual nourishment needed to continue your work.

God, Paul tells the church to keep away from those who are idle. He reminds us that he and others became models for us to follow. He also reminds us that we cannot wait for Christ's return in order to set the world right. There are things we must do here and now! I have found that a structured and directed life is easier to live. Most important, it detracts us from associating with people who are not as spiritually inclined as we are. Paul says to stay away from those kinds of people, to detach from them. I must get busy and prepare for Jesus, now.

MORNING
Dear God, you have taught me so much through all of your
prophets and disciples. I ask you to help me become a model for others.
(Prayers of Intercession)

EVENING
Great Spirit and Creator of us all, idleness and evil are everywhere. Help me
to stay on the path you have determined is mine, so I may witness for others.
(Prayers of Intercession)

"IDLENESS BREEDS ANXIETY AND DEFEAT. PREPARE YOURSELVES DAILY."

MORNING
Great Spirit, I face all directions
this morning with hope and with the
spirit of willingness. In the Savior's
name, I pray. Amen.

EVENING
Holy, holy, holy God. You've kept
me from evil, you've given me a glad
heart to do your work, you've guided
me. Thank you. In the Savior's
name, I pray. Amen.

Monday, November 15

(Read Luke 1:68–79)

MORNING

God of the prophets, thank you for remembering me today.
Shine your light on me, fill me with joy, and give me the words
with which to praise you today.

EVENING

God of the prophets, thank you for remembering me today.

Creator God, I praise you for all you have done for me, your servant. You haven't forgotten me; you haven't left me to wallow in my troubles or to be trapped by those who attack me. You have fulfilled your promise of sending a leader. I will serve Jesus by proclaiming his mercy and righteousness, and I will enjoy the light of God that has been given to me.

MORNING

May your praise burst forth from me today,
proclaiming the fulfillment of your will in my life.
(Prayers of Intercession)

EVENING

God of the ages, thank you for leading me through
another day. If I failed to share with others the story
of what you've done for me, forgive me.
(Prayers of Intercession)

**THANK YOU FOR THE OPPORTUNITIES TO TELL OF THE WAYS
IN WHICH YOU MOVE IN MY LIFE.**

MORNING

I will serve you today
and follow your paths. Thanks be
to Christ. Amen.

EVENING

May I be ready to follow you
wherever you might lead. Thanks be
to Christ. Amen.

Tuesday, November 16

(Read Jeremiah 23:1–3)

MORNING

Almighty God, thank you for stories of your action
and intervention in the lives of your people. I read these words today
with a renewed sense of hope and trust in your guiding hand.

EVENING

Almighty God, thank you for stories of your action
and intervention in the lives of your people.

Dear God, there are people who are abusing positions of leadership and authority. Their idolatry has led those of us under their charge to be removed from your way. Their false instruction has driven us apart and forced us away from our paths. Here our cry, God of wisdom, and bring us back into community with one another. Heal us and let our endeavors develop as you would have them do.

MORNING

May I live this day wary of false voices
and those who misuse their positions.
(Prayers of Intercession)

EVENING

God who knows all things, grant me a night
of renewal and regeneration. If I have followed today
the stray path of false leaders, forgive me.
(Prayers of Intercession)

**THANK YOU FOR YOUR SPIRIT, WHICH GUIDES US
AWAY FROM EVIL AND BRINGS US TOGETHER.**

MORNING

I commit myself to following
only your way, my God. Thanks be
to Christ. Amen.

EVENING

May I be ready tomorrow
to walk in the path you have chosen
for me. Thanks be to Christ.
Amen.

Wednesday, November 17

(Read Jeremiah 23:4–6)

MORNING

God of righteousness, thank you for the assurance that you will
nurture leaders to walk with your people. As I begin this morning,
fill me with confidence in your guiding hand.

EVENING

God of righteousness, thank you for the nurturing of leaders.

I know, Creator God, that you are able to touch me and bring to life my
talents and abilities. Develop my capabilities, that I might provide leadership to your people in whatever form you would have me do so. Enable
me to help your people face new challenges with courage and unity. Make
me like a "righteous branch," and give me the discernment to make wise
decisions and proper moves in the execution of today's responsibilities.

MORNING

May I enter this day with the conviction that you will
give me a spirit of leadership when you would have me lead.
(Prayers of Intercession)

EVENING

Righteous God, who has inspired me this day,
grant me a night of peaceful rest. Forgive me if I failed to take up
the mantle of leadership when you called me to do so.
(Prayers of Intercession)

THANK YOU FOR PROVIDING ME WITH A SPIRIT OF LEADERSHIP THIS DAY.

MORNING

I enter this day looking for areas
in which you call me to lead.
Thanks be to Christ. Amen.

EVENING

May I face tomorrow
with enthusiasm for heeding any call
to leadership you may give.
Thanks be to Christ. Amen.

Thursday, November 18

(Read Psalm 46)

MORNING

Protecting God, I face this day with confidence, knowing
that you are with me as I go through today's experiences. Thank you
for hymns and poems of praise that express my faith in your guidance.

EVENING

Protecting God, thank you for hymns and poems of praise
that express my faith in your guidance.

God of strength, you are our shelter amidst the trials of our life. When problems and difficult situations threaten to engulf us, you protect us and give us what we need to weather the storm. You are with us in the community, making your presence known even through the troubles of our times. We must slow down enough to experience your calming presence in all aspects of life and to witness how you move in this world.

MORNING

May I be still enough today to experience your company
in all the areas of my life.
(Prayers of Intercession)

EVENING

Sustaining God, who has been my sanctuary today,
provide me tonight with rest and the comfort of your guarding hand.
Forgive me if I failed to trust your presence this day.
(Prayers of Intercession)

THANK YOU FOR SENDING YOUR GUIDING AND PROTECTING SPIRIT THIS DAY.

MORNING

I will draw strength from you
today and allow you to be my retreat.
Thanks be to Christ. Amen.

EVENING

I look forward to experiencing your
presence tomorrow and increasing my
faith in your direction and protection.
Thanks be to Christ. Amen.

Friday, November 19

(Read Colossians 1:11–14)

MORNING

Eternal God, who gives us energy to live, thank you for the witness
of your servants, who endured tribulation with long-suffering and praise on their
lips you. As I begin a new day, let that same thanksgiving spring forth from me.

EVENING

Eternal God, thank you for the witness
of your servants' endurance and thanksgiving.

My vigor comes from your wonderful, awesome might, Creator God. Let me tap into your power in order to survive and be strong in whatever situation I find myself; you give me a spirit of perseverance. It's amazing how you empower me to sing your praises with joy and enthusiasm even while I go through the difficulties of life. I know that I walk through the same trials that your servants have endured throughout history, and I am excited to know that, like them, I will receive your blessings! Through your mercy, you have allowed me to dwell in the world of the Christ.

MORNING

May I live this day in a spirit of perseverance and praise to you.
(Prayers of Intercession)

EVENING

Everlasting God, your presence has enabled me to make it through the trials
of the day. Grant me rest along my journey, and forgive me if there were times
when my heart withheld thanksgiving from you.
(Prayers of Intercession)

THANK YOU FOR THE STRENGTH TO LIVE THIS DAY
WITH ENERGY PROVIDED THROUGH THE SAVIOR.

MORNING	EVENING
I receive your power this day, in order to live with vigor and with praise to you. Thanks be to Christ. Amen.	May I continue to draw upon your energy tomorrow, giving all thanks to you. Thanks be to Christ. Amen.

Saturday, November 20

(Read Colossians 1:15–20)

MORNING

Everlasting God, whose presence is in all the universe, thank you
for the way in which your servants have praised you over the ages.
As I begin this day, fill me with the peace and completeness that
come from you through the Christ.

EVENING

Everlasting God, fill me this evening with the peace and completeness that come from you through the Christ.

I am brought to you, Creator God, by the One who is your manifesta-
tion. Through the Christ I can begin to see your wonders and the dy-
namic way in which you move in the universe and in my life. I know
that the eternal Christ is my leader, and the One who brings together
my brothers and sisters in the faith. I come to you, Creator, through the
sacrifice of Jesus: now I am brought back to you, and I am able to experience the abundance of your love and will for my life.

MORNING

May I experience this day the completeness that you offer through
the Christ.
(Prayers of Intercession)

EVENING

Endless God, you have filled me today with the peace that comes
through the Christ experience. Restore me tonight as I rest. Pardon
me for any times that I was not in harmony with you.
(Prayers of Intercession)

THANK YOU FOR THE BOUNDLESS RECONCILIATION I HAVE WITH YOU THROUGH CHRIST.

MORNING	EVENING
I go forward this day in the peace of the Creator, expressed through the Christ experience. Thanks be to Christ. Amen.	May I awake tomorrow knowing that you, Creator, will present yourself to me through my experience with the Christ. Thanks be to Christ. Amen.

Sunday, November 21

(Read Luke 23:33–43)

MORNING
Loving God, you have given us the opportunity to read the story
of those precious moments on the cross, to understand what you have done for us
through Jesus' sacrifice. As I feel the love you demonstrated in the midst
of your pain, my heart cries, "Thank you, merciful God, thank you."

EVENING
Loving God, you have given us the story of your sacrifice
on the cross. Thank you, merciful God.

Somehow, my God, you forgive me. When I crucify you with my
thoughts, my actions, my unfaithfulness, you forgive me. When I gamble away and waste the resources and talents you have provided me, you
forgive. When I taunt you and play games with your love, you still forgive me. Let me not pretend that I deserve your mercy; enable me to
receive your blessings with thanksgiving for your amazing and all-encompassing love, your paradise, your dominion.

MORNING
May I live this day ever mindful of the love you demonstrated for me.
(Prayers of Intercession)

EVENING
Caring God, whose love for me is more than I could sufficiently
praise you for, grant me a restful night. Forgive me if I have lived today without
forgiving others and reflecting toward them the caring you show me.
(Prayers of Intercession)

REMEMBER ME, SAVIOR, AS I ENDEAVOR TODAY
TO LIVE A LIFE WORTHY OF YOUR DOMINION.

MORNING
I commit myself to embrace the
experience of the cross by showing love
to others. Thanks be to Christ. Amen.

EVENING
May I love and forgive tomorrow,
as you have done for me.
Thanks be to Christ. Amen

Monday, November 22

(Read Isaiah 2:1–3)

MORNING

God, I open my eyes this morning to a glimpse of your mountain.
The dreary clouds of November have shifted to reveal your house on the rock,
and I see that it is stable and strong. May I start this new week on a path that
leads to your house; may I follow the winding road up to your mountain.

EVENING

God, I give thanks to you for a day of learning, a day of risks.
Your strength and wisdom nourish me and guide me on the road. Have I inched
closer to you by the day's end? Am I nearer than I was at sunrise? I pray for you
to answer "Yes." For you to say "Come closer still."

Eternal God, I hear the ancient call that beckons, "Let us go up to the
mountain of God, to the house of the God of Jacob." I yearn to share your
home with you, to be with you always. But how scary to make that climb.
What awaits me at the peak? Will I find stability? Or will I need, also, to
face my fear of falling from the cliff? Loving you, dear God, is risky.

MORNING

God, you are always within reach, Help me to be aware of your presence.
(Prayers of Intercession)

EVENING

You ask that I follow your way, O God.
May Christ be with me this evening as my teacher and my guide.
(Prayers of Intercession)

COME, LET US GO UP TO THE MOUNTAIN OF GOD.

MORNING

Thank you, loving and forgiving God,
for this new opportunity to be with
you. Each day you grant me yet another
invitation to visit your house on the
mountain. Thanks be to Christ. Amen.

EVENING

Ever-present God, I know that
our time together does not end when
I sleep. May I wake tomorrow with
the knowledge of your presence.
Thanks be to Christ. Amen.

Tuesday, November 23

(Read Matthew 24:36–39)

MORNING
Powerful God, I am thankful for your presence in my life.
This morning I seem to be especially mindful of your Spirit as it works in me
and through me and reveals your beauty in the people I encounter.

EVENING
Powerful God, may I be awake to your call and stirred
by your voice, each day and every hour.

God, you surprise me again and again. When it seems that I have forgotten you, you rush, like a flood, back into my life. You were never really gone—I was the one who was absent. When I become distracted and busy with details of this crazy world, you and your Child come to me, unannounced, and demand that I turn and look. Help me to remember that daily life has more meaning when I invite you to be a part of it. It is crucial for me to remember you, not only in crisis, but in all times.

MORNING
All-knowing God, grant me the ability to hear your voice
above the noise of life. Grant me the wisdom to respond.
(Prayers of Intercession)

EVENING
I pray for, and with, all of my sisters and brothers who need you
in their lives. We all need you. Please answer our cries. Be with us now.
Help us to welcome you. Help us to work together in peace.
(Prayers of Intercession)

AND THEY KNEW NOTHING UNTIL THE FLOOD CAME AND SWEPT THEM ALL AWAY.

MORNING
I pray that today will be nothing like yesterday. I ask for tomorrow to be new and fresh. I will strive to notice you in all of the beauty and struggle of your creation. Thanks be to Christ. Amen.

EVENING
God, it takes energy and effort for me to be in this relationship with you. Help me to stay on your path. May tonight's rest be fuel for tomorrow journey. Thanks be to Christ. Amen.

Wednesday, November 24

(Read Matthew 24:40–42)

MORNING

Creator God, you have caused the sun to rise once again.
What a beautiful reminder of new birth and resurrection! I praise you
and the new light you bring to the world each day.

EVENING

Creator God, thank you for guiding me through another day.
I am grateful for your forgiveness when I refuse to pay attention
to your coming. You still have not left me behind!

Maker of both darkness and light, I know that each day you will reveal
yourself in a new sunrise. I have yet to find a morning where the sun
refuses to rise or an evening without a sunset in the west. Thank you
for giving me some things that are certain. Help me to respond quickly
to those things that are unexpected, to be like the woman grinding meal
who stopped her work to go with you. I fear that you will come to me
when I am asleep and inattentive. I will attempt to follow the words of
scripture. I will strive to keep awake.

MORNING

God, I pray today for the gift of your presence.
Please, make yourself visible to me.
(Prayers of Intercession)

EVENING

Forgive me, God, if my eyes were closed to you today.
Help me live out my desire to know you.
(Prayers of Intercession)

ONE WILL BE TAKEN, AND ONE WILL BE LEFT.

MORNING

God of us all, today I am willing
to see your light break through in life's
most mundane moments. I will try to
be awake to your unexpected grace.
Thanks be to Christ. Amen.

EVENING

I have been present for another
sunset. I pray that I will see more
vividly the colors of your sun and feel
more deeply the warmth of its light.
Thanks be to Christ. Amen.

Thursday, November 25 · Thanksgiving Day—U.S.A.

(Read Psalm 122)

MORNING
I pray that you will be with me and my loved ones
as we celebrate Thanksgiving.

EVENING
God you provide me with all I need. Grant me the goodness
of heart to pass this generosity on to others.

Sustainer of Life, forgive me when I do not recognize the ways in which you care for me. Teach me to live in a spirit of thanksgiving, not one day each year, but every day. Help me to measure my blessings in peace, good health, and family, rather than by the world's materials standards. On this Thanksgiving Day, may I focus on the themes of Psalm 122: thanks and peace. If I become more aware of the gifts you send then perhaps I will be able to give more to others, and perhaps peace will be easier to achieve.

MORNING
God of all nations, I pray for the strength to say, "Peace be within you," to whomever I meet. I pray for my immediate family, and for families around the world who need you. Touch their lives as you have touched mine.
(Prayers of Intercession)

EVENING
Generous God, I seek to understand more about your peace.
I pray for the places where war and conflict continue to wage.
(Prayers of Intercession)

FOR THE SAKE OF MY RELATIVES AND FRIENDS, I WILL SAY, "PEACE BE WITHIN YOU."

MORNING
Whether I spend my holiday surrounded by loved ones, in an intimate circle of two or three, or alone with my God, bring to my heart a true sense of thanksgiving. Thanks be to Christ. Amen.

EVENING
May this new holiday season be a time of honest reflection and renewal of purpose. Help me to finally understand the messages of goodwill and peace on earth. Thanks be to Christ. Amen.

Friday, November 26

(Read Isaiah 2:4–5)

MORNING
Mother God, I arise and give thanks for your peace,
which extends beyond all human understanding. Show me today how
I can become a more effective witness for peace in your world.

EVENING
Mother God, as another day ends, I celebrate the moments
when I acted in peace. I praise you for showing me the way.

You speak to us, God, in your powerful voice about the ways of your peace. But my sisters and brothers and I still choose war. I continue to live in turmoil instead of reconciliation. How did we learn to make war against ourselves and against you? You created us to live in peace, and we have turned away from your love for us. Guide me back to you, O God. Guide me back to your peace.

MORNING
I pray that your prophecies may come to fruition, that our guns may
be beaten into tools of knowledge and our bombs into creativity's power.
(Prayers of Intercession)

EVENING
God of wisdom, remind me to let you be the judge. Only you have the power
to judge the nations. Only you have the power to judge my neighbor.
(Prayers of Intercession)

NEITHER SHALL THEY LEARN WAR ANY MORE.

MORNING
Strengthen me, God, with the memory of peacemakers who have come before me. May I learn from strides already made and be inspired to put down my own sword and shield. Thanks be to Christ. Amen.

EVENING
As I sleep tonight, may I dream of peace. Wake me in the morning, dear God, with the unquenchable desire to transform the dreams into reality. Thanks be to Christ. Amen.

Saturday, November 27

(Read Matthew 24:43–44)

MORNING
God of love, I drift out of sleep, thankful that you are present
both in my dreams and as I wake. For this, I am grateful.

EVENING
God of love, you may come like a thief in the night, but unlike the thief, you come
to repair, not to destroy. No matter how unexpected, I will celebrate your coming.

God of paradox, you are right in front of me, but I am blinded by your
light. Though you have never left, you must reenter my life again and
again. You come like a flood, like a thief, like manna from heaven. And
I, like so many of your people, am stubborn and not ready for you. But,
God, you keep trying. You have even sent your Child Jesus to us. This
time, may Jesus help me to welcome you in. May I be forced to wake up!

MORNING
Strengthen my heart and energize my spirit, so that I may serve you
and your people today. Open me to opportunities for sharing Christ's love.
(Prayers of Intercession)

EVENING
Gracious God, help me to distinguish
between your Word and those of imposters.
(Prayers of Intercession)

YOU MUST BE READY.

MORNING
This morning I commit myself
once again to walk along the road to
your house. I know that I will stumble
many times before I reach the mountaintop, but I have faith that you will
lead me home. Thanks be
to Christ. Amen.

EVENING
Tomorrow the season of Advent
begins. Christmas will soon be here.
God of understanding and mercy,
I pray that I will awaken to hear your
call, see your face, touch your Spirit,
and say your name. Thanks be
to Christ. Amen.

Sunday, November 28

(Read Romans 13:11–14)

MORNING
Praise God! Soon your Savior will be born again into our world.
The time of waiting has begun. On this first day of the Advent season,
I sit in joyful anticipation.

EVENING
Praise God! Thank you for your salvation, for rescuing me again.
Now is the moment for me to sleep. Now is the time for me to accept your gift.

God Emmanuel, each year you provide me with another chance to grasp the meaning of Christ's birth. Each year you give me a new armor of light for protection and strength. But I am stubborn and refuse to wear it. When will I learn to choose the light? You are so patient with me, Savior God. Help me to be patient, too, as I anticipate the power of your coming. Now is the time for me to wake from sleep! You have warned me to be ready.

MORNING
Guide me, O God, from the depths of this sleep
into the reality of Jesus Christ's coming.
(Prayers of Intercession)

EVENING
During this time of sacred and holy days, lead me to the light
of your star. Open my ears to the voices of your angels.
(Prayers of Intercession)

FOR SALVATION IS NEARER TO US NOW THAN WHEN WE BECAME BELIEVERS.

MORNING
May I live and work honorably in this day. As the night ends and the time of Advent begins, I will sit with the knowledge that a new day is near. Thanks be to Christ. Amen.

EVENING
Help me not to be afraid of the shadows. Your light is always available to me if I choose to see it. As I wait for answers, I have faith that when the waiting is over, there will be joy and peace. Thanks be to Christ. Amen.

Monday, November 29

(Read Isaiah 11:1–10)

MORNING
God, we wait. You fulfill your promises in your time, not in ours.

EVENING
God, fulfill our needs tonight as we rest in your care.

Creator God, you promise a reign of true justice and peace. Help us to hold on to the dream, to work for its fulfilment, to await your intervention, and to share your vision. Show us ways in which we can be instruments in our families, in our communities, in our nations, and in our world.

MORNING
Righteous God, bless us as you have in birthing your creation.
(Prayers of Intercession)

EVENING
God of history, break into ours once again.
Let your Son play with our children, playing "over the hole
of the asp" and trusting in your promise.
(Prayers of Intercession)

THANK YOU FOR THE VISION. HELP US TRUST.
EMPOWER US TO SERVE. SHOW US HOW.

MORNING
Shoot of Jesse, come to us again
that we might cuddle you in our
children and hear your voice and your
teachings. Challenge us.
Thanks be to God.
Amen.

EVENING
Spirit of God, comfort us
in our afflictions and in the change
that swirls around us.
Thanks be to God.
Amen.

Tuesday, November 30

(Read Psalm 72:1–7)

MORNING

God, you formed us from nothing and brought us toward maturity.
Like a loving parent, you hold us in your hands and brood over us.

EVENING

God, we who have received so bountifully await your presence this day
with all your children, whom we call sisters and brothers because you love us all.

Loving God, like a parent you love all your children alike, and favor none. Mario, one of your children, strains to reach the windshield with his squeegee. At the corner, his baby sister strains at the sides of a cardboard box that serves as a playpen. The sun burns. Mario is six. He lives in Phnom Penh, in Madras, in Managua, in Toronto, or in Denver. Give them deliverance.

MORNING

God, help us to love equally. By loving you, we, too, will love Mario.
(Prayers of Intercession)

EVENING

Empower us that we might really be useful, not just to ourselves
and to our families, but to those we step around
because they cry out or smell or look different.
(Prayers of Intercession)

MAY WE BE MINDFUL TO SERVE THE MARIOS IN THE WORLD.

MORNING

God, you bless us with much financial wealth but, more importantly, gifts of faith and of freedom. You expect us to use them to adore you and to serve your children. Please show us how. Thanks be to God. Amen.

EVENING

God, grant that we may rest peacefully this night so that we may awake to serve you and all your children. Thanks be to God. Amen.

Wednesday, December 1 · World AIDS Day

(Read Psalm 72:18–19)

MORNING

O God, new every morning are your acts of re-creation.

EVENING

O God, this day, we thank you for stirring in us
an appreciation of all you do for us
and with us and through us.

We thank you for so may things. Thank you for your acts of creation
and the wonders of nature, and for the faith you have inspired in us.
Your psalm speaks of the promise of justice and peace, and of you,
Wonderful Ruler, who will usher it in.

MORNING

Loving God, we pray for your children even when
we fall away, and for your reign over history. We thank you
that you chose to bring peace to lands locked in conflict
and those once locked in conflict.
(Prayers of Intercession)

EVENING

We pray for our enemies, whom we bring before you this day.
(Prayers of Intercession)

**TO GOD, NOT TO ANY POPULAR OR POWERFUL
CONTEMPORARY LEADER, BE THE GLORY!**

MORNING

We awaken each day bathed
in signs of your love for your children.
Thanks be to God.
Amen.

EVENING

In joy and wonder we greeted
the new day. Now we entrust all that
we have done or thought or spoken in
it to you. May it help build your
realm of peace. Thanks be to God.
Amen.

Thursday, December 2

(Read Romans 15:4–13)

MORNING
God of Steadfastness and Encouragement,
remind us always of your presence in the familiar things of the past
and in the new things to which you call us.

EVENING
God of Steadfastness and Encouragement,
for the night that we have passed we thank you.

Welcoming God, busy people swarmed the airport. Desperate, I led my unknowing senile mother on her last flight to a nursing home across the country nearer to us. An awful trip—though she seemed at peace. Between flights in a busy terminal, her diaper needed changing. Frantic, I sought a private place, a lonely washroom. Travelers packed them all. From the crowds, a kindly older woman who spoke broken English said, "Here, let me help." And she led Mom off. Thank you for that welcoming stranger.

MORNING
If we have rested peacefully we awake to serve you joyfully.
(Prayers of Intercession)

EVENING
You speak to us in familiar ways and we thank you.
We joyfully sing your praises this day.
(Prayers of Intercession)

WE EXPECT GOD'S GRACE IN WELL-WORN, FAMILIAR PLACES. GOD ALWAYS SURPRISES US BY BREAKING IN—IN UNEXPECTED MOMENTS.

MORNING
Thank you for the challenges of this day and for asking us to speak your familiar truth in new ways to those who have not yet heard. Thank you for the challenges of speaking and loving anew. Thanks be to God. Amen.

EVENING
We thank you, too, for calling us to new things—for not letting us bottle it all up inside. Thanks be to God.
Amen.

Friday, December 3

(Read Matthew 3:1–9)

MORNING

God, we awaken once again to seek your will for us.

EVENING

God, this evening, show us what you want us to do tomorrow.
Speak to us to shape us.

God of John the Baptist, of course the cancer would kill her, growing malevolently, malignantly. When she left this time, it would be to die, among her family back home. Today was a good one; we listened to music. Now, branded a revolutionary because of her work with the poor, she had seen friends massacred and others who escaped. "I came to prop up the structures that had formed me as a girl," she said. "These people taught me so much. Thank God for their patience and for changing me."

MORNING

Thank you for the familiar, for all that is good
in what we have received. Now, speak to us afresh again.
(Prayers of Intercession)

EVENING

Still you lead. You call us to new things, new understandings,
and new life. Help us to discern truth through your lens of justice.
(Prayers of Intercession)

YOU SPEAK IN THE RITES THAT WE CELEBRATE
AND IN THE TRADITIONS ENTRUSTED TO OUR CARE.

MORNING

You, the God of our history,
be also God of our todays and of our
tomorrows. Thanks be to God.
Amen.

EVENING

God, we entrust our dreams to you.
Help us to recall your wondrous deeds
in our lives and to dream with you a
future. Thanks be to God. Amen.

Saturday, December 4

(Read Matthew 3:8–12)

MORNING

God of slumber and of waking, let us live this day not fearfully but
rather expectantly, awaiting your in-breaking, your surprise.

EVENING

God of slumber and of waking, thank you for this day
and for the day to come.

Spirit God, the crowds surrounded the airport. Troops lined the runway
and the last plane was loading. What remained of the embassy staff hurried
up the stairway. A woman pushed towards the car with a baby, crying,
"Take her, take her, please. There's nothing for her here." The plane
taxied and the man reflected about his own family, the paperwork, a
strange baby in his world. Of course, he couldn't take her. And then he
thought of who she really is. Not many of us have babies pressed upon
us. But every day circumstance surprise—even amaze—us.

MORNING

Show us today ways in which we can serve.
(Prayers of Intercession)

EVENING

Mold our dreams, God of Samuel,
that we might catch your vision.
(Prayers of Intercession)

**WE KNOW THAT THE WAY WE LIVE REALLY DOES MATTER.
MAY IT MATTER AS MUCH TO US AS IT DOES TO YOU.**

MORNING

God, open us to today's surprise.
Thanks be to God. Amen.

EVENING

Breathe upon us, Spirit of Mary,
that we might accept your will.
What we do matters. Inform our sleep
that we might know what you want.
Thanks be to God. Amen.

Sunday, December 5

(Read Isaiah 11:1–5)

MORNING
Spirit of Wisdom, help us to listen
in hope for your great Gift,
for your day.

EVENING
Spirit of Wisdom,
we praise your wondrous works.

Righteous God, work with us to make what we do conform to your will. We are weak, but you are an empowering God. We come seeking the path to your faithfulness.

MORNING
Spirit of God,
bless those who seek your favor.
(Prayers of Intercession)

EVENING
God, this night, bless those
who seek peace and healing.
(Prayers of Intercession)

"HIS DELIGHT SHALL BE IN THE FEAR OF [GOD]."

MORNING
Mold us and shape us.
We pray for the joy of your presence.
Thanks be to God. Amen.

EVENING
Bless this evening
that we might awake with your spirit
of righteousness.
Thanks be to God.
Amen.

Monday, December 6

(Read Isaiah 35:1–7)

MORNING
Loving and healing God, strength for my fearful heart,
I open the door of my attention to you this day.

EVENING
Loving and healing God, at the close of this day I look to you.
Thank you for being present with loving attention to me and to
this world, even when we are unaware.

God, in this season of Advent waiting, I lose sight of you. I look at all
that needs to be done, and I feel anxious. I look at what others are
doing in preparation for the season, and I feel driven. The holy way of
your coming loses its fragrance, and my heart becomes a dry wilderness
when propelled to rush. But you come to where I am in my fatigue and
fear, and invite me to look to you. When I gaze at you, my eyes are
opened; I see my anxious ways for what they are; and you pour springs
of water on the parched ground of my being.

MORNING
Healing God, you who come to save, open my eyes
to see you in this day in this season of Advent waiting.
(Prayers of Intercession)

EVENING
Dear God, as I reflect over the day, help me to see where
crocuses have blossomed, to notice the springs of water you are giving.
I rest beside the pool of your presence this night.
(Prayers of Intercession)

IN THE PRESENCE OF YOUR LOVE, I PRAY.
(Pray the Prayer of Our Savior.)

MORNING
As I move into this day, God, you are
here. Shape the desires of my heart and
the work of my hands, so that I colabor
with you in the wilderness of this world.
In the mighty name of Jesus. Amen.

EVENING
I rest in you this night.
O God, giver of streams in the desert
and joy on the way. In the mighty
name of Jesus. Amen.

Tuesday, December 7

(Read Psalm 146:5–10)

MORNING
Loving God of Jacob, Yahweh, you made heaven and earth,
the sea, and all that is. I look to you for help.

EVENING
Loving God of Jacob, I come to you, thanking you for watching
over all of creation today and for caring for this tired world.

God, Jacob ran from home in fear. When we lose trust and run, you are with us. You wait to meet us when we pause for weariness and sleep. As I open my heart to receive your help, I discover you are faithful. You help me see your creating and sustaining presence beneath and around the earth, and your faithful love beneath and around those who are lost, oppressed, lonely, and abandoned. You meet us and lift us like a tender parent holding a lost and lonely child.

MORNING
Loving and gracious God, help me to notice your goodness
in this day, and help me to see others—the lost, the unwanted,
and the overlooked—as you see them.
(Prayers of Intercession)

EVENING
God of all Jacobs, as I reflect on this day, help me to see the people
I encountered as you see them. For Jesus' sake.
(Prayers of Intercession)

HUMBLY I PRAY.
(Pray the Prayer of Our Savior.)

MORNING
Jesus, I thank you that as I once again
wait in the Advent of your coming,
your Holy Spirit meets me, lifts me,
and opens my eyes to see your presence
and care. In the mighty name
of Jesus. Amen.

EVENING
Dear God, you watch over
the night with loving, tender care.
In the mighty name of Jesus.
Amen.

Wednesday, December 8

(Read Luke 1:47–55)

MORNING
God, my Savior, I praise you this day.
In you I find the source of all my joy.

EVENING
God, my Savior, help me to notice where you have been
the source of my joy this day.

God of might and mercy, I listen to Mary's song today. As she sings, her song opens a door and allows me to see her heart—that inner continent where we both hide from you and long for your presence. Now you are present in her body, for she carries Jesus. Mary sings, even while she is at risk. Joseph is fearful of this scandal; Herod is violent in his opposition. Embracing the Christ child means being embraced by you. You give joy, for you, God, are ever present.

MORNING
Mighty One, you come to us in the womb of our lives in Jesus.
Grow within me. Scatter those proud thoughts that are against you, and
bring down the powers that wage war against you within me.
(Prayers of Intercession)

EVENING
Savior God, you are at work even as I sleep this night.
Help me to lean into your ways, your coming; to embrace the Christchild
within me; and to risk the security of your embrace.
(Prayers of Intercession)

IN THANKSGIVING I PRAY.
(Pray the Prayer of Our Savior.)

MORNING
Just as Mary sang in the house of Elizabeth, help me to discover persons who acknowledge your presence and work within me and this world. In the mighty name of Jesus. Amen.

EVENING
With Mary, I sing to you, Mighty One, in thankfulness for your help and goodness this day. In the mighty name of Jesus. Amen.

Thursday, December 9

(Read Isaiah 35:3–6; Matthew 11:2–11)

MORNING

Loving and healing God, I look for you this day.
I wait for your coming.

EVENING

Loving and healing God, as I look back over this day, help me to
see your ways, with the loving eyes of Jesus.

Saving God, you don't come the way I sometimes wish you would. You don't come with vengeance, stomping on abusers and war-makers, thieves and murderers, throwing out selfish rulers and putting yourself in charge of governments. Maybe that is why John wavered and wondered, "Are you really the one to come?" Today the world barely notices you. But you still come to us one by one, healing, giving, restoring life, and speaking good news to us who are poor. Help me to see you today as you are.

MORNING

Loving God, help me to notice you this Advent.
And help me to keep you at the center.
May others notice your kindness, and believe.
(Prayers of Intercession)

EVENING

Saving and Healing One, be with your servants
this night who are tired and fearful, who sometimes doubt
your presence and care.
(Prayers of Intercession)

IN CONFIDENCE I PRAY.
(Pray the Prayer of Our Savior.)

MORNING

This day, loving Jesus,
open my eyes and my ears to see and
to hear your presence. In the mighty
name of Jesus. Amen.

EVENING

As I rest this night, I thank you
that you come to be with us in gentle,
healing ways. In the mighty name
of Jesus. Amen.

Friday, December 10 · Human Rights Day

(Read Matthew 11:2–11; James 5:7–10)

MORNING

Present and coming God, as I awake this day,
I look to you and for your coming.

EVENING

Present and coming God, forgive me
for forgetting you and complaining against others.
I thank you for not forgetting me.

Holy One, help me to live in the expectancy of your coming again. My heart grows impatient, turns to other things, forgets the age in which I live: the Advent of your coming. Gentle me into the fruitful rhythm of seedtime and harvest, for you are the owner of the field of this world. Like seed, your loving dominion is planted—oft hidden, sometimes seen.

MORNING

Coming God, I am not patient in suffering.
Help me sit with John the Baptist today and contemplate
the signs of your coming.
(Prayers of Intercession)

EVENING

This night, strengthen and encourage those who speak
in your name and suffer for your sake.
(Prayers of Intercession)

PATIENTLY I PRAY.
(Pray the Prayer of Our Savior.)

MORNING

As I move into this day, dear God,
help me to look for seedlings that are
sprouting, signs of your presence.
In the mighty name of Jesus.
Amen.

EVENING

Your coming is near, Mighty One.
Your presence brings healing,
gentle Jesus. Gentle us into trusting
sleep, renewing rest this night.
In the mighty name of Jesus.
Amen.

Saturday, December 11

(Read Psalm 146:5–10; Matthew 11:2–11)

MORNING

Yahweh, I look to you this day. I am your servant.
You are my help and my hope.

EVENING

Yahweh, as this day comes to a close,
I open my heart to you.

Merciful and holy God, I ask your help as I look back over this week to see as you see. For what am I grateful? . . . (*Pause to reflect.*) In what have I noticed your presence? . . . Where have I doubted your presence? Your love? . . . Where have I responded in trusting faith to your presence? . . . How have I shown your love to others, especially those who are alone, in need, fearful?

MORNING

Freeing God, forgive me for times when I have forgotten you,
for times when I have avoided loving others as you love them and
me. Healing God, open my eyes and ears to see and hear you.
(Prayers of Intercession)

EVENING

Gentle us now into your healing presence. Bring healing
and hope to all who are prisoners of impaired sight, those who are
bowed down, alienated, orphaned, and alone.
(Prayers of Intercession)

IN GLADNESS I PRAY.
(Pray the Prayer of Our Savior.)

MORNING

We cannot love you without your help, or see you without your giving sight, or hear you without your giving us ears to hear with the heart. Be our healer and help this day. In the mighty name of Jesus. Amen.

EVENING

Gentle me now into your healing presence, O God, who uphold the orphan and the widow. Hold all that is orphaned and alone within me in love this night. In the mighty name of Jesus. Amen.

Sunday, December 12

(Read Isaiah 35:1–10; Luke 1:47–55)

MORNING

O Mighty God, my soul magnifies you, and my spirit rejoices
in you. For you have done great things, and holy is your name.

EVENING

O Mighty God, your mercy comes like streams in the desert;
your favor creates pools in the burning sand. I rest with joy,
and my heart is glad as I look to you at the end of this day.

God of goodness, Giver of joy, I thank you for making a way, a holy
way for us to walk. Thank you for your mercy for all that is lowly; you
do not let us go astray. Thank you for your protection from what is wild
and destructive. Thank you for lifting sorrow and sighing from our
hearts and minds. And thank you for your gift of song and everlasting
joy as we walk with you.

MORNING

My soul sings, and my spirit rejoices. Help me to hear the song
you give within my heart, and to walk in joy and gladness this day.
(Prayers of Intercession)

EVENING

As this day comes to a close, I thank you for your great strength
on behalf of all in need this day. How kind you are! I rejoice in your care.
(Prayers of Intercession)

IN YOUR MERCY, I PRAY.
(Pray the Prayer of Our Savior.)

MORNING

Great God, joy that lasts for
all time comes only from you.
I rejoice with gladness and singing
this day. In the mighty name
of Jesus. Amen.

EVENING

This day, Mighty One, you have
lifted those who are low, filled those
who are hungry, and helped those
who serve you. I praise you for your
faithful, loving care. In the mighty
name of Jesus. Amen.

Monday, December 13

(Read Isaiah 7:10–16)

MORNING
God of signs and wonders,
I begin this Advent week with expectation!

EVENING
God of signs and wonders, as a parent cares for children
as they sleep at night, so you care for me in my slumber.

God, you heard the prayers of the people. Through Isaiah the promise was given. A child named Emmanuel was to be born to a virgin. Fulfilling God, you do fulfill your promises and you hear our prayers. We are given signs of your faithfulness in your gifts. Sometimes it is in the new life of a child but more often in new beginnings. You do deliver into our lives blessings of new birth through events, circumstances, or people. Help me to look with anticipation for what you are going to do in my life. Let me see your signs and wonders this week.

MORNING
Morning is about a new opportunity. Be with those who feel
each new day is a burden rather than an opportunity.
(Prayers of Intercession)

EVENING
Tomorrow God, give signs of hope and wonder for those
who need assurance in their daily living.
(Prayers of Intercession)

GOD HAS UNEXPECTED SIGNS OF NEW BIRTH FOR YOU.

MORNING
God, you gave us your child.
May I see you working in my life as I
live with others. Thanks be
to Christ. Amen.

EVENING
God of evening and night,
I trust you will watch over me and
those whom I care for and love.
Thanks be to Christ. Amen.

Tuesday, December 14

(Read Psalm 80:1–7)

MORNING

God, your ears are turned towards my prayer.
May I lift up what is truly in my heart today!

EVENING

God, in this holy season of expectation,
may I be open to your leading for every day!

God, we often ask, "Do you hear me? Do you answer me?" The psalmist in our text cries out in prayer for help in the same way that you assisted Joseph. Centuries later our prayers sound so similar to Joseph's words in seeking direction. We need to be led like Joseph. Prayer gives us that guidance. Not only are our prayers heard but they are also answered by you. Sometimes your answer comes instantly and sometimes it takes awhile. Yet, we can be assured that you hear and answer our prayers.

MORNING

For those who feel their prayers are unheard,
God, give them ears to hear your answer.
(Prayers of Intercession)

EVENING

God, help those to be at peace with the answers
that you provide through prayer.
(Prayers of Intercession)

GOD WANTS TO HEAR AND ANSWER YOU!

MORNING

God of listening and caring,
be with us in our rising. Thanks be
to Christ. Amen.

EVENING

God of answering and caring,
for all who pray to you, be with us
in our resting. Thanks be
to Christ. Amen.

Wednesday, December 15

(Read Psalm 80:17–19)

MORNING

God of sunrise, may your face shine on my life
each and every day with your love!

EVENING

God of sunset, may your face shine on me
as I lie in bed this night!

In the northern hemisphere the days are now at their shortest and in the southern hemisphere they are now at their longest. God, the psalmist prayed for your face to shine upon the people in their distress. Whether we are living in days of darkness or in days of light, Sunrise and Sunset God, your face is always shining upon us. Sometimes we do not always see it but it is there. God, thank you for never leaving or forsaking us. Continue to shine for us.

MORNING

Help me, God, to be your light to others.
Let my face show your light.
(Prayers of Intercession)

EVENING

Comforting God, help me to be a light to those
who are experiencing difficult times. Remind me that I may be
the only smile and the only hug for others.
(Prayers of Intercession)

GOD IS ALWAYS OUR SHINING FACE OF HOPE AND LOVE.

MORNING

God, in Christ you give me light.
Help me to be light to others what-
ever the season. Thanks be to Christ.
Amen.

EVENING

God, in Christ you shone so long ago
in Bethlehem. I praise you for shining
each day in my life. Thanks be to
Christ. Amen.

Thursday, December 16

(Read Romans 1:1–7)

MORNING

Savior God, the newspaper may be full of bad news
but your message is full of the good news!

EVENING

Savior God, we rejoice with the message of your good news.
You loved us and sent your best!

Transforming God, Paul was given the mission of sharing the best news of all. His life served as a gospel messenger for your son. We hear so much that is bad in daily life, but your gospel is about the good news of love and salvation. This time of year reminds us of the blessing of your son. Christ's life is about what is good in life. Yes, Paul had the best message of all to share with the world.

MORNING

God, where there is no hope, I pray that your gospel
will give hope to the hopeless through your love.
(Prayers of Intercession)

EVENING

May our ears be open to hear what is right in life
rather than only that which is wrong.
(Prayers of Intercession)

HEAR THE GOOD NEWS!

MORNING

God of love, may we look
at each day as a gift of Jesus.
Thanks be to Christ.
Amen.

EVENING

God, through all the ups
and downs of this day, thanks for
your undying love in Christ.
Thanks be to Christ.
Amen.

Friday, December 17

(Read Matthew 1:18–20)

MORNING

God of new birth, it is a baby we remember
during this Advent season. I wait for your gift!

EVENING

God of new birth, the excitement of a child
creates feelings of unknown expectations.
We wait for Christ!

What should I do? What is the right thing to do? Joseph's questions can easily be ours too. Creator God, you gave Joseph an answer long ago. Like Joseph, I can come to you for unexpected answers as well. And, like Joseph, I must be willing to come to you in prayer no matter what the problem may be. God, the answer you gave Joseph was not an easy one but it was the right one. May I be open to the difficult as well as the easy answers.

MORNING

We pray for those who are unwilling to take their concerns
to God. May they be open to sharing with you.
(Prayers of Intercession)

EVENING

God, you give courage to those who have difficulty
accepting your answers. Give them the strength to follow you.
(Prayers of Intercession)

GOD IS THERE AND GOD HAS AN ANSWER FOR YOU.

MORNING

God of our questions,
give me direction for the living of this
wonderful day. Thanks be to Christ.
Amen.

EVENING

God, thanks for the answers
you have given me this day.
May I act upon them. Thanks be
to Christ. Amen.

Saturday, December 18

(Read Matthew 1:21–23)

MORNING

God of gifts and delights, may Christ be reborn in my heart today.

EVENING

God of gifts and delights, who cares for me as a parent
does a young child, watch over me tonight.

How do we understand that a child has been born to save his people and to save us today? Savior God, help us to comprehend the miracle that took place in the manger. Such a gift given to each of us seems so incredible. We have done nothing to earn this gift. All we need to do is accept this gift so freely given. This is the miracle of Christmas. God, you cared enough for us to send to earth your very best. May we focus on the heart of Christmas this Advent season—the Child, our Savior, who is the answer to so many prayers and the fulfillment to so many promises.

MORNING

May Christ's birth bring a rebirth to lives that are hurting
and in need of healing this day.
(Prayers of Intercession)

EVENING

May the miracle of Christmas be in our hearts and souls
throughout the year.
(Prayers of Intercession)

THE NAME IS JESUS AND JESUS IS CHRISTMAS.

MORNING

God, thank you for such a great gift.
Help us to take into our daily living
the gift of Christ. Thanks be
to Christ. Amen.

EVENING

Still my heart, O God,
to take in all you have given me.
Thanks be to Christ.
Amen.

Sunday, December 19

(Read Matthew 1:24–25)

MORNING

Loving God, you work in wonderful ways
that we cannot even comprehend or ever fully see.

EVENING

Loving God, may I be open to do your will
even if it seems impossible to understand.

Prophetic God, we picture angels as part of every nativity scene. Children dress up in pageants at this time of year to play the "angelic hosts." Yet, do we really believe in angels? Do we believe they existed and, more importantly, exist today? As Joseph followed the angel's directions, may we also be open to your direction for our lives. You still perform miracles every day. May we have the eyes to see, and the ears to hear, that you are at work in the world today.

MORNING

In situations of trouble and hurting, may you, Loving God,
work in wondrous and miraculous ways to heal those in need.
(Prayers of Intercession)

EVENING

God, your loving presence is always with us.
Touch us with your presence.
(Prayers of Intercession)

THERE ARE STILL THE WONDERS OF GOD'S ANGELS WORKING IN OUR LIVES TODAY.

MORNING

God, as Joseph heard your message
to be with Mary, may we also hear
your message this day. Thanks be
to Christ. Amen.

EVENING

May your angels guard
and look over me this evening.
Thanks be to Christ.
Amen.

Monday, December 20

(Read Isaiah 63:7–9)

MORNING

God of Loving Kindness and Tender Mercies,
it is with gratitude that I awaken with glad joy!

EVENING

God of Loving Kindness and Tender Mercies,
it is with a grateful spirit that I submit to you my offerings
of this day!

Coming Savior, how awestruck I am that you would dare to come again! In just five more days we will celebrate your birth! It's mind blowing! It's mind boggling! And it's the inspiration for my praise. How thankful I am! You came once, saw personally just how awful we are, and even after you ascended back to glory, you returned! Surely, you are our salvation, now and forevermore. Forgive my sin. Let my life reflect your coming into my heart!

MORNING

God who comes, I lift those who need
a fresh experience of your coming.
(Prayers of Intercession)

EVENING

Savior of the world, it is indeed a blessed assurance
that your coming was not in vain.
(Prayers of Intercession)

OUR GOD CAME, IS PRESENT, AND WILL COME AGAIN!

MORNING

In appreciation of your coming
to me, allow me to be fully present to
those I encounter today. In the
matchless name of the Christ.
Amen.

EVENING

In acknowledgement of your being
with me all this day, I offer myself to
your keeping power in the watches
of the night. In the matchless name
of the Christ. Amen.

Tuesday, December 21 · Winter begins

(Read Isaiah 63: 9–11)

MORNING

Remembering God, thank you for the Sonlight that continues to shine this day!

EVENING

Remembering God, your love and your pity carried me all day long!

Angel of Presence, you have allowed yourself to be afflicted with our human afflictions. It was not required that you move into our community, put on our flesh, walk in our shoes, and conquer all of our foes. You decided not only to come to earth, but to die and be buried in the earth so that you might win for us eternal salvation and everlasting life. You chose to be born to die! What a mighty, awesome God you are! Forgive my sin and help me to be prepared, this day, to give evidence, by my life, that I am indeed grateful for your first coming. Help me to be a living testimony, causing others to desire to be made ready to receive you when you come again! For it is certain that you will soon come again!

MORNING

Healing Presence, be with those who come to mind as I pray.
Allow your healing presence to enfold them even now.
(Prayers of Intercession)

EVENING

Carrying God, all day long you have borne me
in your capable arms. Rock me now in the cradle of your love,
especially now as I pray for these:
(Prayers of Intercession)

GOD CREATED. GOD CARRIES. GOD REALLY DOES CARE!

MORNING	**EVENING**
Shine on me! In the matchless name of the Christ. Amen.	Remember me! In the matchless name of the Christ. Amen.

Wednesday, December 22

(Read Psalm 148:1–6)

MORNING
Worthy God, your created order sustains my everlasting praise!

EVENING
Worthy God, the moon and the stars continue to call forth my praise!

Creating God, help me to slow down and to appreciate all that you have ordered in this world. As the hustle and bustle seeks to consume me, allow me the space of these few minutes to remember how you took time to create a beautiful, magnificent, and reproducing world as a birthday gift for ungrateful humans. It was our desire to be you that allowed sin to enter the world and for you to decide to take on our flesh to reunite us through Jesus. You spoke and the world came into being. Yet, you took the time to play in the dirt as you formed us and gave us dominion over your gift to us. As you prepare to come again, forgive my sin and let my deeds today reflect my sincere appreciation for the gift of Jesus Christ.

MORNING
I am the gift you send out into the world this day!
I pray for these:
(Prayers of Intercession)

EVENING
I have encountered many people this day
who need your special attention now:
(Prayers of Intercession)

THE GREATEST GIFT IN THE WHOLE WIDE WORLD IS JESUS!

MORNING
Spirit of the Living God, fall afresh on me! In the matchless name of the Christ. Amen.

EVENING
Spirit of Refreshment, rock me now, in the cradle of your divine love! In the matchless name of the Christ. Amen.

Thursday, December 23

(Read Psalm 148:7–14)

MORNING

Majestic Sovereign, as the whole earth prepares to join in praise to
you this day, I lift my voice in the unending concert.

EVENING

Majestic Sovereign, hail, snow, and clouds might reign outside, but the breath
of your love has hovered over me all day long. I offer grateful praise.

Exalted One, kings, queens, state legislators, men, women, and children are preparing for your coming. Some will never mention your name. Some will never attend a worship service to give you praise. Some will use this season as a time for parties, exploiting others, and providing the rich with "things." In their place, your glory is exalted among the elements you have created. The mighty winds sing praise. The mountains and hills testify to your worthy praise. Fruitful trees, creeping vines, and flying things give honor to the grandeur of your name. For you alone are worthy. Your name is exalted in my mouth. Forgive my sin and renew a right spirit in me, I pray.

MORNING

There are many who have no song of praise on their lips;
I lift them to you.
(Prayers of Intercession)

EVENING

I have encountered many today who are singing
the wrong tunes; for these I pray.
(Prayers of Intercession)

PRAISE THE NAME OF GOD, WHOSE NAME ALONE IS EXALTED!

MORNING	EVENING
Let my life be praise unto your worthy name. In the matchless name of the Christ. Amen.	My soul rests content in the God of creation. In the matchless name of the Christ. Amen.

Friday, December 24 · Christmas Eve

(Read Hebrews 2:10–18)

MORNING

Death-defying Savior, my eyes, my mind, and my spirit
awake in gratitude for this new gift of life.

EVENING

Death-defying Savior, your solicitous help has nurtured
and encouraged us on this busy day.

Helper of the Helpless, we approach you, as the pregnant Mary and anxious Joseph sought refuge in the inn. How great, how wonderful, how awesome it is that you always make room for us! God, like the poor shepherds, tending the needs of lowly sheep, we await the bright stars that will lead us this day to the Hope of the Ages! And, like the heavenly choir that leaned over the banisters of glory to sing songs of praise for the birth of a newborn king, let my life be the song, as you are the melody. Forgive my sin. Fill me with your Holy Spirit. Give me a new song of praise this day.

MORNING

As you have been gracious in aiding me and mine, I pray for these:
(Prayers of Intercession)

EVENING

You have allowed me the privilege of being an aid to others.
I lift their names to you:
(Prayers of Intercession)

**JESUS CAME TO SUFFER, TO BE TEMPTED,
AND TO DIE JUST TO BE OUR CAPABLE HELPER!**

MORNING

I'm leaning on the everlasting arms!
In the matchless name of the Christ.
Amen.

EVENING

I have been carried all day long.
I rest in thee now. In the matchless
name of the Christ. Amen.

Saturday, December 25 · Christmas Day

(Read Matthew 2:13–18)

MORNING
Morning Glory, I awake with joyous expectations and praise.

EVENING
Evening Glory, the day has been filled with joy-filled delights.

Well, the Baby has been born! We thank you that the long wait of Advent has ended. We love you for coming again. In spite of our horrible world conditions and even our bad state of affairs in your church, you dared to come again. Thank you for continued instructions, guidance, and directions on how to avoid death. Forgive my sin and bless me to be just the perfect gift to someone this day. I pray in the name of the God who comes!

MORNING
Babe Born in Bethlehem, many are the forces of death
seeking to destroy these for whom I now pray.
(Prayers of Intercession)

EVENING
Sovereign of Love, for these who may not have experienced
your glory today, I pray.
(Prayers of Intercession)

JESUS WAS BORN TO DIE!

MORNING
Very God of Very God,
live in me this day. In the matchless
name of the Christ.
Amen.

EVENING
Mary's Baby, let the night
lullabyes comfort my spirit now.
In the matchless name
of the Christ.
Amen.

Sunday, December 26

(Read Matthew 2:16–23)

MORNING
Comforter of the Disconsolate, let my life speak peace in the world today.

EVENING
Comforter of the Disconsolate, thank you for staying around,
even as the tinsel begins to fade.

As I approach your throne of grace, God of infants, aged, and all in between, it is with full certainty that the spirit of Herod lives today. There are simply too many mothers—Rachels—in too many places around the world, lamenting lost children. Christmas is not always a happy time. There is the reminder of those small gifts called children who were snatched away by death way before their divine potential could be developed. I pray for every Rachel. I add my lamentations, tears, and great mourning with theirs. Send the power of comfort this day, I pray. Let me be an agent of healing as I encounter an undercover Rachel!

MORNING
Great God who is mother, father, sister, and brother,
we need your comfort as we pray for all mothers.
(Prayers of Intercession)

EVENING
Nurturing God, we have witnessed your concern
for Rachel this day and call her name before you now.
(Prayers of Intercession)

**GOD CARES AND KNOWS ABOUT THOSE HANDS THAT ROCK CRADLES
AS WELL AS THOSE HEARTS THAT ARE BROKEN!**

MORNING
Spirit of Compassion, let me be a healing balm today. In the matchless name of the Christ. Amen.

EVENING
Spirit of Compassion, thank you for allowing me to offer you the work of my hands. In the matchless name of the Christ. Amen.

Monday, December 27

(Read Isaiah 9:2–7)

MORNING

Brightness of the Noon Day Sun, we approach these awakening hours
with hope in our hearts. Thanks for the gift of your only begotten Son.

EVENING

Twinkling of the Midnight Moon, we come to these hours
of rest with gratitude for your keeping power all day long.

Giver of every good and perfect gift, as the trees come down, the wrapping papers are thrown away, the day-after sales are slowing, and the goodwill of the previous week is fading fast, I come to you with joy. Thank you for the gifts of family, friends, and community. Thank you for angels, hourly workers, little children, and those who share their gifts. Thank you for the quiet hours, the sweet melodies of carols, and the memories that bring both tears and smiles. Thank you for the abundance of food that you provided and for those with whom I have broken bread over these holy days. Forgive me of the sin that would keep me from you. Allow the light of your presence to make my heart a prepared home for you to remain all the year. For unto us a child has been born. Unto us your Son has been given. Thanks be unto a generous God.

MORNING

For those who have little to remember with joy, I pray.
(Prayers of Intercession)

EVENING

For those who have made too few good memories, I plead.
(Prayers of Intercession)

JESUS IS A WONDERFUL COUNSELOR!

MORNING

For the living of this day, I offer
myself as a gift. In the matchless name
of the Christ. Amen.

EVENING

For the rest of this night, I offer what
I have given in your name. In the
matchless name of the Christ. Amen.

Tuesday, December 28

(Read Isaiah 9:2–7)

MORNING

God of every nation, I lift my eyes and my voice
in a chorus of praise.

EVENING

God of every nation, I close my weary eyes with thanks
for your never slumbering or sleeping.

Peace Giver, how soon we forget your reign of loving shalom. How soon
we return to our ugly ways. How soon we go back to war, rumors of war,
and hostility towards one another. For a couple of days there are sweet
sounds of harmony. For a couple of days there are the cords of community. For a couple of days it seems as if we have almost understood your
message sent in Jesus Christ. Then, the afterglow fades. The music of
peace dies. The smiles disappear. The sounds of war grow louder. God,
forgive the sin in me. I want there to be peace on earth. And I do want
it to begin with me. Work through me this day, is my prayer.

MORNING

For those who have had little peace, I pray.
(Prayers of Intercession)

EVENING

For those who don't know the meaning of inner peace, I plead.
(Prayers of Intercession)

JESUS IS THE PRINCE OF PEACE!

MORNING

I offer myself as a bearer
of your shalom this day. Use me.
In the matchless name
of the Christ. Amen.

EVENING

I bring all the scattered pieces
I collected this day. Restore me.
In the matchless name
of the Christ. Amen.

Wednesday, December 29

(Read Psalm 96)

MORNING
Music Maker God, I awake with a psalm of praise on my lips.

EVENING
Music Maker God, I offer my closing anthem
of thanksgiving to you.

Coming One, thanks for the gift of yet another day. Thanks for a song of gratitude in my heart. Thanks for the opportunity to join in the great and varied halleluias that will be offered in praise of your creation today. The winds sing. The snow and rain offer their own distinct tunes. The flying birds and creeping wild animals are in one accord. Help me to be a bringer of joyous sounds to all those I meet today. Let the discord in my life be silenced as I think of all the wonder you have set before me to discover this day. Honor, majesty, strength, and beauty are yours. Yet, you have given me eyes to behold the glory of your creation. Let me add my voice in exalted hymns of delight. Forgive me of the sin that tells me to sing the blues! Play a new song upon the strings of my heart.

MORNING
For those who sing the blues, I pray.
(Prayers of Intercession)

EVENING
For those who feel they have no song, I plead.
(Prayers of Intercession)

LET THE WHOLE EARTH BRING FORTH NEW SONGS OF PRAISE!

MORNING
As morning gilds the sky,
my heart's awakening cry is,
"Let Jesus Christ be praised!"
In the matchless name of the Christ.
Amen.

EVENING
As the moon mounts its pulpit
and shines forth its glorious note,
I rest my weary soul in the anchor
that holds. In the matchless name
of the Christ. Amen.

Thursday, December 30

(Read Titus 2:11–14)

MORNING

Great God and Glorious Savior of Grace,
thank you for another fresh opportunity to get it right!

EVENING

Great God and Glorious Savior of Grace,
with gratitude I approach the ending of another day.

Daily Provider, this is another year drawing to a close. My heart offers thanks for the living of these days. For many who began the journey of this year have been called home for eternal rest. Many, who are in pain and distress, are longing to be with you before the ending of this year. The days seem to rush past. The weeks are over too soon. There is so much I had planned to do. There are so many I had planned to visit, send a card to, call on the phone. Yet the days of this year are closing on us. You have been so faithful, so loving, and so kind. I ask forgiveness for the sin that lives in me. For you were gracious enough to send Jesus as a role model of a self-controlled, upright, and godly life. As I take stock of my days, I find myself so short of his mark. Help me to take stock of this year and to make better use of my life.

MORNING

For those who need the knowledge of Jesus Christ, I pray.
(Prayers of Intercession)

EVENING

For those who have tried to make a permanent and positive impact
on the world, I pray.
(Prayers of Intercession)

JESUS IS OUR BLESSED HOPE!

MORNING

Manifest yourself through
my life this day. In the matchless
name of the Christ. Amen.

EVENING

May God be glorified in my living
of this day. In the matchless name
of the Christ. Amen.

Friday, December 31 · New Year's Eve

(Read Luke 2:15–20)

MORNING

Great Shepherd of the Sheep, I offer my treasures to you this day.

EVENING

Great Shepherd of the Sheep, another year of my life
is offered as my testimony to you.

Record Keeping God, the pages of another year are drawing to a close. The ledgers will be balanced. I will be found wanting, lacking, and short! For I did not do all the things you gave me as an assignment. I made excuses. I was scared. I didn't know how to accomplish all the great tasks. Then, the things you told me not to do, I did. I didn't sin boldly, but I didn't love others as you had commanded. I didn't really give sacrificially; rather, I offered you less than I give a good waitress or waiter! Some of my gifts, I hid. For I was too tired to add one more project to my list of things to do. Yet, the year is closing. And I have to offer you an accounting. Forgive me of my sin. I have no other excuse. Restore me, I pray in the name of Jesus Christ.

MORNING

Gift of All, this is the last day of the year
and I am prayerful for your world.
(Prayers of Intercession)

EVENING

Yesterday, today, and tomorrow, you are God,
and many need you now!
(Prayers of Intercession)

I'M DETERMINED TO WALK LIKE JESUS, YES, I AM!

MORNING

Today is the end of another yearlong gift of life. Thank you! In the matchless name of the Christ. Amen.

EVENING

This night folds one year into another and a fresh beginning is mine. In the matchless name of the Christ. Amen.

CONTRIBUTORS

Kathleen Crockford Ackley—Rev. Ackley is an ordained United Church of Christ minister. She is the executive for Volunteer Ministries in the Global Sharing of Resource Ministry Team, Wider Church Ministries, United Church of Christ.

Stephen Wentworth Arndt, Ph.D.—Dr. Arndt is an educator who has taught all age levels. His fields of study are theology, philosophy, and literature.

David Bahr—Rev. Bahr has served churches in North and South Dakota and is currently pastor of Archwood United Church of Christ in Cleveland, Ohio.

Douglas B. Bailey—Rev. Bailey is a retired United Church of Christ minister. He is the former training program administrator for the Franklin County Children Services.

Cathy Barker—Rev. Barker is senior minister of Magnolia United Church of Christ in Seattle, Washington. She formerly served churches in Oregon, Michigan, and Minnesota.

Dorothy H. Bizer—Mrs. Bizer, a former Latin and English teacher, is a published poet and writer of devotional prose. She and her husband, Robert, are active members of Trinity United Church of Christ in Quincy, Illinois.

Ronald S. Bonner Sr.—Rev. Bonner is an ordained United Church of Christ minister. He is the Multicultural Resources and Service Manager at Augsburg Fortress Publishers in Minneapolis, Minnesota.

Dallas A. Brauninger, D.D.—Dr. Brauninger is an ordained United Church of Christ minister. She is a prolific writer and author of resources such as *Lessons from a Dog Guide* and *Lectionary Worship Aids.* Dr. Brauninger is also the editor of the United Church of Christ, UC News Insert, "That All May Worship and Serve."

Kenneth R. Brown II—Rev. Brown, an ordained minister in the United Church of Christ, is the Associate for Youth/Young Adult Empowerment, Justice and Witness Ministries, United Church of Christ.

Gerard John Bylaard—Mr. Bylaard, born in the Netherlands, came to Canada as a teenager. He was educated in the United States and currently lives in Toronto. He is married and the father of two grown children.

Michael C. Carson—Rev. Carson is the senior pastor of historic Wayman Chapel African Methodist Episcopal Church in Kokomo, Indiana.

Laurie Ruth Colton—Ms. Colton is a member of the United Church of Christ.

Barbara R. Cunningham—Rev. Cunningham is an ordained minister in the United Church of Christ.

Rose Ferries—Rose Ferries is a lay pastoral minister in the United Church of Canada and is currently serving at Westminster United Church in Winnipeg, Manitoba. Mrs. Ferries, a seasoned author, has penned *Rainbows and Crosses,* a Lenten devotional for her congregation. She is married with two grown children and three grandchildren.

L. Wayne Ferguson—Mr. Ferguson teaches mathematics at a community college in Mississippi.

Rich Foss—Rev. Foss is pastor of Plow Creek Mennonite Church in Tishilwa, Illinois. He is an author and leadership trainer.

Tom T. Fujita—Rev. Fujita is pastor of Nu'uanu Congregational Church, United Church of Christ, in Honolulu, Hawaii.

James C. Gill—Rev. Gill, pastor of a suburban Canadian congregation, recently completed the second building project of this thriving church. He also trains student ministers.

Stephen C. Gray is the Conference Minister of the Indiana-Kentucky Conference of the United Church of Christ.

Cynthia L. Hale—Rev. Hale is senior pastor of Ray of Hope Christian Church (Disciples of Christ) in Decatur, Georgia.

Juanita J. Helphrey—Ms. Helphrey is the minister and team leader of the Racial Justice Ministry Team, Justice and Witness Ministries, United Church of Christ.

Linda H. Hollies—Rev. Hollies is an ordained United Methodist clergy-woman, best-selling author, retreat leader, and transformational agent, residing in Grand Rapids, Michigan.

Ina Jones Hughs—Ms. Hughs is a full-time columnist for Scripts Howard and author of two recent publications, *A Buyer for Children* and *A Sense of Human*. She lives in Knoxville, Tennessee, and is an active member of New Providence Presbyterian Church in Maryville, Tennessee.

Darryl Farrar James—Father James is rector of Messiah Saint Bartholomew Episcopal Church in Chicago, Illinois.

Marilyn Kreyer—Mrs. Kreyer is a widow who is a retired secretary, semi-retired mother, full-time writer, and lover of books—especially the Bible.

Monty S. Leitch—Ms. Leitch writes a weekly feature column for *The Roanoke Times,* in Richmond, Virginia. She is an elder in the Presbyterian Church (USA).

Kevin C. Little, M.T.S., M.Div.—Rev. Little, a native of Halifax, Nova Scotia, has served on the boards of many nonprofit organizations that have assisted the poor. He has been a columnist and ran for Parliament. At present, Rev. Little is minister at MasKay United Church of Canada in Ottawa, Ontario.

Michael E. Livingston—Rev. Livingston is a seasoned author and the former campus pastor at Princeton Theological Seminary.

Derek Maul—Mr. Maul is a newspaper columnist living in Tampa, Florida. He worships with his family at First Presbyterian Church in Brondon, Florida, where his wife, Rebekah, is pastor.

Charles McCaskey, D. Min.—Dr. McCaskey is senior pastor of First Cumberland Presbyterian Church in Cookville, Tennessee. He is married to Wanda Low and the father of two children, Michael Charles and Mary Catherine.

Joseph Turner McMillan, Jr., Ed.D.—Dr. McMillan is the immediate past president emeritus of Huston-Tillotson College. He remains active in civic, cultural, religious, and educational organizations in the city of Austin, Texas, where he resides.

Alan McPherson, D.D.—Rev. Dr. McPherson is senior minister of Central Presbyterian Church in Hamilton, Ontario and a former moderator of the General Assembly in the Presbyterian Church of Canada.

Wendy J. Miller—Rev. Miller is campus pastor and assistant professor of Spiritual Formation at Eastern Mennonite Seminary in Harrisburg, Virginia.

Marilyn Pagàn—Rev. Pagàn is an ordained minister in the United Church of Christ. She is pastoring in Chicago, Illinois.

V. Steven Parrish—Rev. Parrish is an ordained minister in the Cumberland Presbyterian Church. He is also a professor of Old Testament at Memphis Theological Seminary. He is married and the father of two daughters.

Patricia Vincent Pickett, D. Min.—Dr. Pickett is a chaplain for differently able persons. She is a mother, grandmother, and artist. More importantly, she is challenged to become the woman God means for her to be.

John C. Purdy—Rev. Purdy is a retired minister in the Presbyterian Church and a freelance writer. He was an editor of educational resources for twenty-six years.

Frank Ramirez—Rev. Ramirez is pastor of Everett Church of the Brethren in Everett, Pennsylvania. He is also the author of several books.

Thomas Ratmeyer—Rev. Ratmeyer is an ordained minister in the United Church of Christ. He is associate pastor at Mystic Congregational Church in Mystic, Connecticut.

Joseph W. Reed—Rev. Reed has ministered in New York state and Quebec. He served as the director of Inner City Mission in Montreal, taught English in West Africa, and served as a missionary in Central America. Rev. Reed also served as moderator to the 127th General Assembly of the Presbyterian Church in Canada.

Betty Lynn Schwab—Rev. Schwab is a liturgical minister at Meewasin Valley United Church of Canada and professor of World Religions. She is a writer with the Prairie Centre for Ecumenism and a spiritual retreat facilitator.

Jack Smith, D. Min.—Rev. Dr. Smith is an ordained United Church of Christ minister. He provides spiritual direction for clergy, is a church consultant, and serves in event management as a pathfinder for clergy and congregations.

Ozzie E. Smith, Jr., D. Min.—Dr. Smith is senior pastor of Covenant United Church of Christ in South Holland, Illinois.

Martha Evans Sparks—Ms. Sparks, the first ordained elder at Trinity Avenue Presbyterian Church (PCUSA) in Durham, North Carolina, is a journalist with master's degrees in psychology and library science. She has also taught Bible studies for many years.

Barbara Sutton—Ms. Sutton is an elder at Westminster Presbyterian Church in Belleville, Illinois. She has completed Commissioned Lay Pastor training. Ms. Sutton is employed in the Medical Library of the St. Louis Veteran's Administration Medical Center.

Hamilton Coe Throckmorton—Rev. Throckmorton is the senior minister of Barrington Congregational Church in Barrington, Rhode Island.

Harry Uthoff—Rev. Uthoff is an elder at Grace Presbyterian Church and is a former school administrator and professional college football referee. He and his wife Jean, live in Victoria, Texas.

Albert L. Williams—Rev. Williams is a teacher and minister in the United Church of Christ.

Beverly Williams—Rev. Williams, a poet and photographer, is an ordained minister in the United Church of Canada. She has also served in long-term café settings.

Rebekah Woodworth—Ms. Woodworth is a member service representative for Vantage Healthcare Network, Inc. She is a member of the Associated Reformed Presbyterian Church.

Flora Slosson Wuellner—Rev. Wuellner is an ordained United Church of Christ minister, author, and retreat leader.

Robert Lyman Yoder, D. Min.—Dr. Yoder is minister at Bluff Presbyterian Church. He is married to Lina Yoder and the father of one son, Jay. He is active in the Academy of Parish Clergy.